RED BOOK SERIES™

Shield & Liberty Head Nickels

SECOND EDITION

Q. David Bowers

Whitman™
SINCE 1934

Shield & Liberty Head Nickels

SECOND EDITION

Whitman
SINCE 1934

4001 Helton Dr., Florence, AL 35630

whitman.com

Correspondence concerning this book may be directed to the publisher, Attn: *Shield and Liberty Head Nickels*, at the address above.

ISBN: 978-07948-51248 / WW1447-0425 / Ebook ISBN: 978-07948-51798
Printed in the United States of America.

The Red Book Series™ builds on the historic *Guide Book of United States Coins* (popularly known as the *Red Book*). Each numbered volume takes a deeper look into a *Red Book* topic, with more history, more images, more data, and updated valuations from the *Greysheet* pricing team. Volume 5, *Shield and Liberty Head Nickels*, is just one of nearly 30 volumes in the encyclopedic Red Book Series.

Liberty Head Nickel
Collection 1883 to 1912
OFFICIAL WHITMAN COIN FOLDER
9007
Native American Dollars
Lincoln Memorial Cents
Collection 1999 to 2008
Number Two
8196

Contents

Foreword

This latest edition of *Red Book Series: Shield and Liberty Head Nickels* is an essential reference guide to the first two 5-cent coin series our nation to be struck from this peculiar metal. A year after the nickel three-cent piece was introduced, five-cent pieces went into production. Although silver coins of the same nominal value, half dimes, would continue to be struck until 1873, the five-cent nickel has endured to this day.

Author Q. David Bowers extensively covers the history of how these two coin series came about, from their initial discussion and legislation to their design, production, and distribution. This in-depth background information adds rich context for anyone who pursues building a collection of these coins, and certainly adds to the enjoyment of holding them in your hand.

Some of the most important and valuable information contained in this book pertains to how to understand and evaluate the quality of Shield and Liberty Head nickels. These coins, especially Shield nickels, suffered various problems due to the hardness of the composition, resulting in widely variable strike quality. With this book, you can learn positive strike characteristics, accurate grading, and how select the best coin for the grade and your budget. This is even more important in today's numismatic marketplace where many coins that are traded are already in third-party certified holders. Learning how to evaluate the "grade within the grade" is an important step in building a collection.

The date-by-date analysis given to each coin will reveal which coins are the key dates and why, going beyond the simple mintage figure. It will also show which coins are scarce at a particular grade level, so that condition rarity may be better understood. In addition, up-to-date pricing is given for each coin, along with pricing and information on select varieties, of which there are many within these series. Our unique Greysheet Identification (GSID) numbers have been added to all coins in this edition as well. The GSID allows an item to be referenced and tracked across all Whitman Brands products, allowing the user to quickly look up pricing, catalog, and even auction sales data. Our Collector+ subscription package gives users access to not only Shield and Liberty Head nickels, but the entire range of United States coinage, along with paper money and world coins. It is an unbeatable value for the amount of data available. We sincerely hope you enjoy this latest release in our Red Book Series™!

Patrick Ian Perez

Introduction

I have always enjoyed nickel five-cent pieces, or nickels, as everyone calls them. Part of this affection has to do with the interesting coins themselves, but equally important to me is their place in the American way of life. It was recently suggested to me that the regular (non-numismatic) word *quintessential*, meaning *fifth* essence or element—a will-o-the-wisp, an aura—could be used to describe five-cent pieces. Hmm. Nice thought.

I am old enough to remember when a nickel would buy a bottle of Coca-Cola or pay for a local telephone call. At the time, Buffalo nickels were common and probably even in the majority of five-cent pieces in pocket change. The occasional—very occasional—Liberty Head nickel could be found, usually worn nearly smooth. As to Shield nickels, I never saw one in circulation, and likely these faded from the scene in the 1930's.

When I first became a numismatist and could pronounce that word correctly, I was a young teenager. The world of rare coins beckoned, with minor coins being particularly affordable. However, *information* about coins was just as fascinating, and ever so much more affordable. I soon learned that old issues of the *American Journal of Numismatics*, dating back to 1866, *The Numismatist* back to 1888 (although my earliest copy was from 1893), and the *Numismatic Scrapbook Magazine* were in many instances free. At coin-club meetings and conventions, old-timers were more than happy to give me copies they no longer needed. In writing to the American Numismatic Society in New York City I learned that they had copies of every issue from 1866 onward, except for a few popular issues with studies on California gold, pattern coins, and New England coinages. The ANS sent me bundles of these, year by year, each wrapped in a pinkish paper tied with string, and with the date scribbled in crayon.

Through these magazines I learned all about nickels. By happenstance, the *American Journal of Numismatics* was present at the creation of the series, with its first issue appearing in May 1866, the same month that the Shield nickel became a reality! From that point, magazine by magazine, I learned of rare dates, patterns, and, eventually, the coming of the Liberty Head nickel.

In the 1950's (my years as a budding numismatist), the be-all and end-all for price information was *A Guide Book of United States Coins*. Other useful data could be found in the occasionally published *Standard Catalogue of United States Coins*. Walter Breen was a wealth of knowledge and was the one person I could write to and ask technical numismatic questions.

The late John J. Ford Jr. was another mentor, perhaps the most important of all, for he combined a deep knowledge of numismatics with a keen sense of business. I recall finding an 1866 Shield nickel with a wildly repunched date, mentioning it to Ford (who edited the *Standard Catalogue*), and then mailing it to him at his request. Apparently, he had never seen such a thing. This was in the twilight of the old *Standard Catalogue*, and he was considering listing it. Somehow, it got lost in his office or house (to this day it has not surfaced)—a great frustration to John, who prided himself on being a perfectionist. At one time, John and Olga Raymond (Mrs. Wayte Raymond) wanted me to take over the *Standard Catalogue*, and we talked at length about it, but no arrangement was ever perfected.

A particularly wonderful book for the field of nickel-ania in the 1950's was *United States Pattern, Trial, and Experimental Pieces, Being a List of the Pattern, Trial, and Experimental*

Pieces Which Have Been Issued by the United States Mint from 1792 Up to the Present Time, by Edgar H. Adams (primarily the photographer) and William H. Woodin (author), published by the ANS in 1913. In coin talk the book was simply referred to as *AW* or *Adams and Woodin*. As much as for any other series, nickels have a rich background of pattern issues, the first made with the date 1865 (rather late in the time-line for patterns at the Mint)—a panorama of interesting designs, mottoes, conceptions, and more. Catching my eye in particular was the 1882 pattern Liberty Head nickel without CENTS on the reverse, a coin in all ways similar to the famous 1883 of the same design, but virtually unknown to collectors (today, this is the variety known as J-1690). In 1957, collector Bernie Marshfield took a solitary example of this 1882 pattern, put it in an exhibit case at the Central States Numismatic Society convention, and took home a prize ribbon. I thought this was neat! With fewer than 100 known, it makes the similar 1856 Flying Eagle cent (also a transitional pattern) look common!

After poring through old auction catalogs, listings, and other sources in the early 1950's, I concluded that the 1867 Shield nickel With Rays on the reverse was a great rarity in Proof format—well recognized as a key issue, but, to me, even rarer than supposed. At the 1955 American Numismatic Association convention held that year in Omaha, Nebraska, the auction was conducted by Aubrey and Adeline Bebee. Among the items listed was a Proof 1867 With Rays. I bid it up to the amazing record price of $610, which became the talk of the show! To put matters in perspective, at the same show Aubrey Bebee showed me a prooflike gem 1796 quarter dollar (today worth well over $100,000), and commented that he had just bought it for $200, saying in effect, "I know the price is very high, but it is so beautiful."

Of course some *Proof* nickels went directly into the dark drawers of coin cabinets maintained by numismatists such as T. Harrison Garrett, Lorin G. Parmelee, and a string of others in the hobby. However, most *circulation strikes* were launched into the real world, where they were spent in the pursuit of an endless variety of products and pleasures.

To me, a single nickel can offer a "program" of delights if contemplated: how was it designed and minted, how many were made, how rare is it today in a given grade, and how was it used?

In 1960 I bought an antique music box made at the turn of the 20th century by the Regina Music Box Company of Rahway, New Jersey. I soon became fascinated with automatic musical instruments, delved deeply into their history, and tried to learn as much as possible about a field that had been largely unexplored. Among the favorites I added to my collection were coin-operated music boxes, pianos, and orchestrions (self-playing orchestras), which played melodies when a nickel was deposited. I wrote *Put Another Nickel In*, a history of such instruments (published in 1966), followed by *A Guide Book of Automatic Musical Instruments* (in two volumes), and then, in 1972, *The Encyclopedia of Automatic Musical Instruments*. This *does* have something to do with nickels. Read on! Of course, if you are interested solely in the coins themselves and not their aura or quintessence, just skip this!

In the field of coin-operated musical devices, the nickel was king. Similarly, in the early 20th century a nickel was the passport to many pleasures for young and old—the 5¢ cigar, the 5¢ glass of beer, a chance at hitting the jackpot in an ornate Caille-brand slot machine, and admission to a nickelodeon theater. My 1979 book, *Adventures With Rare Coins*, began with a chapter about the romance of nickels. The present edition of this book discusses the era and its fascinations in the context of the history of the nickel, but readers can learn more from my other books and articles (mentioned previously) if they wish.

The famous 1913 Liberty Head nickel, featured in *Adventures With Rare Coins*, also gets its share of attention here. There are just five known; of these, I have bought, sold, or been involved in the transfer of four. When the first U.S. coin ever to cross the auction block for more than a million dollars was sold, it was a 1913 Liberty Head nickel, from the Eliasberg Collection. The year was 1996, and I was the auctioneer at the podium, calling for bids. Regarding this particular rarity, ever since I was a teenager, Eric P. Newman (who once owned all five of these coins) has been a personal friend, and in 1957 he was among the organizers of the Rittenhouse Society. Emery May Holden Norweb, the doyenne of American numismatics in her day, was also a fine friend, and I was instrumental in having her 1913 nickel donated to the Smithsonian Institution.

This book was originally envisioned as beginning with Shield nickels in 1866 and concluding with the Westward Journey issues in the Jefferson series. However, reality intervened with two choices: condense the book to exclude about half the information, or create two volumes. I opted for the latter, and the companion bears the title *A Guide Book of Buffalo and Jefferson Nickels*.

Thus, I left nothing out. As a result, you have the opportunity for total immersion in Shield and Liberty Head nickels in the present book—possibly more than you need to know. However, as Michael Korda once wrote in a piece in the *New York Times*, there is no such thing as too much information. This was a generation ago, before the Internet. Perhaps today he would modify that by stating that there is no such thing as too much *useful* information.

Shield and Liberty Head nickels are very egalitarian—anyone can collect them, with no insurmountable rarities save for the 1913 Liberty Head, which has its own special context. If you are a typical reader you will probably opt to acquire one of each date and mint, in a collection to suit your tastes and budget. However, the Shield nickel series in particular opens a panorama of wonder to anyone caring to use a magnifying glass to study the many die varieties. Perhaps the ultimate reflection of this is the comment made by Ken Hill, a contributor to this book: "My personal collection of 1868 nickels approaches *900 pieces*." Studying die varieties can become addictive, so watch out! Just ask Bill Fivaz. Fivaz has had a lifelong passion for studying interesting die varieties in all series, and with coauthor J.T. Stanton compiled those varieties in a series of books.

"There are more things in heaven and earth, Horatio, than are dreamt of in your philosophy," Shakespeare wrote. He could have been discussing nickels. There are more things about nickels that the average numismatist knows or dreams about, and doubtless new varieties remain to be discovered. For you this means a lot of opportunity.

In *some* areas of nickel-ania, such as price listings, we all probably have more information than we need. No doubt a search on the Internet for information about the 1901 Liberty Head nickel, a common date, would yield hundreds of listings and scraps of essentially repetitive information. Yet there are many other *market concepts* that, amazingly, have not been closely examined and are scarcely mentioned on the Internet or in auction catalogs or popular reference books. The marketplace virtually ignores the concepts of sharp details and eye appeal—important considerations if you want to acquire some fine coins.

In the quest for useful, accurate, meaningful, and interesting information to create the pages you are about to read, I have drawn upon fine sources from the past and tapped the knowledge of present-day specialists, collectors, and dealers (check the impressive list of contributors!). To this information has been added a generous helping of nostalgia and Americana, and data reflecting rarity and market values. I have tried to distill all of this into text that I hope will share the enthusiasm I have had for nickel five-cent pieces for all of my numismatic career.

For the astute buyer, there are many opportunities to cherrypick (to borrow a favorite Bill Fivaz word) great rarities for reasonable prices. In addition, you might find a rare or even new variety. If you *use* this book, I rather imagine that it will pay for itself right away, and will help you earn great profits in the future. However, that is not my main purpose, which is to help you *enjoy* this fascinating American series.

Nickels can be your friends, so to speak, and in the following pages you will experience some of the warmth I have enjoyed with the study and appreciation of these wonderful coins—little messengers from the past, from a bygone era, but fascinating to own and enjoy today.

How to Use This Book

Key to Notations and Abbreviations

The following notations, abbreviations, and references are among those used in the text. For others, see the endnotes and the selected bibliography.

Rarity Scales

The *Universal Rarity Scale* (URS) is used by Bill Fivaz and others for rarity and is employed in several places in the present book. URS-0 = None known.

URS-1 = 1 known, unique
URS-2 = 2 known
URS-3 = 3 or 4
URS-4 = 5 to 8
URS-5 = 9 to 16
URS-6 = 17 to 32
URS-7 = 33 to 64
URS-8 = 65 to 124
URS-9 = 125 to 249
URS-10 = 250 to 499
URS-11 = 500 to 999
URS-12 = 1,000 to 1,999
URS-13 = 2,000 to 3,999
URS-14 = 4,000 to 7,999

URS-15 = 8,000 to 15,999
URS-16 = 16,000 to 31,999
URS-17 = 32,000 to 64,999
URS-18 = 65,000 to 124,999
URS-18 = 65,000 to 124,999
URS-19 = 125,000 to 249,999
URS-20 = 250,000 to 499,999

URS-21 = 500,000 to 999,999
URS-22 = 1,000,000 to 1,999,999
URS-23 = 2,000,000 to 3,999,999
URS-24 = 4,000,000 to 7,999,999
URS-25 = 8,000,000 to 15,999,999
URS-26+ = same progression

Attributions and Numbering Systems

Certain coins and varieties are cross-referenced to standard works (see the selected bibliography). Frequently used references include the following:

Breen or ***Breen Encyclopedia***—Refers to *Walter Breen's Complete Encyclopedia of U.S. and Colonial Coins*, 1988, or, as noted, *Walter Breen's Encyclopedia of United States and Colonial Proof Coins, 1792–1977.*

F or ***Fletcher***—Refers to listings by Edward L. Fletcher Jr. in *The Shield Five Cent Series, 1994.*

FS or ***Fivaz-Stanton***—Refers to listings by Bill Fivaz and J.T. Stanton in *Cherrypickers' Guide to Rare Die Varieties, sixth edition, volume 1*, 2015.

J or ***Judd***—Refers to pattern coins described by J. Hewitt Judd in *United States Pattern Coins, 10th edition*, 2024.

PM or ***Peters and Mohon***—Refers to references by Gloria Peters and Cynthia Mohon in *The Complete Guide to Shield and Liberty Head Nickels*, 1995.

P or ***Pollock***—Refers to pattern coins described by Andrew W. Pollock III, *United States Patterns and Related Pieces*, 1994.

Style Notes

Nomenclature: In text, quoted and original, *dentil*, for toothlike projection on the inside rim of a coin adjacent to the field, has been changed to *denticle*. Instead of *business strike*, referring to a coin made for circulation, *circulation strike* is used.

Proof is capitalized in numismatic usage, as are grades such as *Mint State*, *Very Fine*, and so on. The term *Full Details* is capitalized, similar to *Full Head*, *Full Bands*, and the like, that are capitalized in other series. For the nickels of 1873, *Closed 3* has been used instead of the former *Close 3*.

Minor typographical errors in quoted text have been corrected, thus avoiding the repeated use of [*sic*]. Minor editing has also been done for clarity. Generally, spelled-out numbers in government reports, such as "fifty-seven thousand and six hundred dollars," are given here as $57,600.

GSID Numbers

The *Greysheet* Identification system represents unique catalog numbers for more than 275,000 items of U.S. and world coinage and paper money, and it is the bedrock of the vast CDN–Whitman database. Comprising tens of millions of records of pricing, auction prices realized, metadata, and images, it grows and changes on a daily basis. The GSID number allows the user to quickly search this database, and enables seamless identification across Whitman's family of products.

1

The Story of the Nickel

Prelude
The Gathering Storm

The nickel five-cent piece, which debuted in 1866, was spawned by national events several years earlier. Absent these, the silver half dime would have continued in circulation, and there would have been no need for a nickel coin.

In 1860 all was well on the American financial and monetary scene. The political landscape was something else entirely—with the North challenging the South over the slavery question and President James Buchanan endeavoring to please both, but satisfying neither.

The decade of the 1850's had been very prosperous, fueled by the building of railroads, the development of western lands, easy credit, and busy stores and factories. Then came the Panic of 1857, precipitated by excessive speculation and the expectation that the good times would never end. They did, and quickly. In October in New York City all but one bank (the Chemical Bank) ran short of gold and silver coins and stopped redeeming its notes. Anxiety spread, credit tightened, and across America there were many bank and business failures. The echoes resounded through most of 1858.

In 1859, enthusiasm was on the rebound, and signs of prosperity were just about everywhere, although a coolness remained in banking circles. Mills and factories in the North registered excellent profits, while the products that comprised the "wealth of the South" (as per the inscription of a popular token of 1860 made in Cincinnati)—cotton, corn, rice, and tobacco—found ready sale.

Then came the presidential election of 1860, with campaigning throughout the summer. Four candidates were in the running. The burning issue of the day was the abolition of slavery. Many Northerners, championed by Republican candidate Abraham Lincoln, wanted the practice stopped, or at least prevented from expanding into new territories. In the South and middle districts, many citizens simply wanted to preserve the status quo. Slavery made possible the wealth of the South through cheap labor, and it was hard to envision a viable economy if workers had to be *paid*.

The question was hardly a new one, and echoes went back several decades. In the 1820's and 1830's slavery was a pressing issue, often defended under the umbrella of "states' rights"—which simply meant that states should be free to do as they wished. In the 1820's, in a move that became known as the "American System," new protective tariffs were enacted that encouraged mainly Northern industries—much to the aggravation of the South. If South Carolina, the most vocal advocate of states' rights through Senator John Calhoun, wanted slavery to be maintained, or sought to end the tariffs through its own actions, it was not the business of politicians in Washington to interfere. At times, this situation threatened to tear the United States apart. "The Union must and shall be preserved," a statement adapted from an 1830 comment by Andrew Jackson, referred to this threatened division and became a motto later used on many tokens that are of numismatic interest today.

Abraham Lincoln.

When the November 1860 election results were tabulated, Abraham Lincoln garnered 40% of the popular vote and 180 electoral votes, while his main opponent, John C. Breckenridge, got only 18% of the popular vote and 72 electoral votes. Stephen A. Douglas had 30% of the popular votes but just 12 electoral votes. John Bell gained 12% of the popular votes and 39 electoral votes.

The outcome was unacceptable to many Southerners, who despised Lincoln and all he stood for. On December 20, 1860, the South Carolina legislature voted 169 to 0 to secede from the Union.

The Crisis of 1861

In short order, Alabama, Arkansas, Florida, Georgia, Louisiana, Mississippi, North Carolina, Tennessee, Texas, and Virginia also withdrew. Delegates from six of these states met in Montgomery, Alabama, on February 4, 1861, to form the government of the Confederate States of America. Jefferson Davis was named president on a provisional basis (in October he was confirmed in a general election).

In American commerce there was great confusion. No one knew what would come next. In the meantime, business between the North and the South continued unabated among the uncertainty. The Confederacy called upon the American Bank Note Company in New York City to print bonds and the National Bank Note Company to print Confederate paper money.

Howell Cobb was secretary of the Treasury from March 6, 1857, until December 8, 1860, joining Confederate Army. In 1861, New York City die sinker George H. Lovett produced a medal titled "Gallery of Traitors No. 1," apparently one of a projected series. Cobb is among those listed in the medal inscription.

Robert Lovett Jr., a Philadelphia die sinker and token maker, designed a one-cent coin for the Confederate States of America. Lovett created a French Liberty Head obverse in combination with a distinctive reverse showing cotton, corn, tobacco, rice, and barrels (of molasses?). By his own account, he struck just 12 of these, all in copper-nickel metal.

Southerners (including Howell Cobb, who had been secretary of the Treasury) withdrew from federal positions and took up posts in the Confederacy. Many envisioned that the Confederacy would simply operate as a separate country, enjoying fine relations with the Union, but without Union interference.

Lincoln, in his inaugural address on March 4, commented: "This country, with its institutions, belongs to the people who inhabit it. Whenever they shall grow weary of the existing government they can exercise their constitutional right of amending it, or the revolutionary right to dismember it or overthrow it." The revolutionary right was very much in progress. There was no going back.

On April 11, Major Robert W. Anderson, in command of Fort Sumter in the harbor of Charleston, South Carolina, was ordered by Confederate General P.G.T. Beauregard to evacuate his troops from the facility. He refused, and early on the morning of April 12, Confederate batteries at Fort Moultrie on the shore opened fire. On April 14, Major Anderson left the fort, now reduced to rubble, and fled with his men on a steamer to New York City.

The Monetary and Numismatic Scenes

In early 1861, commerce in the North and South was mainly conducted through coins and paper money. Coins included the Indian Head cent, silver coins from the three-cent piece (or trime) to the dollar, and gold coins from the dollar to the double eagle. Five mints were in operation: Philadelphia, Charlotte, Dahlonega, New Orleans, and San Francisco (three of these being in the South).

Paper money in circulation was nearly entirely in the form of notes issued by state-chartered banks. There was no federal paper in general use, and no widespread issues had been produced since the ill-fated Continental Currency issues of the 1770's. These had depreciated to be worthless. Even by 1860 there was no public desire to use government paper.

The collecting of coins, tokens, medals, and paper money formed a fine hobby for thousands of numismatists who were riding a wave of enthusiasm that had been spawned by the discontinuation of the "large" copper cent in early 1857. By 1860, several numismatic societies had been formed, and auctions were conducted regularly; at least a dozen dealers were in business in the larger cities, and several reference books had been published.

As to current coinage, interested collectors bought specially prepared Proofs from the Mint each year, paying a premium for them. No one sought coins with Charlotte (C), Denver (D), New Orleans (O), or San Francisco (S) mintmarks, as having a coin to represent a *date* was sufficient. Current bank bills were ignored by collectors, but there was quite a bit of interest in colonial and provincial notes, as well as the old Continental Currency issues.

The Civil War

On April 15, 1861, President Lincoln assembled a special session of Congress. War was declared against the Confederacy, and a call was issued for 75,000 troops to enlist for a period of three months. In the North, the War of the Rebellion, as it was generally designated, was expected to be over in a short time. Parades and parties were held in New York City, Philadelphia, and elsewhere, as soldiers marched off to the game of war, expecting victory in short order. The South was viewed as having very little in the way of military capability or industrial strength. It would be an easy win.

The first Battle of Bull Run in July changed all that, with a decisive victory for the Confederacy. Both sides settled in for a longer conflict. In the meantime, the Union was short of money and issued Demand Notes (redeemable in gold coins, to pay debts). By December of 1861, it was quite unclear as to which side would win. The situation was going from bad to worse. At the end of the month, banks in larger cities stopped paying out gold coins in exchange for bank notes. Frightened, the public began hoarding coins—first gold, then, in the spring of 1862, silver. The government's issue of large quantities of Legal Tender Notes—paper money with no redemption privilege in coins—did not help matters and made coins seem all the more precious to hold.

By the second week of July 1862, even one-cent pieces had disappeared from circulation. To fill the gap, various privately made tokens with political or advertising messages flooded commerce, as did paper scrip bills in denominations from one cent upward, with 3¢ and 5¢ being the most popular. Postage stamps were allowed to be used as money, per Congressional authorization, engendering John Gault's innovation of the encased postage stamp. Then came Postage Currency, followed by Fractional

Encased postage stamp of the 5¢ denomination issued by Burnett's Standard Cooking Extracts, Boston.

This scrip note for 5¢, dated November 12, 1862, was issued by William M. Weed of Sandwich, New Hampshire, and honored by the Carroll County Bank. Thousands of varieties of scrip notes were issued as substitutes for coins during the Civil War.

James D. White, a grocer in Albany, New York, issued this 5¢ scrip note dated November 6, 1862. Each note was serially numbered in ink and signed by White.

Currency bills in the denominations of 3¢, 5¢, 10¢, 15¢, 25¢, and 50¢, issued by the Treasury Department. Many different five-cent substitutes were issued in the several years before the birth of the nickel five-cent piece.

In 1864, the coin shortage eased somewhat, and cents were again seen in circulation; many of the two-cent coins, a new denomination, were also seen. Silver coins remained hoarded, as did gold. The traditional five-cent coin of the realm, the half dime, was no longer seen in circulation.

Birth of the Nickel Five-Cent Piece

Joseph Wharton in Action

The ways of those who controlled the destiny of the Mint in yesteryear are beyond the understanding of present-day numismatists and historians, nor were they clear in the 1860's. In particular, Joseph Wharton (1826–1909) was a strong and persuasive advocate for the use of nickel in coinage. His nickel mine at Lancaster Gap, Pennsylvania, purchased in 1863, was America's foremost producer of this metal. Under his direction the American Nickel Works went into operation in Camden, New Jersey, and was the first truly successful such enterprise in the United States.

Unrelentingly in the early 1860's, Wharton solicited, cajoled, and otherwise influenced politicians and Mint officials to make increasing use of the metal. In the next decade, his campaign went worldwide as he endeavored to interest foreign countries in using nickel as a substitute for silver denominations. Much of Europe abandoned silver in the 1870's and adopted gold as the single standard.

In the United States in the late 1850's and early 1860's, nickel was employed as a component of an alloy for coinage, but it did not work well. At the Philadelphia Mint, many problems were encountered with die wear and breakage of the copper-nickel Flying Eagle cents of 1857 and related later issues. In 1863, Mint Director James Pollock endeavored to get rid of nickel, stating this in a letter to Secretary of the Treasury Salmon P. Chase, December 8:

> It is not proposed to change the size and devices of the cent, only the weight. The weight of the new coin would be 48 grains or 1/10th of an ounce Troy. Enclosed I send you specimens of the bronze cent, which is very superior in every respect to the *slumpy* nickel.

Exactly what Pollock meant by the word *slumpy* is not known today, but it certainly was a negative. In any event, the dislike by Pollock and others for nickel was an element in the Act of April 22, 1864, which discontinued the copper-nickel alloy for cents and substituted "French bronze." French bronze was 95% copper and 5% tin and zinc, a tractable alloy that was also used in the newly authorized two-cent piece. This act was passed despite the bitter opposition of many legislators who had come under the influence of Wharton.[1]

On April 15, 1864, in face of the impending legislation, Wharton published a pamphlet titled "Project for Reorganizing the Small Coinage of the United States of America," which recommended that the use of nickel be *increased*, and denominations of 1, 2, 3, 5, and 10 cents be made with an alloy of 25% nickel and 75% copper. Incredibly, this was *twice* as much nickel as had been in the difficult copper-nickel cent (12% nickel and 88% copper)!

Bronze was immediately used to strike cents and two-cent pieces, and the metal proved to be all that was hoped for. Die damage decreased, the new coins were struck up with sharper detail, and all else was in good order.

Events of 1865

In March 1865, *Banker's Magazine* reiterated the positive aspects of the new bronze alloy:

> The substitution of the bronze alloy for the nickel mixture, as authorized by Congress, has been highly successful. The demand for the one and two-cent pieces has been unprecedented, and every effort has been made to meet it. The demand still continues, although the number daily issued largely exceeds that of any former period. Large quantities are hoarded, and thus kept from circulation. They have also been bought and sold by small brokers at a premium; this has induced individuals to collect them for the purpose of sale, thus producing a scarcity and inconvenience of the public that ought not to exist. . . .
>
> The two-cent piece is a most convenient and popular coin. Its size and weight contribute to its usefulness. The motto, "In God we trust," stamped upon this coin, has been highly approved by the public, not only as improving the artistic beauty of the piece, but also as expressive of our nation's reliance upon the "God of Nations" in this hour of peril and danger.

Switcheroo

We can only guess what happened behind the scenes, but in 1865 Mint Director James Pollock had a change of heart, and all of a sudden nickel was back in the limelight, now championed by the director as a very desirable coinage metal! The Honorable John A. Kasson, chairman of the Committee of Coinage, Weights, and Measures in Congress, viewed nickel with favor as well. Kasson proposed a new three-cent piece of nickel alloy, in the 25% to 75% proportions recommended by Wharton, as a way to redeem worn Fractional Currency. These small paper bills were detested by the public. With virtually no opposition and no debate, the nickel three-cent piece was authorized under the Act of March 3, 1865 (which had the unusual distinction of being introduced and passed into law on the same day).

Although the Mint had great problems with striking the new three-cent coins, which entered circulation that summer, the public loved them. They became popular immediately and largely superseded the bronze two-cent piece.

In his *Annual Report* for the fiscal year ended June 30, 1865, Director Pollock, now an ardent believer in nickel for coinage, suggested creating another coin containing this metal:

> From this nickel alloy, a coin of the denomination of five cents, and which would be a popular substitute for the five cent note, could easily be made. This suggestion, however, is respectfully submitted in view of the probable withdrawal of the smaller denomination of the fractional paper currency, and as preparative and aid to its accomplishment. This to continue only until the resumption of specie payments, or for a fixed and limited period.

In a country abounding in the precious metals, and with silver generally in excess, in time of peace, of all demands for coinage or other purposes, tokens or coins of inferior alloy should not be permitted to take the place permanently of silver in the coinage of pieces above the denomination of three cents.

Authorizing the "Nickel"

In the next year, Pollock's comments were translated into the Act of May 16, 1866:

> **SEC. 1.** *Be it enacted by the Senate and House of Representatives of the United States of America in Congress assembled,*
>
> That, so soon as practicable after the passage of this act, there shall be coined at the Mint of the United States a five-cent piece composed of copper and nickel, in such proportions, not exceeding twenty-five per centum of nickel, as shall be determined by the Director of the Mint, the standard weight of which shall be seventy-seven and sixteen hundredths grains, with no greater deviation than two grains to each piece; and the shape, mottoes and devices of said coin shall be determined by the Director of the Mint, with the approval of the Secretary of the Treasury; and the laws now in force relating to the coinage of cents, and providing for the purchase of material, and prescribing the appropriate duties of the officers of the Mint and the Secretary of the Treasury, be, and the same are hereby, extended to the coinage herein provided for.
>
> **SEC. 2.** *And be it further enacted,* That all laws now in force relating to the coins of the United States, and the striking and coining of the same, shall, so far as applicable, be extended to the coinage herein authorized, whether said laws are penal or otherwise, for the security of the coin, regulating and guarding the process of striking and coining, for preventing debasement or counterfeiting, or for any other purpose. And the Director of the Mint shall prescribe suitable regulations to insure a due conformity to the required weights and proportions of alloy in the said coin, and shall order trials thereof to be made from time to time by the assayer of the Mint, whereof a report shall be made in writing to the Director.
>
> **SEC 3.** *And be it further enacted,* That said coin shall be a legal tender in any payment to the amount of one dollar, and it shall be lawful to pay out such coins in exchange for the lawful currency in the United States, (except cents, or half cents, or two-cent pieces, issued under former acts of Congress,) in suitable sums, by the treasurer of the Mint, and by such other depositories as the Secretary of the Treasury may designate, and under general regulations approved by the Secretary of the Treasury. And under the like regulations the same may be exchanged in suitable sums for any lawful currency of the United States, and the expenses incident to such exchange, distribution, and transmission may be paid out of the profits of said coinage; and the net profits of said coinage, as ascertained in the manner prescribed in the second section of the act entitled "An act relating to foreign coins and the coinage of cents at the Mint of the United States," approved February 21, 1857, shall be transferred to the Treasury of the United States:
>
> *Provided,* That from and after the passage of this act no issues of fractional notes of the United States shall be of a less denomination than ten cents; and all such

> issues at the time outstanding shall, when paid into the Treasury or any designated depository of the United States, or redeemed or exchanged as now provided by law, be retained and cancelled. . . .
>
> **SEC. 5.** *And be it further enacted,* That it shall be lawful for the Treasurer and the several assistant treasurers of the United States to redeem in national currency, under such rules and regulations as may be prescribed by the Secretary of the Treasury, the coin herein authorized to be issued when presented in sums not less than one hundred dollars.

In *Fractional Money*, 1930, Neil Carothers commented concerning the coin:

> The fractional weight of the new piece, 77.16 grains, calls for explanation. The original bill, probably drawn up by Pollock, made the weight 60 grains, and the House passed the bill in this form. In the Senate the Finance Committee amended the bill, Senator [John] Sherman reporting that the committee, after conference with Pollock, Secretary McCulloch, and the House committee, had decided to change the weight to 77.16 grains. The Senate accepted this incomplete explanation and the House concurred.[2]
>
> The purpose of the amendment was to give the coin a metric weight. Since the time of Jefferson there had been an intermittent interest in the matter of a universal system of coins and measures. Senator Sherman was a leader in the movement. The Senate committee wished to give the new coin a weight of 5 grams, but could not bring themselves to use the metric term. They adopted, therefore, the awkward fractional figure of 77.16 grains, which is approximately the equivalent. Inasmuch as there was not anywhere else in Treasury or mint [Mint] operations any use of the metric system the provision was an empty gesture. It has never been changed, and our present day 5 cent piece still has a metric weight.[3]

Thus, the nickel five-cent piece became America's first metric coin, the precursor of a movement that would gain much momentum in the next decade and result in the production of pattern coins across several denominations.[4] The diameter of 20.5 mm also had metric connections.

Throughout these enactments, Joseph Wharton remained a stalwart figure in the advocacy of nickel usage in U.S. coins. If a special-interest numismatic group is ever formed for the study and appreciation of this denomination, it could well be named the Wharton Society, for without his influence it is likely that the coin never would have been born.

Preparing Designs

On May 28, 1866, Director Pollock wrote a memorandum to Secretary of the Treasury Hugh McCulloch, to accompany several patterns that had been prepared by Chief Engraver James B. Longacre and his staff. As the large 5 number-punch for the reverse of No. 1, below, was furnished to the Mint by S.E. Adamson on May 19, it is evident that this pattern, at least, was prepared in a hurry.

Likely, this message was delivered personally by Pollock, who traveled to Washington about that time:

Sir,

I have the honor to forward for your selection and approval specimens of the five-cent piece, the coinage of which has been recently authorized.

No. 1: Obverse, the "Union Shield resting on tied arrows," &c. Motto, "In God we trust," and date. Reverse, 13 stars set in rays, U.S. of America, and figure &c. "5 cents." A neat and unique design, and differs from the devices on all of our other coinage. This specimen is in my opinion before all the others in artistic beauty, significance, and diversity. I would respectfully recommend its adoption.

No. 2: Obverse, "Head of Washington," Motto, "In God we trust," and date &c. Reverse, same as No. 1; a neat and elegant design.

No. 3: Obverse, "Head of Washington," U.S. of America and date. Reverse, Wreath and figure &c. "5 cents."

No. 4: Obverse, "Head of Washington," Motto, "In God we trust," and date. Reverse, Wreath and figure "5."

The above are respectfully submitted for your consideration. Be pleased to notify me of your decision as early as convenient, so that the dies may be prepared for the coinage of the specimen selected.

Pollock's recommended No. 1 design was accepted forthwith by Secretary McCulloch, and what we now call the Shield nickel soon became a reality. Incidentally, McCulloch had a strong background in banking and finance before he came to Washington, but he is not known to have had numismatic inclinations.[5]

Overview of the Shield and Liberty Head Nickels

As extensive information concerning the several designs and many varieties of nickel five-cent pieces minted in the early range of the series, 1866 to 1913, is given in detail in the following chapters, I give only a brief overview here.

While the nickel five-cent piece may have been born in a scenario of graft and influence peddling, it went on to become very popular with the public. In time the anti-nickel (metal) sentiments were forgotten.

It is unknown when these coins were first called *nickels.* The copper-nickel cents introduced in 1857 had been called *nicks* for a long time. The composition of 75% copper and 25% nickel gave five-cent coins in the new alloy a silver appearance. Technically, perhaps these should be called *coppers*, as nickel is the minority element. However, nickels they are—even those made with *silver* content for a short time in the 1940's.

As described above, the first nickels were designed by James B. Longacre and employed a shield design on the obverse, taken from Longacre's motif on the bronze two-cent piece introduced in 1864. The reverse depicted the large numeral 5 with 13 stars surrounding. Between each pair of stars a ray was inserted, creating what is known as the *Shield nickel With Rays* type today. In the 19th century, certain numismatists called this the *stars and bars* design.

Difficulties arose in striking these pieces with Full Details, and in February 1867 the rays were eliminated, creating the Shield nickel Without Rays type. That design was coined through 1883.

In 1883 a new motif, the Liberty Head (by Charles E. Barber, who had been chief engraver at the Mint since 1880), was introduced for the nickel five-cent piece. The obverse featured Liberty facing to the left, stars surrounding, and the date below. On the reverse the denomination was simply stated by the Roman numeral V, a tradition following the use of III to designate the value of the nickel three-cent and silver three-cent pieces. The word CENTS did not appear. Certain miscreants and sharpers gold-plated the new nickels and passed them off as $5 gold coins, the diameters of the two denominations being the same.

Realizing the omission, Barber added the word CENTS to the reverse, ending the deception. Liberty Head nickels without CENTS were coined only in 1883, and those with CENTS were coined from 1883 through 1912, plus a small mintage (estimated at just five coins) in 1913. Accordingly, in 1883 there were three different nickel types made: Shield, Liberty Head without CENTS, and Liberty Head with CENTS. In 1912, nickels were struck at branch mints for the first time, at Denver and San Francisco.

Although today it is difficult to envision anyone becoming tired of the Liberty Head design, such was a reality, and beginning in 1911 serious thought was given to replacing it. Enter sculptor James Earle Fraser—and, lo and behold, in 1913 the Indian Head or Buffalo nickel was first minted, bringing down the curtain on the series studied in this book.

Although no readers of this text will have had first-hand experience with Shield nickels in pocket change, some may remember when Liberty Head nickels were fading rapidly from the scene in the early 1950's, to become extinct by 1960.

Fortunately these coins, once made by the tens of millions, were saved by youngsters with piggybanks and numismatists with coin cabinets, with the result that excepting the 1913 Liberty Head, which was not an official issue, all dates are collectible today, and most are affordable.

SHIELD NICKELS:
The 1866 (shown) and 1867 had the With Rays design; from 1867 to 1883 (1868 shown here), the Without Rays design was used.

LIBERTY HEAD NICKELS:
The 1883 (shown) lacked the word CENTS on the reverse; from 1883 to 1913 (1903 shown here), CENTS did appear on the reverse.

2

The Minting of Nickel Five-Cent Pieces

Making Obverse and Reverse Dies

Creating Working Dies

Each nickel was and still is produced by striking it in a high-pressure coining press, using an obverse or front die with the date, in combination with the reverse die, bearing the denomination. The dies come together with force, and transform a planchet into a finished coin.

By the time the first nickel five-cent pieces were struck for circulation, the Philadelphia Mint was very sophisticated in its procedures. Almost everything—from die making to stamping out coins—was mechanized; there was human oversight, but the work was largely that of mechanical devices.

For the Shield and most of the Liberty Head series, *working dies* used in coining presses were made from *working hubs.* The process of making a working hub is delineated in detail in chapter 4, the introduction to Shield nickels. In brief, the working hub was made of hardened steel, one hub for the obverse and one for the reverse. All features were raised or in relief, appearing quite like those on an actual coin.

Working dies were created by use of a hand press (and later, beginning in the 1890's, by use of a hydraulic press) to force the working hub into a shank or cylinder of soft die steel. Afterward, the soft working die was inspected, and then given additional impressions to bring out all the details of the designs.

Adding the Date

The working die in soft steel was then taken to the Engraving Department, where a workman took a four-digit logotype punch dated, say, 1866, and drove it by hand into the die in the proper position, near the bottom of the obverse. Once that was done, the die was heated to a high temperature (turning cherry red), sustained at that temperature, and then quickly quenched in water. The sudden change of temperature crystallized and hardened the steel. The die at this point was somewhat brittle, so it was heated again, now to a medium temperature, causing a slight discoloration, after which it was slowly cooled. The die metal was then fit for coining use.

At this time, the face of the working die was rather rough, sometimes with scale or flakes from the heating and quenching process, so it was finished by filing and grinding (usually laterally), which often imparted countless tiny parallel die striae into the face. There were exceptions, and on occasion a rotating tool was used, leaving curved marks. Sometimes the die was given a light polishing to remove the striae, and other times it was not. Some dies for Shield and Liberty Head nickels were basined, giving a curvature to the fields. Policies in this regard varied over a period of time. Ready to be used for coinage, the obverse die was given a light coating of grease, to keep it from rusting due to humidity, and put in a vault.

Each year, beginning in the autumn, obverse working dies were created with the next year's date, so that coinage could begin in early January. In its unfinished state, each working die was complete with all features except the date. The steel was still soft (unhardened).

Many obverse dies were made, based upon the anticipated use for them. If the demands for coinage were to be extensive, dozens would be kept on hand, with more made throughout the year. If the coinage proved to be small, as it was from 1879 through 1881, no doubt the several dies made in the latter part of the previous year sufficed for the coinage year in question, and no others were made.

Reverse dies were created the same way, except that larger quantities could be made and stored, as, bearing no date, they did not become obsolete.

Die-making techniques evolved over the years, and no single commentary can cover all possibilities. However, in the second decade of the 20th century, the date for a given year was put on a hub, which then created a master die, with the result that the master dies were dated—thus, when working dies were made, dates did not have to be added separately. In the Liberty Head nickel series, there are slight date position differences for 1911, but none for 1912. Accordingly, it can be assumed that dated master hubs were put into use in late 1911 or in 1912. In other series, the changeover was made in 1907 or 1908.

The numismatic implication of the earlier hand-punching of the date is that Shield nickels and Liberty Head nickels can be collected and studied for minute differences in date positions or, in the Shield series, misplacements and many errors. In particular, the earlier dates in the Shield series are a playground for anyone having both a sense of curiosity and a low-power magnifying glass. Later repunchings and the like are common, but are usually slight and are not as spectacular to view.

The last year of the Liberty Head nickel saw the Denver and San Francisco mints used for the first time to make coins of this denomination. Appropriate reverse dies were hand-punched with the distinguishing letter D or S.

THE COINING PROCESS

Preparing the Planchet

Nickels are struck on planchets. For nickels, blanks were cut out of long strips of copper-nickel alloy, much as cookies are punched out of pieces of dough by a cookie cutter. Sometimes this was done at the Mint, first by using narrow strips and punching out one planchet at a time, and later (in the Jefferson series, beyond the purview of this book) by using gang punches that made a tremendous noise and stamped out multiple blanks in one blow. At other times it was the practice simply to order finished blanks from suppliers, removing the planchet-cutting process from Mint supervision. Each blank had to be of a specified diameter and with a weight of 77.16 grains, with two grains' variation (about 2.5% up or down, or about 5% overall) allowed. The diameter of a *finished* Shield nickel was 13/16ths of an inch, or 20.6 mm. The Liberty Head nickel, introduced in 1883, was slightly larger—5/6th of an inch, or 21.2 mm.

After the disk or blank was ready, it would be put into a milling or upsetting machine and run at high speed between a roller and an edge, in an area in which the diameter decreased slightly, forcing the metal up on ridges on both sides of the coin. This process created what is called a *planchet.* The resultant planchet was blank on both sides but had a raised rim.

Although processes varied over a period of years, it was customary to soften the planchets by annealing them (heating, then cooling slowly). This permitted better metal flow in the coining process. Next, the planchets were cleaned in a soapy or acidic mixture, rinsed, and then dried by tumbling in sawdust or exposing them to currents of air.

At the end of this, the dry planchets would be ready for coining. Tumbling around in a cleaning machine imparted countless nicks and marks to both sides. It was hoped that the squeezing and compression of the planchets in the coining press would obliterate these marks. In practice, as discussed below, for many coins the dies did not come completely together in the coining press, and the deepest areas of the dies, representing the highest areas on the finished coins, were not completely struck—with the result that marks from the original planchets were still visible.

Punching blanks from strips at the Philadelphia Mint. While this was sometimes done in the process of making nickel planchets, oftentimes planchets were bought ready-made from outside suppliers.

A lady (second from left) operates the milling machine while other employees deliver blank discs and take away planchets, now with raised rims on both sides.

Striking the Coins

The working dies were fitted to a coining press, at first driven by pulleys powered by steam, then in the 1890's converted to electrical operation. The typical press was vertical with more or less an elliptical frame, with an area at the center to hold the dies. The anvil, or bottom, die (sometimes the obverse and sometimes the reverse in the nickel series) was fixed firmly in position. The top, or hammer, die was fixed to a matrix that moved up and down as the flywheel on the press rotated and actuated a cam. This general type of press was called a *knuckle press*, from the mechanism's resemblance to a finger knuckle. On the top of the anvil die was mounted a collar—a flat piece of steel with a circular hole the diameter of the finished coin.

In the coining press, the obverse and reverse dies were oriented 180°. However, sometimes the anvil die would become loose and turn slightly or come out of alignment, producing coins that were different from the standards. Still other times, a die would be slightly loose in the press and would "chatter" during the coining process, producing what is called *machine doubling* on the finished coins.

During the production process, blank planchets were fed by an attendant into a tall tube mounted at the left front of the press, not far from the die. Each planchet would be grasped by mechanical fingers, taken to position, and dropped into the collar. The fingers then retracted automatically; the hammer die came down and stamped the coins, which were forced from the collar; and mechanical fingers then ejected the finished product. At that point each coin went down a slide at the back of the press that fed into a little hopper or bin.

At the Philadelphia Mint, one coining press was located so that visitors behind an iron railing could see the process. At the left, the drive belt connects to a wheel below the floor, which in turn is connected to a steam engine. The lady attendant takes planchets from the box on the pedestal to her left, and drops them into a vertical brass tube near the center of the press. After the top die comes down to strike the planchet, the new coin is ejected out the back and falls into a small box.

Why "Full Details" Coins Are Scarce

It was the intention of the Philadelphia Mint, later joined by the Denver and San Francisco mints, to produce the largest number of nickel five-cent pieces possible in the shortest amount of time and with the least amount of effort. In fact, minor coins were held in generally low regard at the mints, and less attention was paid to them than to denominations struck in precious metals. There was no consideration whatsoever to pleasing numismatists who might later collect such coins.

The sharpness of a finished nickel five-cent piece depended on the technician who adjusted the press as well as on the weight and preparation of the planchet. If the dies were fit precisely the right distance apart, and a planchet was of precisely the correct weight and annealed to ideal softness, a coin with every detail needle sharp would be the result. However, the authorization for the nickel five-cent piece permitted a 5% latitude in weight, as noted previously. If a pair of dies was adjusted perfectly in the matter just mentioned, for a planchet weighing the authorized 77.16 grains, this would result in the striking of a perfectly detailed coin on such a planchet.

If a slightly overweight, but still legal, planchet is fed into the press, the metal will have nowhere to go into the dies and will be forced out the edge, creating a wire rim (called a *fin* in mint jargon) and wearing the die in the process, or worse, cracking the die.

The obvious answer was to space the dies slightly farther apart than optimum, so that slightly overweight planchets could be accommodated and coined at high speed without attention. Under this arrangement, only overweight planchets produced perfectly struck coins, while correct-weight and underweight planchets created coins with areas of weakness.

In addition, the hardness of the planchets (resulting from poor annealing processes, poor metal flow, and design peculiarities) contributed to strike weakness in some cases. Walter Breen, Cindy Mohon, and Gloria Peters give this as a reason for the unsatisfactory surfaces of certain Proof nickels of the late 1880's.

Why Quality Is Elusive

With this information, you now know that whether coins with Full Details (FD) exist for a given variety depends on two factors: first, the weight and preparation of the planchet; and second, the spacing of the dies.

Fortunately, in the Shield and Liberty Head series the problem of strike weakness is not as severe as in the Buffalo and Jefferson series. In the companion volume to this study, *Red Book Series: Buffalo and Jefferson Nickels*, you will learn that this was a major problem on those designs—so much so that certain issues are hardly ever found sharply struck. To be sure, many if not most circulation strikes have lightness in one area or another, but few are as flat as the proverbial pancake. Not true with the Buffalo (especially) and Jefferson designs.

While it was a general rule that planchets were bright and clean, although nicked and marked, in some instances the quality of the finished nickel was poor—discolored, stained, or irregular. Again, while planchets can be a problem, the situation with Shield and Liberty Head nickels is minor compared to that with later issues. Improvements in mint technology produced the opposite effect in the quality of coins produced. Some of the most miserable nickels are Jeffersons from the 1960's!

After the box that received newly minted Shield or Liberty Head nickels at the back of the coining press was filled, it was taken by an attendant and dumped into a hopper with other nickels. Afterward, the coins, still mixed together, were run through a mechanical counting machine, then put into cloth bags and tossed into a vault, to be shipped away. At no time was any care taken to prevent nicks, marks, or other damage, including during the bagging, shipping, and delivery process.

The result of this is that very few production-run nickel five-cent pieces survived in high Mint State (MS) grades such as MS-65, 66, or 67 after such handling. A banker viewing a bag of nickels might find few coins nicer than MS-63 or so.

Producing Proof Nickels

Proof coins were made in a different manner. The die production was essentially the same, except the face of each was given a high degree of polish to create brilliant or mirror Proofs. A pair of dies was fitted into a hand-fed press located in the Medal Department of the Mint. A planchet was placed into the collar, the press actuated, and a coin struck. In most years, including in recent times, the press struck each coin twice in quick succession to bring up all details sharply. The finished coin was then removed by hand, and a new planchet inserted.

In 1893 the director of the Mint announced that the hand presses in the Medal Department had been replaced by hydraulic ones. Proof coins of 1894 and later are generally sharper and of higher quality than those of earlier years. The planchets for Proof coins were always inspected (although sometimes not carefully) to be sure they did not have chips, flakes, discoloration, or damage. They also went through a special cleaning process, after which they were dried.

After striking, Proofs in the 19th century were sometimes jumbled together in trays awaiting sale. However, the majority seem to have been treated with care. The typical Proof struck in the 19th and 20th centuries reached its intended recipient in virtually perfect condition, with few if any marks and also well struck. However, there are many exceptions, and it is somewhat of a shock to see a Proof Liberty Head nickel with several flatly struck stars or other details.

Minting and Distribution of Nickels

Quantities Minted

Nickels cost less than five cents each to produce, and, accordingly, they were continually a source of profit for the Mint, as were other coins in nickel alloy or bronze. The profit, called *seignorage*, contributed heavily to the operating profits of the various mints and, accordingly, the production of such pieces was highly encouraged. This was quite unlike the situation for silver and gold coins in the early days, when gold was of full intrinsic value, and for a long time silver was likewise, resulting in little if any profit to the mints.

The aspect of seignorage profits has been largely overlooked in numismatic accounts, but is it a major factor affecting the mintage quantities of cents, two-cent pieces, three-cent pieces, and nickels. In the five years immediately prior to the introduction of the nickel five-cent piece, the revenue from this source not only paid many Mint expenses, but returned to the Treasury a profit exceeding $1,000,000.[1] So as not to disturb this situation, Mint Director James Pollock was uncertain as to how worn minor coins should be redeemed in the future. Exchanging them for *paper money* would be more profitable than giving new coins. Eventually, redemption was made in any form the depositor requested, to the extent that minor coins or paper notes were available. It was not until 1876 that they could be swapped for silver coins, as noted below.

Over the years, demand varied for new nickels. In robust economic times new coins would be needed in quantity. Typically, during recessions or slow times, supplies on hand would fill all needs.

Mintages of Shield nickels were substantial in the late 1860's, but dropped in the next decade. There was little call for them from 1877 through 1881 because silver coins of all denominations, hoarded by the public since spring 1862, suddenly became available in commerce in quantity, the pivotal date being April 20, 1876. Vast quantities of half dimes, dimes, and the like, not seen for years, flooded banks and merchants, neutralizing any demand that might have arisen for new nickel five-cent pieces. In 1877 and 1878 only Proofs were made for collectors, and from 1879 through 1881, production was small for the reasons just stated. In the latter year, as the reserves ran low, large-scale production resumed. Political pressure applied by Joseph Wharton contributed to the Mint's output as well. In 1881 he engineered an attempt once again to have nickel used for one-cent pieces.

In April 1883, *Banker's Magazine* reported that nickels were scarce in California. In the South, the smaller-denomination minor coins were not popular, despite many attempts to get the population to use them. Further:

> Daily newspapers in the South, which in New England would sell for a penny or two, go for five cents. To buy a three-cent stamp a two-cent stamp must be accepted in change. New York manufacturers of penny wares put them into five-cent packets for most of the trade below Mason and Dixon's line. Nearly everywhere there a cent piece is a rarity, and in some of the towns not reached by a railroad it is a curiosity.

A real demand for five-cent pieces all across the nation took place when coin-operated devices, mostly using nickels, became popular in the 1890's. The need for nickels grew with the increased number of nickelodeon theaters, vending machines, and amusement machines made in the early 20th century.

From that time until the end of the Liberty Head nickel series, officially in 1912, mintage quantities were in the millions each year.

As you can see from the preceding, an "ordinary" nickel can be quite complex if the various aspects of die making, planchet preparation, striking, market demand, and distribution are considered! This is what has made the series fascinating to so many enthusiasts.

The Philadelphia Mint

From 1866 through 1911, nickel five-cent pieces were made only at the Philadelphia Mint. From the 1860's through the 1880's, there was not much demand for nickel five-cent pieces in the Midwest or West. Silver coins, which had been hoarded in the East and Midwest since spring 1862, were not hoarded in the West, and half dimes, dimes, and other denominations continued to circulate freely. More important, westerners simply did not like "small change." Indian Head cents were not popular there either, as reflected in many Mint reports. In the early 1880's, there was a great deal of interest in the new Liberty Head nickels, and supplies were sent to the Pacific states. Beginning in the 1890's, coin-operated machines and, later, theaters and amusement devices became as popular there as anywhere else.

All 19th-century nickels were coined at the second Philadelphia Mint, the cornerstone of which had been laid on January 4, 1829, in a ceremony in which silver half dimes were given out. By the time that the nickel five-cent piece became a reality in 1866, many improvements had been made, including in the processes used to create dies and in the use of steam power to drive presses and other machines.

In late 1901, coinage operations were transferred to the new, larger third Philadelphia Mint, equipped with new apparatus mostly driven by electricity. This building remained in use until the fourth Philadelphia Mint was inaugurated in 1967.

During these transitions the Philadelphia Mint remained the center for creating designs and making dies. The Engraving Department was and is headquartered there. The Mint Collection was also on display at this facility.

In 1912, the Denver and San Francisco mints produced nickel five-cent pieces for the first time. Information concerning them is given in chapter 7.

The second Philadelphia Mint opened in January 1833.

3

How to Be a Smart Buyer

Focusing on Nickels

Introduction

So many nickels and so little time. Actually, I suppose that no numismatist ever lacks time to buy another coin or two or even a few hundred. However, the nickel five-cent series from 1866 to date has *so many* pieces that forming a collecting strategy is a good idea.

No matter how you decide to build a collection, you will be *buying* most of the pieces. There is no hope of finding a Shield or Liberty Head nickel in pocket change, although perhaps one or two are among family heirlooms. Accordingly, aspiring to be a "smart buyer" is a worthwhile endeavor. First, the more you know, the better position you are in to cherrypick for the best values in an arena where the vast majority of your competitors are not smart! Second, being a smart buyer increases the challenge and therefore the enjoyment of the series. Third, you will be completely free of aggravation because you will avoid buying coins that are not worthwhile. They will not become annoyances later. It is always easy to buy nickels or anything else in haste and to repent in leisure. Buy with knowledge, and you will not have to repent.

Further, smart buyers enjoy themselves more. Try it and see!

Ways to Collect Nickel Five-Cent Pieces

Nickel five-cent pieces, from day one (1866) to the present time, neatly break down into four major categories, including the Shield, Liberty Head, Buffalo, and Jefferson series. The Shield and Liberty Head series are discussed in the following text with three chapters devoted to each, the first in each instance being the history of the type, the second containing numismatic information and suggestions, and the third being a listing of dates and varieties.

For the two motifs now under consideration, a type set consists of just four coins:

- 1866 and 1867 Shield With Rays
- 1867 to 1883 Shield Without Rays
- 1883 Liberty Head Without CENTS
- 1883 to 1913 Liberty Head With CENTS

None of the above types are at all rare, although the first type of the Shield nickel can be expensive if you desire a gem Mint State or Proof example. Building a type set is a fine way to get acquainted with nickel five-cent pieces. If you later decide to expand and build a date set, the type coins can be used in it. The later Buffalo and Jefferson nickels are very inexpensive for type pieces.

Before starting your type set, check market prices in current listings to determine the grades you want and the money you wish to spend for them. This is important for the first several coins, as examples in high grades beyond MS-65 can be very expensive.

For the Shield nickels, choice or gem Mint State or Proof would be going first class, but, certainly, there is nothing wrong with a pleasing Very Fine (VF) or Extremely Fine (EF). It is your choice.

Liberty Head nickels are less expensive, and even the fascinating 1883 Without CENTS is abundant. I recommend MS-60 as a minimum, but if it is in your budget, then buy gem Mint State or gem Proof for each of these two types.

Even a basic type set can be spiced with interesting pieces. For example, you could pick a Shield nickel that displays many die cracks—most of the early years have such. Perhaps for the 1883 to 1913 Liberty Head series, a fine choice would be a 1912-D—an unusual mintmark as well as a variety that seems to be somewhat overlooked in the marketplace. Read about the possibilities, then pick coins you find to be interesting.

Picking a Nickel Specialty

While the following chapters provide as much information as you probably want, and perhaps even more than that, here is an overview of collecting each of the two motifs covered in this book.

Shield nickels, made from 1866 to 1883, offer a veritable wonderland of curious die varieties, particularly repunched dates, doubled dies, misplaced dates, and other mistakes and sloppy practices of making the working dies. Of course, whenever the Mint makes a mistake about anything, collectors rejoice! Just about any Shield nickel specialist will say that he or she would rather spend an hour with a magnifying glass looking at two dozen assorted Shield nickels to find doubled dies, repunched dates, die cracks, and other things, than looking at 200 Jefferson nickels. However, the latter design also has its attractions.

One beauty of Shield nickels is that there are no "impossible rarities." Each basic date is easily obtainable. As to the minor varieties, they are legion. No collector ever has or ever will get one of each unusual variety, so you simply pick up pieces here and there as opportunities present themselves.

Liberty Head nickels from 1883 to 1912 can be collected easily enough, although 1885, 1886, and 1912-S examples are elusive. The 1913, of which just five are known, is in a different category. I personally like Liberty Head nickels because they invoke an incredibly romantic era. Examined carefully, Liberty Head nickels have their own secrets—such as the little-known aspects of sharp striking. Already you know why some nickels have Full Details (FD) and why others do not.

Authenticity

In the marketplace, particularly on the Internet, in antique shops and shows, and at gun shows, there are many fakes, alterations, and other non-genuine coins. The 1913 Liberty Head nickel has been faked countless times, by altering a 1903, 1910, or some other coin. However, no one in his or her right mind would buy a 1913 Liberty Head nickel without first having it checked out. Or would they? Actually, *many* have been sold, usually on the Internet, or in antique shops, or in other venues, where such coins are offered with a comment such as, "I know nothing about old coins, but someone said this one is rare. I didn't pay much, so I offer it as-is for $500."

The leading grading services often guarantee *authenticity* of what they encapsulate, but policies are subject to change, and I am not aware of any single source where you can keep tabs on changing grading policies. My advice is to contact your favorite service and ask for a written copy of any guarantees the service provides. There have been more than 100 grading services in business since the 1980's, and some have sold fakes and/or vastly overgraded coins. Stick with your pick among the top several leaders, but ask around among dealers and collectors before making a choice.

Fakes and alterations will be no problem at all if you follow the above guidelines, and if you can resist buying "bargains."

Four Steps to Success

Beyond the Numbers

Another aspect of logical decision making that is important for you to know, but that is not discussed in the wide marketplace, is that for any Proof Shield or Liberty Head nickel to be other than gem grade, say PF-65 or better, it has to have been subject to some handling. If it has hairlines, this is because the coin has been cleaned. However, the grading services are inconsistent as to how they handle such situations. Generally, a Shield nickel with, say, hairlines, will be graded less than PF-65—perhaps PF-62 or PF-63. If the cleaning is severe, it might be called PF-60. A correct listing would be as follows: "PF-62 due to hairlines from cleaning." Some services will return a coin ungraded if it has been *severely* cleaned, others may put a "net grade" on it, and the like. There is little consistency in this regard. However, most coins in the numerical ranges of 60 to 63 have not been submitted to the grading services, as the market values of these coins are not high for most varieties.

Any Shield or Liberty Head nickel, if as brilliant as when first minted, including a bright edge, is a coin that has been dipped (immersed in a liquid silver cleaner or chemical metal brightener). Conversely, Shield or Liberty Head nickels that have been held until the present day by the most careful of numismatists and their successors will *always* show some light toning. I know this from great experience in having handled some of the finest collections ever—including those that were assembled when Shield and Liberty nickels were being struck, and that have been carefully preserved as family heirlooms or in museums ever since.

Then there is the matter of sharpness of strike. Some nickels are flat in areas, while others have Full Details (FD). Most circulation-strike nickels are a compromise, this being especially true for high-mintage dates. In the Shield and Liberty Head nickel series, needle-sharp pieces can be found for every issue except 1912-S. Your challenge is to find them, a pleasant endeavor.

You can see that the nomenclature, such as MS-63, PF-67, or whatever, doesn't tell you much if you really want to be a connoisseur. Instead, you need to apply your own expertise and thinking. Suggestions are found in the chapters that follow. Among the nickel series, no single rule fits all—and what I might say for an 1866 Shield nickel, which usually has problems, would not be appropriate to an 1883 Shield nickel, which is usually very well struck, on a good planchet, and with excellent eye appeal.

Some time ago, for Whitman Publishing, LLC, I devised the following four-step process. It has caught on with a number of readers who have applied it to their own fields of interest. Adapted for the present text, here it is.

Step 1: Numerical Grade on the Holder

You are holding a coin in your hand. Should you buy it? Your first step is to look at the assigned grade of the coin, or, if you are familiar with grading, to assign your own number. Experienced collectors and dealers will often share their opinions with you—without being an annoyance, see if you can ask around for help.

If you are just entering numismatics, you would do well to consider only those coins that have been certified by the four leading grading services (listed alphabetically): ANACS, Independent Coin Grading (ICG), Numismatic Guaranty Corporation (NGC), and the Professional Coin Grading Service (PCGS). ANACS, NGC, and PCGS each publish population reports delineating the coins that have passed through their hands. There are other grading services, and you might want to check them out. At present, however, the companies mentioned above seem to be the most widely used by advanced collectors, with NGC and PCGS capturing the lion's share of the business. Price information for many commercially graded coins can be found in numerous places, in particular the *Monthly Greysheet.*

The grade listed on a certified coin holder (popularly called a *slab*) is simply the *starting point* in the buying process. *This is one of the most important concepts for success.*

When you visit a coin shop or a convention, or contemplate a catalog or Internet offering, have an approximate grade in mind for each coin you are seeking. If you are looking for an 1867 Shield nickel of the scarce With Rays variety, and have $200 to spend, there is not much sense asking to see MS-65 or other high-grade coins, nor is there any reason to waste your time looking at well-worn pieces in G-4 or VG-8 grades. These are the prices for an 1867, With Rays nickel, from the 2026 *Guide Book of United States Coins*: G-4, $36; VG-8, $49; F-12, $75; EF-40, $210; AU-50, $265; MS-60, $420; MS-63, $725.

At a coin show, or when sending a "want list" to a dealer, if your budget is about $200, ask to see coins in the range of EF-40 to AU-50, as these are more or less in the price range you want to pay.

No matter what grades you ask for, reject any that seem to be overgraded. This comment is with the realization that you will need some experience, for lacking this, you will not know. The best way to gain experience is to visit a coin show or a coin shop and look through as many Shield and Liberty Head nickels as you can (perhaps a few to several dozen or more). Few dealers have deep inventories in Liberty Head nickels, and fewer yet in the earlier Shield series. Today the Internet offers some at-home opportunities. While the grade may be hard to figure out from a low-resolution Internet image, and the angle of the light on a coin can make it look more attractive than it really is, other aspects, such as sharpness, can be discerned.

Read *The Official American Numismatic Association Grading Standards for United States Coins.* Spend time looking at nickels, preferably in person, perhaps with this book in your hand. If you do this at a show or in a shop, it is good form to advise the dealer what you are doing—seeking education—and to make a courtesy purchase of a coin or a book or two. In less time than you realize, you will learn the fundamentals of grading.

Step 2: Eye Appeal at First Glance

Now, the process becomes easier! At this point take a quick glance at the coin. Is it pretty? Is the toning (if present) attractive, or is it dark or blotchy? Is the coin stained? If it is brilliant, is it attractively lustrous, or is it dull and lifeless? Are there black spots on the surface? Here the Internet can offer many opportunities for education. While writing this book, I viewed hundreds of nickels on the Internet—and found that most pictures posted by sellers and auctioneers are quite good. However, it is common to adjust the light or exposure, or to change the color of a digital photograph, to make a coin look nicer than it really is. Because of this, Internet photographs, as well as photographs in dealers' printed catalogs, are just a starting point. You should make your final decision only by inspecting a coin in person. If you buy on the Internet or by mail, insist on a return privilege if *for any reason* you do not like the coin. If the vendor will not extend you this courtesy, find another seller.

If the coin is not attractive, then reject it and go on to look at another. Even if the price seems to be a super-bargain, cast the coin aside. Stop right here, and go back to step 1 with another coin. An ugly coin graded as MS-65 is still ugly, and if it were my decision I would not buy it for *half* the current market price! Do not be tempted by overgraded and/or ugly coins offered at "below wholesale" prices. Keep your wallet in your pocket. The good news is that Shield and Liberty Head nickels are easier to find with good eye appeal than are Indian Head cents, two-cent pieces, and Liberty Seated and Barber silver coins from the same era. Among certified coins, eye appeal rises with the numerical grade. A PF-64 is more likely to have spots or discoloration than a PF-66. However, there are many exceptions in the marketplace.

If the coin is attractive to your eye, then in some distant future year when the time comes to sell it, the piece will be attractive to the eyes of other buyers, an important aspect. Now, with an attractive coin in hand, you have a candidate *for your further consideration.*

Step 3: Sharpness and Related Features

At this point you have a coin you believe to be more or less in the numerical grade assigned on the ANACS, ICG, NGC, or PCGS holder, or if you are in the fast lane, determined by your own experience. You also have for consideration one that has passed your test for excellent eye appeal.

The next step is to take out a magnifying glass and evaluate its sharpness. Here, no one rule fits all, and for a given nickel, check out the specific listing for it in this book. You will learn what to look for—the horizontal lines on the obverse of a Shield nickel might be weak; on a Liberty Head nickel, there is that all-important ear of corn on the reverse to the left of the ribbon bow—these are just a couple of the guidelines you will use. The grades on certified holders are of no help at all regarding sharpness of details. A Liberty Head nickel can be certified as MS-66 or MS-67 and have flat areas in the design.

To determine sharpness, you must examine the coin! There is *no* alternative unless you enlist a trustworthy dealer or friend to do this for you. By reading this book you will know how easy or how difficult it is to find a Full Details example for a given variety—if it's difficult, you can compromise slightly.

Also check for surface quality. Is the luster satiny (or frosty), with full sheen—or is the coin struck from overused dies showing metal flow and granularity? Again, certified holders reveal nothing about this. Is the planchet of good quality, or is it rough? Generally, Proofs are more sharply struck and present fewer difficulties than do circulation strikes, this being particularly true for early dates in the Shield nickel series.

If the coin you are considering buying has passed the preceding tests, it is ready for further consideration. Chances are good that you are holding a very nice coin in your hand!

Step 4: Establishing a Fair Market Price

You've done everything right; you have a coin that is correctly graded, of superb eye appeal, and sharply struck (a realistic goal for all basic dates in the series except the 1912-S). Now, to the price you should pay.

For starters, use one or several handy market guides for a ballpark estimate. Unlike many other specialties, nearly all issues in the Shield and Liberty Head series are actively traded, and there is no lack of information. For pattern coins (see appendix A) the situation is quite different, and offerings can be infrequent.

Now comes the fun part: If the coin is common enough in a given grade, with sharp strike, with fine planchet quality, and with good eye appeal, then the market price is very relevant, as you can shop around. If a coin is common in the grade you want, and with all other desired features, and you have ascertained that the market price level is about $700, then there is no sense paying $800 or $950. Wait until you find one at or near $700. On the other hand, chances are good that you will not find a problem-free coin for, say, $500 or $600. If something is offered to you for below wholesale, this simply means that any dealer wanting to buy a choice coin will not buy *this* one—and, accordingly, it is available for less!

You are very lucky in that, for Shield and Liberty Head nickels, hardly anyone looks at sharpness and overall quality. This is amazing, but true. You are also lucky that each and every issue does exist with Full Details, save for the 1912-S. Bide your time until you find them. When you do, the market premium will be modest or even nonexistent over a typical coin of lower quality.

Also consider what might be the optimal collecting grade for the issue. That is, in instances in which a very small difference in grade makes a very large difference in price, opt for the lower grade. If a nickel is priced at $1,000 in MS-65 and $2,000 in MS-66, the MS-65 might offer you the most coin for the money, as grading is a matter of opinion anyway, and there is little difference between the two levels.

Taking Your Time

If you follow these steps, each coin you acquire for your collection will be a very nice example of its date and, for 1912, branch mint, from an aesthetic viewpoint. In terms of the price you pay, it will be a worthwhile purchase, as you will know what is rare and what is not, and what degree of striking sharpness is available (the subsequent chapters give details).

The negative, if it could be called that, is that connoisseurship takes time. You cannot simply go to a convention, walk by bourse tables, write checks willy-nilly, and come home with a decent set of Shield or Liberty Head nickels. It has never happened.

At the outset, buy the less expensive varieties. It would be a mistake to start out with the rarities, for if you make mistakes, and you probably will, they will be more expensive. Start slowly and before you know it, you will become confident in your abilities.

Buy each coin carefully, keeping in mind the value received. If a coin is common in MS-63 or MS-64 but an ultra-rarity and super-expensive in MS-66 to MS-69, buy a nice MS-64 or thereabouts, and use the extra money to add other varieties. (At least, that is what I would do.) Also be aware that population reports keep enlarging as more coins are certified. I have seen time and again the situation in which a coin was a supposed rarity in, say, MS-67, with just one certified years ago, but now there are dozens.

Also remember that basic scarcity and rarity never go out of style. Such issues as 1867 With Rays, 1877, 1878, 1885, 1886, and 1912-S were rare 20 years ago and will be rare 20 years hence. On the other hand, that "rare" common-date Liberty Head nickel from the early 1900's, now standing as the only MS-68 certified example, might have dozens of companions 20 years hence!

Time Yields Quality and Enjoyment

At this point you can adopt your own mindset. You can either do as 90% of purchasers do and "buy the slab," which means simply buy the coin because it has been commercially graded at a certain level. In that way you can tell a friend, "I have an MS-64 1886 Liberty Head nickel," or "I have a rare 1912-S MS-65 nickel." By this method you will able to breeze through all of the nickel series and have a complete collection in just about any grade you want and spend little time building it. After that point, you can go on and collect Morgan dollars, commemoratives, or whatever.

Alternatively, you can savor the experience, like being at a royal banquet rather than a drive-through fast food restaurant. Contemplate each variety one by one, selecting for your plate the pieces that seem to be very special. Just as the royal banquet might well occupy an entire evening as opposed to five minutes driving through a hamburger stand, collecting a set of sharply struck Mint State Shield nickels will take time; ditto for Liberty Head nickels. The experience of searching for the right coins—the pursuit of excellence at a reasonable price—can bring much satisfaction.

My estimate is that it will take a year or two to assemble a set of 1866 to 1912 nickels in choice or gem Mint State and Proof preservation, mixed with some of one style and some of the other. A full set of Proofs is doable, except for the 1867 With Rays, which is rare and expensive—but does come on the market now and again. Completing a set of Mint State nickels in choice or gem preservation will be harder to do, as really nice examples of such issues as 1867 With Rays, 1880, 1885, and 1886 are very hard to find.

4

Shield Nickels 1866–1883: History and Background

The Shield Nickel Design

Patriotic Motifs

Without a doubt, the Shield nickel design is one of the most patriotic motifs in American coinage. Douglas L. Kurz, who has spent many enjoyable years collecting the series and communicating with others of like interest, gives this view:

> The shield motif is patterned after the "Union Shield" that appears on the Great Seal of the United States of America. The elements of the shield are meant to represent the American flag, with its colors of red, white, and blue (represented in heraldic engravure by vertical lines, clear areas, and horizontal lines, respectively).
>
> The 13 vertical stripes on the shield thus alternate red (*gules* in heraldry) and white (*argent*). Vertical stripes are called *pales*, and this area of 13 stripes is called the *paleways*, which represents the 13 colonies. The area of horizontal stripes above the paleways is called the *chief*. It is the color blue (*azure*) and is meant to represent the Congress of the United States.
>
> There is so much American history implicit in the shield design, it really needs to be brought to light. Many criticisms of the obverse seem to be a lack of understanding of the symbolic significance of the motifs.

General Comments

In some instances Chief Engraver James B. Longacre copied and adapted his earlier work and the artistry of others. It was easier to use an old motif than to create a new one. His Flying Eagle cent of 1856 combined Christian Gobrecht's eagle (after a sketch by Titian Peale) from the reverse of the 1836 silver dollar with Longacre's own "agricultural" wreath used on the gold dollar and $3 coin of 1854.

So it was with the Shield nickel. The obverse is essentially a copy of the two-cent piece of 1864, while the reverse is a mechanical, rather than artistic, work—made by punching symbols and letters into a steel hub. Early issues had rays between the stars, a feature discontinued in early 1867. Today, the With Rays style is capitalized in listings, as is Without Rays (alternatively, No Rays). With Rays is sometimes abbreviated as WR and the other as NR. In the 19th century, the designation *stars and bars* was given for the With Rays type (e.g., in J.W. Scott & Co. catalogs). The stars-and-bars nomenclature, with the significant number of 13 each, could well be added to Douglas Kurz's comments about the patriotic obverse—the reverse was patriotic, too!

The reverse is quite similar to that used on certain tokens made by John Stanton, die cutter and operator of a Cincinnati shop that turned out many Civil War tokens and other issues. It is likely that Stanton simply copied the Shield nickel design of 1867 without rays on the reverse—making it likely that they technically are not part of the Civil War series (since that conflict lasted from April 1861 to April 1865).

This was an era of similarity in coin designs. Silver coins from the half dime to the dollar all used the same Liberty Seated design; $1 and $3 gold pieces each had the Indian Princess motif; and $2.50, $5, and $10 coins depicted the same Liberty Head. As will be seen under the history of the Liberty Head nickel, in 1881 thought was given to standardizing the designs of the cent, three-cent, and nickel five-cent pieces (the trime having been discontinued in 1873). Just the opposite occurred in the early 20th century, when a passion arose for artistry in coinage, with most denominations being changed to distinctively different designs.

The Life of James B. Longacre

Chief Engraver James B. Longacre had a profound influence, not only as the creator of the Shield nickel but also as the originator of the majority of regular-issue and pattern coins from the late 1840's until his death on January 1, 1869.[1]

James Barton Longacre was born in Delaware County, Pennsylvania, on August 11, 1794, son of Peter Longacre. Of Swedish ancestry, he descended from a family originally known as Longaker (Longker in some citations). At an early age he developed an interest in art and literature and demonstrated skill in sketching. In his youth, he entered the family of John F. Watson, a Philadelphia bookstore owner, for whom he served as an apprentice in the book shop. (Today, Watson is remembered for his *Annals of Philadelphia.*)

From there, he became apprenticed to George Murray, a Scottish immigrant who was a partner in Murray, Draper, Fairman & Co., bank-note and scenic engravers located at 47 Sansom Street. Principals included George Murray, John Draper, Gideon Fairman, and Jacob Perkins. Perkins was prominent in both bank-note and coin engraving and was a predecessor to Longacre in this pattern of activity, except for the coin dies, which preceded bank-note plates for Perkins.

Watercolor self-portrait of James B. Longacre, circa the 1840s. Longacre, designer of the Shield nickel, served as chief engraver at the Mint from 1844 to 1869.

Murray, Draper, Fairman & Co. was preeminent in the bank-note field and had customers from the Atlantic coast to the prairie lands west of Pennsylvania. In 1819 Longacre established his own business, emphasizing the engraving of portraits. His first important commission was plates for the 1820 edition of S.F. Bradford's *Encyclopedia.* A print of Andrew Jackson, from a portrait by Thomas Sully, achieved wide sales. In the 1820's, Longacre acquitted himself well in the making of portrait plates, from the original art of others, to illustrate John Sanderson's nine-volume *Biographies of the Signers of the Declaration of Independence.*

About 1830, in partnership with John Herring, he began the *American Portrait Gallery*, better known later as the *National Portrait Gallery of Distinguished Americans.* Published in four volumes from 1834 to 1839, its 147 biographies of prominent Americans were accompanied by a portrait of each and was recognized as one of the most important historical publications of the time. Longacre did 24 of the engravings himself, in the stipple or shaded manner, and created sketches or preliminary artwork for many of the others. In the meantime he took on other commissions. On February 25, 1832, *Niles' Register* included this singular tribute to his ability:

> The first volume of the new edition of Marshall's life of Washington—written by the celebrated judge—has just been completed by the publisher at Philadelphia. The *National Gazette* states that the portrait of Washington, engraved for this work by Mr. Longacre, is one of the finest specimens of American advancement in the art. In Europe, it would be deemed worthy of the reputation of any engraver of London or Paris.

Circa 1833 he became a partner with John Draper, Charles Toppan, and Marcus Bull in the short-lived firm of Draper, Toppan, Longacre & Bull, maker of bank-note plates and other engravings on metal. In 1834 he joined two of the same men to form Draper, Toppan, Longacre & Co., where he remained until 1839. His period of activity there coincided with a great rush of business for bank-note firms, precipitated by the demand for bills to take the place of hoarded coins during the Panic of 1837. At the time, his company had its main office at 60 Walnut Street, Philadelphia, and a branch at One Wall Street, in the heart of New York City's financial district. The output of Draper, Toppan, Longacre & Co. was of very high quality and also extensive. Today, the numerous bills of this firm are highly appreciated by numismatists. In the meantime, his *National Portrait Gallery* continued to sell well through several editions and bindings, and became a necessity for public and college libraries as well as a fine addition to private bookshelves.

On September 16, 1844, through the influence of Senator John C. Calhoun of South Carolina, Longacre was named chief engraver at the Philadelphia Mint, succeeding the late Christian Gobrecht. He soon found that he had entered a hornet's nest of intrigue, politics, and infighting, dominated by Franklin Peale, the chief coiner since 1839, who used Mint men, dies, and equipment to run his own private medal business, and who even sent Mint personnel to do work at his private residence.[2] Peale controlled access to many, if not most, of the hubs and master dies for coins and medals, and in other ways was in a position to stymie the work of the chief engraver. To make matters worse, Peale was close to the Mint director, Robert M. Patterson, although no evidence has been found to indicate that the latter participated in Peale's private entrepreneurial activities. Longacre was widely criticized by Peale and Patterson as being incompetent or worse, the usual thread being that while he may have been a superb engraver of illustration and bank-note plates, he had no abilities as a coin-die engraver.

When Longacre experienced difficulties, such as in bringing the portrait on the pattern 1849 double eagle up to the proper relief, this criticism was used against him. Complaints of Longacre's so-called incompetence reached the Treasury secretary, William Meredith, to whom Longacre was forced to defend his position in the face of Patterson's threats to replace him. Indeed, Patterson is said to have offered the position to Charles Cushing Wright, a well-known engraver and portrait artist of the time, before approaching the subject of Longacre's dismissal! After successfully defending himself, Longacre began significant experimentation with coinage beginning in 1850. A wealth of Longacre's designs sprinkles numismatic history through 1869. The paper trail of all of this created the Longacre stigma, which was advanced in July 1883, long after Longacre's passing, when Patterson E. DuBois contributed a biographical sketch to the *American Journal of Numismatics*, including this:

> Mr. Longacre was appointed Engraver of the Mint, Sept. 16, 1844. He found himself in a new field of labor, as the art of die-sinking is quite distinct from that of plate-engraving. The result was that the double-eagle obverse was severely criticized, upon the ground that the relief was too high.

In the 1950's, numismatic historian Walter Breen excoriated Longacre many times, calling him responsible for the various blunders in date-logotype punching during his tenure, but overlooking the fact that, for example, on the 1843 quarter-eagle dies, the 18 and 43 are from two different-sized fonts, this happening before Longacre was appointed! In any event, the punching of date logotypes into dies was likely done by assistants (under the direction of Franklin Peale), as the work required no artistic talent.

In December 1854, Director James Ross Snowden kicked Franklin Peale out, engendering a huge storm of protest. The Senate mounted an investigation, and Peale submitted testimony and a memorial on his own behalf, seeking $30,000 compensation for certain of his inventions, and other redress.[3] However, Director Snowden examined the claims, and in a letter to Treasury Secretary James Guthrie, July 29, 1856, he demolished many of Peale's assertions by identifying other people who'd accomplished much of what Peale had claimed for himself. Peale never returned. After that time, life at the Mint was easier for Longacre. Still, Peale's memory seemed to pervade the Mint. Years later, in March 1861, when *Harper's New Monthly Magazine* treated its readers to an illustrated tour of the Mint, Peale was mentioned in a favorable light.[4] Excerpt:

> We can not conclude without a tribute to the skill and genius of Mr. Franklin Peale, brother to the late Rembrandt Peale. In 1833 he was appointed assistant assayer, and ordered to spend two years in examining the European mints, which he did, returning in 1835 laden with plans of improvements much needed in our then very imperfect Mint. In 1836 he was appointed melter and refiner; and while performing those duties introduced the beautiful process . . . of precipitating chloride of silver by means of common salt—a much quicker and cheaper process than the old one, requiring the use of copper. He is not the discoverer of this method, but the first to apply it to a practical use on a large scale. In 1838 [*sic*; actually 1839] Mr. Peale was appointed chief coiner, and we have seen traces of his skill in the various machines employed. It is safe for the visitor to ascribe to his ingenuity—either in design, improvement, or construction—almost any machinery in the Mint which is finished, complete, or compact. In 1854 Mr. Peale was removed by the President.
>
> This removal was certainly unfortunate, as mainly to the efforts of Mr. Peale America is indebted for the finest mint in the world. An attaché of the Royal Mint, London, recently visited ours at Philadelphia. As he was leaving, he remarked to the coiner, "When you come to London, I beg you not to visit our mint. You are a hundred years in advance of us."

Today, Peale is one of several Mint people who can be viewed from many different angles, each perspective leading certain writers to draw widely differing conclusions.

Returning to Longacre's biography, prior to his creation of the Shield nickel in 1866, the chief engraver had posted a long string of accomplishments in 22 years of Mint service. His first important work involved the gold dollar and double eagle, authorized under the Act of March 3, 1849. Although the gold dollar design required adjustments, and the double eagle was a great challenge, the final coins were well received. The gold dollar was modified in 1854 and again in 1856. The 1857 Flying Eagle and 1859 Indian Head cents were Longacre's work, as were the 1864 two-cent piece, the 1851 trime, the 1865 nickel three-cent piece, and the 1854 $3 gold coin. The Flying Eagle cent obverse utilized an earlier motif by Christian Gobrecht.

At the behest of various Mint directors, Longacre prepared dozens of different pattern coins from the late 1840's onward, some for true pattern and experimental purposes, but most for the private profit of those in charge at the Mint. I have located no evidence that Longacre was involved in such illegal actions, other than carrying out orders. Indeed, Longacre is reputed to have been of a quiet demeanor, task oriented, and strictly ethical in the duties of his office.

As Longacre had every right to do, he often copied his own work in regular issues as well as patterns. The facial features of the Indian Head cent and certain of his gold coins are identical, although the headdresses are different. Certain of his Liberty heads, wreaths, and the like are similar. From time to time, he was aided in his work by Anthony C. Paquet, Peter Cross, and William H. Key, among others.

Longacre continued as chief engraver until his death, on New Year's Day, 1869. On January 21, 1870, the numismatic part of his estate was auctioned by Thomas & Sons, 139 and 141 South Street, Philadelphia. Included in the sale were many patterns and regular coin issues that he had kept as souvenirs. Certain of Longacre's designs were continued at the Mint, including on new die combinations of patterns, into the early 1870's.

In 1928 Longacre was recognized in an exhibition of 100 notable American engravers at the New York City Public Library. Today, Longacre is widely admired by numismatists, several of whom—most notably R.W. Julian, Thomas DeLorey, and John Dannreuther—have endeavored to clarify the record of his accomplishments.[5]

Obverse Design of the Shield Nickel

Description

As noted, the obverse of the Shield nickel loosely copies the motif used on Longacre's bronze two-cent piece of 1864. On the nickel, a shield dominates the center and is composed of a frame made of scrolls to the sides and bottom, parallel lines at the upper left and right, and scrolls at the top. Within the shield are finely spaced horizontal lines filling the top, below which are six groups of closely spaced lines with seven vertical empty areas, together constituting 13 vertical stripes. David W. Lange suggests *Baroque shield* as a description for this design.[6]

Above the top center of the shield is a ring-shaped ornament or annulet over which is a cross-like ornament with a dagger-point base, called by some a *pattee cross* (a cross with triangular arms that are widest at their tips) touching the top of the annulet. Regarding this attribution, Howard Spindel gives a broader view:

> There are differences of opinion as to whether the cross is really a pattee cross (cross patté) or not. According to Wescott's book, the pattee cross is not strictly correct. He says a pattee cross is supposed to have three lobes on each end resembling a lion's paw (*patté* being French for *paw*). Walter Breen thought it possibly a Cross of the Order of Calatrava, but it doesn't look like that to me either. Perhaps it is simply a cross that Longacre liked, and not intended to be a specific type of cross. Without knowing Longacre's thinking, we can't know for sure.
>
> Perhaps it is best simply to document it as a cross without calling it a specific kind of cross. There is a great deal of information in print and on the Web about crosses, often conflicting.[7]

To the left and right, outside the shield, are clusters of laurel leaves in groups of (from top to bottom on either side) three, four, four, and three leaves, along with five berries per side. The curved ornaments at the top of the shield are properly called *curlarms*. Below the bottom scroll frame of the shield to each side is an arrow feather and, below it, an arrowhead; curved projecting ornaments (with no specific agreed-upon term to describe them); and, at the bottom tip of the shield, a rounded cartouche with a raised rim, elongated and slightly elliptical to left and right (usually referred to as a *ball*). Below the ball is space for the four-digit date logotype punch to be stamped. Along the top border in small letters is the motto IN GOD WE TRUST. Denticles decorate the inner rim.

From Model to Working Die

Likely the shield design was created by James B. Longacre in the form of a large, raised wax model, perhaps four to six inches across, carefully sculpted. This probably consisted of the shield frame elements, curved projecting ornaments below the shield, and the ball, *but not the arrow elements.* At the top, the wax model included the pattee cross, the annulet below it, and leaves to each side. All features were in relief (raised above the surface).

Not included were the horizontal and vertical lines within the shield, the lettering IN GOD WE TRUST, or the date. The berries may have been omitted as well.

In the mid-1860's there were several ways of using wax models to create coins. A probable scenario was that Longacre used the wax model to make a plaster impression, which would have had the design incuse, or intaglio (carved below the surface), in the plaster. Then the plaster mold was filled with molten metal (iron, copper, or brass), and a casting, positive with the features in relief, was made. Alternatively, the electrotype process could have been used to make a copper impression.

1. The Master Hub (Positive, in Relief)

The finished metal model, several times the size of the final product, was then examined by Longacre, and any roughness was smoothed or cut away. The metal model was then placed in a Contamin transfer lathe (a.k.a. *portrait lathe*). The model slowly rotated in synchrony with a soft steel hub rotating a short distance away. Connecting the two rotating surfaces was a pantograph arm; at one end of the arm, a stylus traced the surface features of the metal model; at the other end, a tiny cutting head worked the hub, duplicating the features on the model in miniature, creating a master hub. The process usually took more than a day, sometimes two. All of the features were raised, as on the larger version. The small version in soft steel was examined and, if necessary, touched up. It was then heated to a sustained high temperature, after which it was suddenly quenched, to harden the molecular structure. Again examined and finessed to remove any scaling or debris, the master hub was now almost complete.

2. The First-Generation Master Die (Negative, Incused)

The next step was to press the master hub, with its raised features, into a soft shank of steel to create the master die, with the features incuse (recessed). When completed, this soft master die was given to the engraver, who punched IN GOD WE TRUST at the top, letter by letter, then scribed the horizontal and vertical lines (probably with the aid of a ruling machine, not with a hand instrument), and possibly punched in the berries and stems. The vertical line groups on the shield were not carefully spaced, and it can be seen that the ones to the left are closer together than the ones to the right. Denticles were added to the border. This incuse master die was then heated, quenched, and again inspected and finessed.

Reducing lathe at the Philadelphia Mint, late 19th century. This was the Hill portrait lathe, developed in England in 1858. Its design was based on Contamin principles, but was not as effective (per Mint correspondence of the era). In 1906 a Janvier lathe was installed, and was a great improvement.

3. The Second-Generation Master Hub (Positive, in Relief)

The second-generation master hub was made in the same way—by pressing the master die slowly into a soft shank of steel and creating a master hub with all features in relief, in effect a representation of the obverse of the coin, but without a date.

The second-generation master hub then went through the hardening process. Afterward it was cleaned, and any scale or debris was removed.

4. The Second-Generation Master Die (Negative, Incused)

Repeating the transfer process, the second-generation master die was created. These could be made at will from the first-generation master hub. The second-generation master die was then finessed by the addition of an arrowhead, arrow feathers, and, possibly, the decorative cross above the shield. At any later time, finessing could be done to the second-generation master die, resulting in appropriate changes to other hubs and dies later in the sequence. As an example, on a later second-generation master die, an extra leaf was added on the outside of the second clump at the upper right.

The second-generation master die was then used to create working hubs.

5. The Working Hub (Positive, in Relief)

Repeating the transfer process, the working hub was created—in relief, a copy of the finished coin with all details except the date. After hardening, the working hub was used to make as many working dies as needed.

6. The Working Die (Negative, Incused)

The working die, completed in soft steel, was then inspected, and a four-digit date logotype was punched into it below the ball. This was a hand process that resulted in slightly different date positions from die to die, and, sometimes, doubling of features when the logotype was punched more than once, slightly off-register the second time.

The working die was then hardened by the usual process, then dressed by grinding or lapping the field. For Proof coins, such a die was given a high polish. The die was then ready for coining use.

Life of the First-Generation Obverse Master Die

Master dies usually lasted a long time. Master dies usually lasted a long time. Master dies usually lasted a long time. Master dies usually lasted a long time. The entire Liberty Head nickel series of a later era, 1883 to 1913, used only one *obverse* master die, in combination with three *reverse* master dies (one of the Without CENTS type and two of the With CENTS type, the last change being made in 1901). In addition, for early Proofs of the Without CENTS type, another die was made by hand, with no master die involved.

In the Shield nickel series, it seems that just one first-generation obverse master die was made. This is verified by comparison of the obverses of the first and last coins in the series (1866 and 1883). The placement of the letters, the arrangement of the leaves, the shield scrollwork, and other features are identical.

However, as described by Edward L. Fletcher Jr., Bill Fivaz, Douglas L. Kurz, and other students of the series, some modifications were made. These were probably done to a second-generation master die, as described above.

Obverse Style 1

There is but one obverse master die, designated Obverse Style 1.[8] This was adjusted to create subvarieties of working hubs, but the original or master die was never changed.

Nomenclature note: Using a number for the obverse and a letter for the reverse follows long-established American numismatic tradition (e.g., S.S. Crosby, *Early Coins of America*, 1875). A designation such as 1-B refers to Obverse Style 1 in combination with Reverse Style B. This deviates from the designations used by Edward L. Fletcher Jr. in *The Shield Five Cent Series* (letters for obverse, Roman numerals for reverse) and Peters-Mohon in *The Complete Guide to Shield and Liberty Head Nickels* (Roman numerals for the obverse, letters for the reverse). Also, I have hesitated to call them all *hubs*, as some dies may have been made directly from the first master, as explained under the reverse styles.

Obverse Style Modifications

Obverse Style 1. The first-generation master die for the obverse was used in sequence to make at least three second-generation master dies, by the process described previously. These, in chronological order, are called Style 1a, 1b, and 1c here.

Although these minor differences are not widely collected, they are highly useful in the study of varieties in the regular series, as well as for patterns and restrikes, to help identify the time period in which certain pieces were made, which in some instances was later than the date on the coins. In particular, such fine points have enabled Andrew W. Pollock III, Saul Teichman, John Dannreuther, and other students of patterns to answer a lot of questions.

Obverse Style 1a. The top barb on the left arrow has a notch in it. On certain obverse dies of 1866 to 1868 and some of 1869, the outer leaf in the second cluster at the upper right varies in appearance. Edward L. Fletcher Jr. demonstrates that this particular leaf was added by hand to each die, or sometimes omitted, a procedure seconded by Douglas L. Kurz, who has studied dies carefully.[9] The Fivaz-Stanton *Cherrypickers' Guide* details certain of the variations known. The Fletcher text devotes a chapter to the subject of missing-leaf varieties. In addition, the highest inside leaf at the upper right is detached. This is Fletcher Obverse Hub A. For the most comprehensive coverage of varieties of this and other styles see www.shieldnickels.net.

Obverse Style 1b. The top arrow barb on the left arrow is sliced off. In 1869 it seems that a new second-generation master die was made, but imperfectly, as certain details are blurry, as in parts of the shield frame. The top inside leaf has been strengthened, and the outside leaf in the second cluster is now part of the master die. Related dies were used for part of the production of 1869 nickels, all of 1870 and 1871, and about 10% of those of 1872. Fletcher calls this Obverse Hub B.

Obverse Style 1c. The top arrow barb on the left arrow is full and complete save for a tiny clip at end of the barb. The final adjustment, called Obverse Hub C by Fletcher, was employed beginning partway through 1872 and was used through the end of the series. The scroll details are again strong. The second leaf on the third cluster at the upper right is slightly irregular, and there are some minor differences in the arrow details at the lower left.

Reverse Design of the Shield Nickel

Description

The reverse of the Shield nickel displays the large numeral 5 at the center, surrounded by a circle of 13 stars with rays between each star. Around the border is UNITED STATES OF AMERICA / CENTS. Denticles circle the inner rim, adjacent to the field of the coin. The Mint had great difficulty striking the coins sharply with Full Details on both sides.

Early in the year 1867 the rays were dropped, leaving just a circle of 13 stars inside the lettering and around the 5. A précis of the situation is provided by R.W. Julian:

> The chief coiner, A.L. Snowden, who was directly responsible for the output of nickels, approached Chief Engraver J.B. Longacre in the latter part of 1866 in order to see if some solution could be found to the excessive die wear for the Shield nickel and the resulting low quality of many of the pieces issued by his department. The result of this conference was a joint decision that Longacre redesign the reverse of the nickel in order to eliminate the rays.
>
> Snowden felt that there was simply too much metal that had to flow into the reverse design elements for it to come up properly. This in turn affected the metal flow on the obverse. The pressure on the dies had to be increased in order to bring up the design, especially on the reverse, and increased die breakage then resulted. The greater striking force not only cracked and shattered dies, but also wrought havoc with the coining presses, creating fresh problems for the chief coiner. It was a vicious circle. . . .[10]
>
> The first pattern pieces with the redesigned reverse were struck towards the latter part of 1866 or very early in 1867. It is thought that the new director of the Mint, William Millward, was not consulted about the proposed change and that Snowden actually approached the secretary of the Treasury directly rather than going through the usual channels. (However, Millward was in a delicate political position because of the struggles then going on between President Andrew Johnson and the congressmen determined to impeach him. Millward wound up not being confirmed by the Senate and Henry R. Linderman was to assume the post in April 1867.)
>
> At the same time that Snowden was writing directly to the Treasury with his ideas for improvement of the five cent design, he and Longacre collaborated on an extensive test of the new design to see how it would improve die life. Results of the test have not been found, and may no longer exist, but it is clear that both men saw a definite improvement in the number of five cent pieces that could be struck from a pair of dies with the revised design.[11]

On January 21, 1867, Secretary of the Treasury Hugh McCulloch wrote to Director Millward to officially notify him of the change. The transition was to take place on February 1, but it is not known if that date was observed. It is likely that leftover With Rays dies were used up in the interest of economy.

From Master Die to Working Die

Due to the quantities of dies needed for production runs of various Shield nickel dates, it is likely that the sequence from master hub to working die described below was followed.

In addition, there seem to have been limited-use dies, such as Reverse Dies A and C, that were made by punching elements directly into a working die.

The reverse of the Shield nickel consists simply of ornaments (stars and a dot or period), letters, and the numeral 5. There is no artistic motif, no Liberty head, and no wreath. These letter punches, all of the same font, with serifs, and larger than used on the obverse, consisted of A, C, D, E, F, I, M, N, O, R, S, T, and U.

1. The Master Die (Negative, Incused)

Likely, the master die, of soft steel, was created by placing a compass point at the center and scribing two circular lines around, one for aligning the tops or bottoms of the letters and the other for the center line of the stars. There was no master hub made from a transfer machine, and no first-generation master die. Instead, a master die was created by hand. This sequence is different from the processes used to make the obverse.

The inscription UNITED STATES OF AMERICA was probably punched first into the master die. That done, the die was reviewed, and CENTS was placed in a central position at the lower border, after which a dot was punched to each side of CENTS. Arranging 13 stars evenly around a circle is not easy to do, as the number is an odd one. Longacre did it visually, probably punching the first star below ES in STATES, then two more above E and T in CENTS, then adding five more to the left and five more to the right. His spacing was not accurate, and a comparison of the separation between adjacent stars will show distinct differences on each of the master hubs described below.

Then came the punching of the large numeral 5 at the center—or perhaps this was done before the stars were added. Uniform, well-spaced denticles were added around the border.

Next, the master die was heated for a time, then suddenly quenched to harden its structure. The die was then ground down slightly to remove metal pushed up at the edges of the punch impressions as well as scale and dirt from the hardening process. The face of the die was then smoothed.

All of the features in the finished master die were incuse (recessed).

2. The Working Hub (Positive, in Relief)

The hardened master die was placed in a powerful press, which drove the master die into a shank of soft die steel, creating a raised impression resembling the relief of a finished coin; the result was known as a *working hub*. This process hardened the working hub somewhat, requiring it to be annealed (softened), after which it received another impression from the master die. In some instances, this process was repeated a third time.[12]

This working hub was then heated, maintained at a high temperature, and quenched in water. After hardening, the working hub was cleaned, but not resurfaced, as this would have damaged the areas in relief. The working hub was ready to create any number of working dies.

3. The Working Die (Negative, Incused)

The working hub was put in the powerful press mentioned above and was driven into a shank of soft die steel. The new die, in soft steel, had all of the features recessed or incuse. This process was usually repeated at least once, sometimes twice, with annealing each time to soften the die. This die was then heated and quenched in water, and became very hard.

The next step was to lightly grind the surface to make it smooth. In the case of a die intended to strike Proof coins, it was given a high polish. (However, the vast majority of dies were simply smoothed.)

The working die was now ready to be placed into a coining press to strike coins. Dozens of working dies would be made in this manner. All were exactly alike, except for microscopic differences in surface preparation visible in the form of tiny lines or striae.

Life of Reverse Hubs and Dies

In the Shield nickel series from 1866 to 1883, several master dies were made for the reverse, as described below. Why this was necessary is not known. Likely, as several master dies cracked during use, or perhaps became damaged, or were rusted, new ones were made.[13] In addition, two reverses seem to have been made by hand, probably for use on patterns, then employed on regular coinage.

Reverse Styles

Although there are other differences, the known reverse styles can easily be identified by the position of two of the star points: one varies its location beneath the ES in STATES, either under the E or under the bottom left serif of the S; and the other varies its location beneath AM in AMERICA.

With Rays

Reverse Style A (Handmade Die), With Rays. The first star points under the bottom left serif of the second S in STATES. There is a prominent center dot from a compass point, and the 5 is slightly doubled at upper left. The innermost ray of the star above the E in CENTS is repunched at the tip. This die was used for regular-issue Proofs of 1866, and for the following patterns of 1865:[14] Judd-416 (Pollock-488), J-417 (P-489), J-473 (P-564), J-474 (P-565), J-497 (P-583), J-498 (P-584), and J-574 (P-630).

Reverse Style A.

The numeral 5 for this die was made from a punch furnished to the Mint on May 19, 1866, by S.E. Adamson, a Philadelphia letter cutter who often provided punches for coinage dies. Accordingly, this die was made after that time. As this die was made very early in the sequence and seems to have been used for a limited number of Proof strikings and patterns, not for circulating coins, the working die was probably fashioned directly with punch elements, rather than through the master-die-to-working-hub process. As the 1865-dated patterns have an obverse style not used until 1872, it seems evident that this reverse die was kept on hand and used at least until that year.

This die is not listed by Fletcher. Its use on patterns of 1866 (J-513 to J-515 [P-540 to P-542]) has not been confirmed, and the specific reverse die used for them is unknown.[15]

Reverse Style B (Multiple Dies From Master Die), With Rays. The star below ES in STATES points under the right serif of the E. This style was used for regular-issue circulation strikes of 1866 and 1867 With Rays, for Proofs of 1867 With Rays, and for pattern J-572 (P-648) of 1867.

This is Fletcher's Hub I.

Reverse Style B.

Without Rays

Reverse Style C (Handmade Die), No Rays. Called "Style C" for purposes of discussion of all six reverse dies, this is more commonly known as the Pattern Reverse. The stars point under the upright of the E in STATES and at the center of the A in AMERICA. There are two center dots from a compass point, and evidence of repunching on the upper and lower left sides of the numeral 5. This limited-use die was likely made by hand. It was used on regular-issue Proofs made early in 1867; it was also used on the following patterns: in 1866, J-500 (P-585), J-507 (P-591), J-508 and 509 (P-592), and J-509a (P-593); and in 1867, J-573[16] (P-649). The pattern P-598 is not listed in Judd and is not confirmed to exist; the reverse die is unknown, and if it does exist, it would have been made outside the Mint.[17]

Reverse Style C.

This die is not listed by Fletcher.

Reverse Style D (Multiple Dies From Master Die), No Rays. This list's "Style D" is best known simply as the normal reverse. Its stars point under the right serif of the E in STATES and between the A and M in AMERICA. The stars are in higher relief on this style, and thus required more care to have them strike up fully (this problem was solved on styles E and F with smaller, shallower stars). Reverse Style D was used for regular issues from 1867 to 1869 (although about 10% of 1868 are of Style E). It was also used in 1870, but appears only as a doubled-die reverse (Style D doubled with Style F, an unusual situation). In addition, the style was used on 1866 pattern J-533 (P-unlisted), likely a restrike; 1867 patterns J-573[18] (P-650), J-575 (P-631), J-582 (P-642), and J-583 (P-643); and 1868 patterns J-635 (P-707, not illustrated) and J-636 (P-708, not illustrated).

Reverse Style D.

This is Fletcher's Hub IIa.

Reverse Style E (Multiple Dies From New Master Die), No Rays. For this style, widely called the Reverse of 1868, the stars point under the bottom left serif of the S in STATES and at the right edge of the leftmost upright of the M in AMERICA. The working hub of Style E failed progressively, as letters chipped away in sections. This progression can be seen in varieties of coins struck from working dies made from this working hub and are illustrated and described in detail in the Fivaz-Stanton *Cherrypickers' Guide.* Apparently, this master hub was used for only a short time—part of 1868 (on about 10% of the regular issues; the others are of Style D)—after which the master die, working hubs, and working dies were discarded. Dennis Paulsen (later cited by Fivaz-Stanton) estimated that only about 10% of the 1868 Shield nickels are of the Reverse Style E.

Reverse Style E.

This is Fletcher's Hub IIb.

Reverse Style F (Multiple Dies From New Master Die), No Rays. The stars for this style point under the right serif of the E in STATES and at the interior of the M in AMERICA just left of center. Reverse Style F is found on regular issues from 1869 to 1883. It is likely that this master die was created in late 1868 (when dies for 1869 were being prepared). Accordingly, it's likely that patterns using this reverse, but dated earlier, are all restrikes. Those bearing this style reverse are 1865 patterns J-418 (P-490) and J-419 (P-491); 1866 patterns J-476 (P-566), J-477 (P-567), J-478 (P-568), J-479 (P-569), J-516 (P-543), J-517 (P-544), J-518 (P-545), J-519 (P-546), J-520 (P-547), and J-532 (P-597); 1869 patterns J-687 (P-768, not illustrated), J-688 (P-769, not illustrated), and J-689 (P-770, not illustrated); and all patterns of this general design, 1870 and later.

Reverse Style F.

This is Fletcher's Hub IIc.

Die Pairings and Cross-References

Howard Spindel has supplied a handy guide to the various combinations of obverse and reverse dies for Shield nickels, as well as a cross-reference of the different names that have been given these dies over the years. See tables 4.1 and 4.2, respectively.

Life Expectancy of Working Dies

R.W. Julian suggests that the average pair of Shield nickel dies used for circulation strikes made somewhat fewer than 20,000 impressions for the 1866 and 1867 With Rays type, improving to about 20,000 to 21,000 for the Without Rays nickels of the earlier years, and rising to about 26,000 by 1882.[19] Such official figures are subject to wide latitude in interpretation and study today; however, in general, and across many series, early-period dies had shorter production lives (smaller numbers of impressions taken from the dies) than did later ones.

In 1868 the mintage of circulation strikes totaled 28,817,000. Assuming 20,000 impressions per die pair, this yields 1,441 die pairs. In his 1994 study, *The Shield Nickel Five Cent Series*, Edward L. Fletcher Jr. identifies 109 different varieties with repunched dates and other unusual characteristics, including about 25 doubled dies. The latest word comes from Ken Hill, who has made Shield nickels a specialty and who was an essential contributor to the Fletcher work:

> Today the CONECA files have 63 doubled dies listed for 1868. As for repunched dates, for 1868 I have 184 listings from my personal collection, plus 18 missing-leaf varieties, plus over 50 that I have yet to attribute. This will give an idea of the extent of varieties for this particular year in the series. My personal collection of 1868 nickels approaches 900 pieces.[20]

Not accounting for varieties yet to be discovered by the indefatigable Hill and other specialists, this would indicate that at least one die in every six for the 1868 year had doubling, repunching, a missing leaf, or some other error!

For 1880 we know that two die varieties exist for a mintage of 16,000 coins, or a die life of 8,000 per coin. As there was no call for a mintage beyond 16,000, both dies were retired in excellent, serviceable condition (no coins with die cracks have been seen). One of the two dies may have even been a backup in case the other broke. Also noteworthy for this particular date is the fact that the same two obverses were used to make both Proofs and circulation strikes (see 1880 listing).

Observation of the coins themselves suggests that the dies of the earliest few years failed more quickly, as more cracks and damage are apparent. Various factors apply to die use and deterioration, including the hardness of the die steel, the quality of the planchets, and the number of coins made.

If a general observation can be made, it is that in the past two decades more attention has been paid to Shield nickels and their dies than ever before. It is rather amazing that this playground of numismatic delights was mostly unknown to numismatists of a generation or so ago!

The Shield Nickel in Circulation

Commenting on new coin designs has been a national pastime for generations. The numismatically loved 1793 Chain copper cent was reviewed in its year of issue as having Liberty "in a fright," and the chain reverse as being "an ill omen." The presently appreciated Morgan silver dollar was roundly condemned by just about everyone in its own day. In the present era, the state-reverse quarters have been fair game, and many hunters are out there firing potshots.

Designs, like prophets, are frequently unappreciated in their own time and place. Such is the case with the design of the Shield nickel. One comment, printed in the September 1866 issue of the *American Journal of Numismatics*, included the following:

On the obverse of this remarkable coin, the first *thing* that attracts the attention, is a very elaborate and highly ornamented gridiron, the clumsy handle of which appears to be broken from the body, thus rendering this culinary utensil almost useless. The upper part and sides of this gridiron are hung with leaves of some sort, strongly reminding one of the savory bunches of herbs displayed in a market-house in autumn, or of a green grocer's sign in huckleberry time. Perhaps the same accident that severed the handle of the gridiron also fractured the lower part, for we notice that it is there skewered by two arrows, pointing in opposite directions. The motto "In God we Trust," is very opportune, for the *inventor* of this coin may rest assured that the devil will never forgive him for such an abortion.

Table 4.1. Known Design-Style Pairings for Shield Nickels

Year	Strike	Obverse	Reverse
1866	Proof	1a	A
	Circulation	1a	B
1867, With Rays	All	1a	B
1867, No Rays	Proof	1a	C
	Circulation	1a	D
1868	Proof	1a	D
	Circulation	1a	D
		1a	D
		1a	E
1869	Proof	1a	D
1869	Circulation[a]	1a	D
		1a	F
		1b	D
		1b	F
1870	Proof	1b	F
	Circulation[b]	1b	D
		1b	F
1871	All	1b	F
1872	Proof	1c	F
	Circulation	1b	F
		1c	F
1873–1883	All[c]	1c	F

a. 1869 circulation strikes with Narrow Date logotype use 1a/D pairing only. b. 1870 1b/D pairing (only) is known as a Doubled-Die Reverse D over F hubbing. c. All Proofs for 1873 are Closed 3 logotype only.

Table 4.2. Cross-Reference for Shield Nickel Obverse and Reverse Design Styles

This Book	Fletcher	Spindel	Peters & Mohon	Other Terms
Obverse Style 1a	Obverse A	Obverse A	Obverse Type I	Notched arrow
Obverse Style 1b	Obverse B	Obverse B	Obverse Type II	Sliced arrow
Obverse Style 1c	Obverse C	Obverse C	Obverse Type III	Full arrow
Reverse Style A		Reverse Ip		
Reverse Style B	Reverse I	Reverse I	Reverse Type A	With Rays
Reverse Style C		Reverse IIo		
Reverse Style D	Reverse IIa	Reverse IIa	Reverse Type B	Reverse of 1867 (r67)
Reverse Style E	Reverse IIb	Reverse IIb	Reverse Type C	Reverse of 1868 (r68)
Reverse Style F	Reverse IIc	Reverse IIc	Reverse Type D	Reverse of 1870 (r70)[a]

a. *Reverse of 1870* is a misnomer, as the reverse first appeared in 1869.

Years later, in 1877, even Joseph Wharton, who had benefited handsomely from the use of nickel metal, expressed his displeasure with the motif in his *Memorandum Concerning Small Money and Nickel Alloy Coinage, with Illustrations and Descriptions of*

Existing Alloy Coins, saying that the Shield design was "awkward and humpy [in] appearance, and . . . entirely devoid of resonance. [Its design] strongly suggests the old fashioned pictures of a tombstone surmounted by a cross and overhung by weeping willows. . . . It is a curiously ugly device."

Planning Ahead

In his *Annual Report* for the fiscal year ended June 30, 1867, Mint Director Henry R. Linderman, who had been in office only since April 2, commented on the need for the government to enact legislation for the redemption of worn minor coins. It seems that banks continually ordered new coins from the Mint, as their customers preferred them, but that there was no clear policy as to what to do with the expanding supply of cents (in particular) in circulation as they became worn. Small cents had been in use since May 1857.

In his 1868 report, Director Linderman stated that he had redeemed about 13 million copper-nickel cents of the 1857 style (Flying Eagle design) by exchanging new nickel three- and five-cent coins for them, although this was in violation of at least two laws.[21] By this time, Shield nickels were a common sight in circulation.

Spinner's View of Nickels

Francis E. Spinner, treasurer of the United States, is numismatically remembered for many things, not the least of which is his florid signature, printed on paper money of the 1860's. It was Spinner who investigated the possibility of (and was instrumental in the issuing of) Postage Currency notes in 1862, followed by Fractional Currency paper, which in 1868 was still being produced in large quantities.

It seems that to him, nickels were interlopers or intruders on the American financial scene, per a report he issued in 1868:

> This convenient small change [Fractional Currency], that was in various ways receivable for public dues, and at the same time convertible into lawful money of the United States, has been replaced, under the specious plea of a "speedy return to specie payments" by an almost worthless irredeemable, poisonous, and stinking copper and nickel token currency. The five cent tokens are made a legal tender for $1, and are redeemable in sums of not less than $100. All the others, including the one cent, the two cent, and the three cent tokens, and whether made of copper alone or of copper and nickel, are entirely irredeemable, and, as irredeemable currency, have already become a nuisance by their great accumulations in the hands of small dealers.
>
> Officers engaged in government collections, especially those connected with the Post Office Department, suffer in consequence. Postmasters are by law compelled to receive these government tokens in payment for postage stamps, and are then immediately liable to the government for the amount of such sales in good money. But the government that sold these tokens at par for their face value, or paid them as money to its creditors, now turns round and refuses to receive them back in payments from its own officers, who were by law compelled to receive them on account of the government.

> Postmasters who were so obliged to receive these tokens have offered them by the bagful in payment of their post office receipts at the counter of the Treasury, and have been compelled to carry them home again, because the Treasurer cannot receive over 60 cents in three-cent pieces, nor over four cents in one or two-cent pieces in one payment. Was there ever an act of the government of a respectable people, that, for meanness, can compare with this? An individual that would practice such a confidence game would be branded as a two-penny thief, and would soon be consigned to a house of correction.
>
> A government that practices such frauds upon the people cannot hope long to retain the respect of anybody. It has been intimated, and there are those uncharitable enough to believe the story, that the ownership of an unprofitable nickel mine had something to do in influencing the passage of these "speedy-return-to-specie payment" laws.[22]

In the last paragraph, Spinner refers, of course, to none other than Joseph Wharton and his profits from nickel metal. The Civil War was over, yet the public was still hoarding silver and gold coins, and these traded at a premium on commercial exchanges. Lip service was paid to "speedy return to specie payment" and to the return of silver to circulation—but so long as Wharton had any influence in Congress, this was not going to happen anytime soon!

Today, numismatists are grateful for Wharton's political maneuverings, just as we are thankful that most of the senior Mint officials were grafters and reaped private profits from making rarities and restrikes. Morally, however, most of this was very wrong in its time.

Counterfeits Appear

Counterfeiting federal coins and paper money was quite a sport in the era of the Shield nickel. Contemporary newspapers as well as issues of *Banker's Magazine* are filled with stories of cat-and-mouse games between Treasury operatives (as they were called) and those who sought to make or pass fake money—not always large denominations, either. Many forgeries were produced of Fractional Currency bills.

This account in the *American Journal of Numismatics*, March 1870, tells of false nickels:

> *Counterfeit Five-Cent.*—The Sub-Treasury lately found they were redeeming counterfeit nickel "fives." A lot was assayed at the Philadelphia Mint, and proved to be deficient in nearly eleven percent of nickel, being about 14 instead of 25, and only 70 instead of 77 grains in weight. Zinc was added, making a "German silver," and the counterfeits very naturally turned yellow.
>
> This and a certain coarseness of finish, coupled with an undue size in the motto "In God We Trust," first led to suspicion. The specific gravity is also about 8.72 when it should be nearly 9 in the genuine. This counterfeit, like some other "good things," seems to be a New York institution. Thus far it has been found with the dates 1867, '68, and '69.[23]

Then, beginning in 1873, a nest of counterfeiters in New York "flooded the city with five-cent pieces," according to a lengthy account in the *Brooklyn Eagle*, August 25,

A die-struck counterfeit of the 1867 Without Rays nickel. Many counterfeit Shield nickels were produced of various dates.

1875.[24] The culprits were John S. and Thomas Loughery and a partner, Philip Lewinski, along with 61-year-old A.C. Taubert (a German immigrant who also went under the surname of Seigel).

According to the *Eagle*'s December 2, 1875, coverage of their trial, Taubert originally got involved when he answered an ad in a German-language newspaper for an "engraver in metals." Believing, he said, that he was dealing with government employees, he entered their employ at $18 per week making metal dies. He eventually even moved into an apartment in the Loughreys' house for a time. During his tenure with the Loughreys, he witnessed both of the brothers, as well as Lewinski, at the work of making planchets and stamping them with the Taubert's dies—at one point, he said, the threesome entered his apartment in the Loughreys' house, and that "one of them had his hands full of the coins which they had manufactured." Eventually the spurious nature of the coins was detected, however, and all four counterfeiters were indicted.

The Later Years

By the early 1870's, the nickel five-cent piece was firmly entrenched as a useful denomination in American commerce. Fractional Currency bills—including those of the five-cent denomination—continued to be produced and to circulate, but the public was not fond of them. The Treasury Department endeavored to restore the circulation of silver coins in 1873. The advent of certain coins sparked this commentary in the *New York Times*, October 29, 1873:

> The low price of silver has brought a large amount of it into circulation. Silver dimes, half-dimes, quarters, half dollars, and even dollars, are given out in change for currency over bar and restaurant counters with the utmost nonchalance by the attendants. The coin is generally fresh from the Mint, and examined critically and with curiosity by many who have never seen [a silver] American coin before.[25]

However, the effort was not successful on a sustained basis, and silver remained scarce in commerce for the next several years. After April 20, 1876, silver coins returned in quantity to circulation, having been hoarded by the populace since the spring of 1862. The premium charged for silver coins in terms of paper money by exchange brokers had been diminishing gradually over a long period of time, and in 1876 silver and paper achieved parity. After that time, Fractional Currency notes were quickly retired. So many old, silver three-cent pieces, half dimes, and other denominations appeared in commerce that no new nickels were needed. Accordingly, production quantities fell sharply, and in 1877 and 1878, only Proofs were made for collectors. From 1879 to 1881 mintages remained modest. In the autumn, the Treasury reserves of nickels were nearly depleted, and on November 12 the secretary of the Treasury directed that production be resumed. In 1881 Joseph Wharton's influence prompted changes that eventually resulted in the Liberty Head nickel, which is discussed in later chapters.

History of Proof Shield Nickels

Proof Shield nickels, specifically made for collectors, are an important part of the chronicle of this series. These were first struck in the summer of 1866. As many collectors had already ordered Proof coins for the year (such sets lacked the nickel), the Mint made single examples available for 10¢ each. The number struck is not known, nor are mintage figures known for any other dates until 1878.

Normal practice was to sell the Shield nickel as part of a minor Proof set, with other denominations such as the Indian Head cent, bronze two-cent piece, and nickel three-cent piece. The two-cent piece was discontinued after 1873.

Proofs were produced by the Medal Department at the Mint, using a hand-operated press. Dies were given a high polish to create a mirror surface in the fields. The nickel planchets are said to have been selected with care, and cleaned to remove dirt and spots. Conventional wisdom has it that Proofs were struck twice, to fully bring up the design details. It is likely that in most instances one strike sufficed. Although a few Proofs show weak details in selected areas, such as at the top of the shield and on one or a few star centers, most seen today are sharply struck.

The quality of "proofness" varies from deeply mirrored, to a combination of deep mirror and slight graininess (this being usual), to fully lustrous with no mirror surface at all (as with many 1878 nickels). Some especially deeply polished Proof dies (such as for 1870) have certain low-relief areas missing on the final coins, such as the thin parts of the letter S near the border—giving the appearance of a "broken" S. Such differences in finish have no impact on market values and are mainly of interest to specialists.

Proofs were struck in several separate runs during a given year, providing some differences upon close inspection, and accounting in part for the presence of sharp details on some pieces while others of the same date had weaknesses. The edges, viewed edge-on, have a mirror finish.

In recent years the close study of dies by various scholars has revealed many situations not disclosed in official Mint records and correspondence. Probably, if you are a typical numismatist, you will view the following as esoteric. Fair enough—just skip over it! On the other hand, this information does give an insight into the workings of the Mint. More on the subject of dies, restrikes, and the like will be found in appendix A, which deals with patterns.

The Proofs of 1866

Proof Shield nickels of 1866, all With Rays on the reverse, were first struck in the summer of that year. The number made is not known, and modern estimates have ranged from about 175 to 1,000 or more. Low guesses are the most popular. My own estimate is about 800 to 1,200—which is considerably more than I would have suggested as recently as a year or two ago. However, the more I investigated this date, the more I realized that quite a few are around.

R.W. Julian gives this scenario:

> There has been considerable collector interest in the number of Proof nickels struck in 1866 and, especially, in 1867. The number actually struck in either year is

unknown and likely to remain so since the records of the Mint for sales of Proof sets and individual coins were mostly destroyed in 1925 due to an excess of records and lack of storage space. However, we can make some educated guesses concerning the Proof coinages of these years.

It was standard practice by the Mint to sell sets of silver Proof coins to collectors, and had been since 1858. The so-called silver set always contained the minor coins (which meant only the cent until 1864), so the known mintages of silver Proof sets after 1858 always show the *minimum number* of minor Proof coins struck as well. The difficulty is that, beginning in 1864, the Mint also made up sets of minor Proof coins for sale just a few cents over face value.[26] No useful records have been found for the sales or striking of minor Proof sets in 1866 or 1867, and the overall data for such coinage prior to 1878 is fragmentary.

There were 125 silver Proof sets of 1866 produced after June 1 of that year, and all contained the new five-cent piece. By coincidence, the first delivery of Proof coins in June was on June 11, the same day that regular striking began for the nickel. It might not, however, be a coincidence as the coiner may not have wanted to deliver the Proof nickels before business coinage commenced. Such a practice appears to have been general Mint policy at the time.

In addition to the known 125 pieces in the silver sets, there may well have been another 75 or 100 pieces struck for the minor sets. Those having purchased silver sets earlier in 1866 (some 600 sets) would surely have wanted Proof nickels to complete their sets.[27]

In addition to Proof nickels sold in minor and full sets, single coins were available from the Mint for 10¢ each.

The problem of estimating the number of known Proofs is complicated by the frequency of market appearances. A generation ago it was fairly unusual for a Proof 1866 nickel to be in a dealer's stock or in an auction, although the issue was hardly considered a great rarity. After the advent of encapsulation (PCGS 1986), coins changed hands much more frequently, in and out of dealers' stocks and collectors' holdings. As it was easier for a casual buyer to gain comfort with grading, more people came into the marketplace. Soon, the passion for ownership faded, and coins were back on the market. This general scenario has played out dramatically in the offering of rarities such as 1913 Liberty Head nickels, 1804 dollars, and Sand Blast Proof gold coins.

1866. Graded PF-65.

In his *Encyclopedia of United States and Colonial Proof Coins*, 1977, Walter Breen stated, "The number made is possibly nearer to 175 than to 125." Gloria Peters and Cynthia Mohon, in *The Complete Guide to Shield and Liberty Head Nickels*, suggest "375+."

Further, without facts on hand, catalogers and other writers are often prompted to emphasize rarity. Today, the certification population data are very useful. Make your own estimate as to the Proof mintage. I think that 800 to 1,200 or so might be in the ballpark. If this is inaccurate, then Proof 1866 nickels have a way of running in and out of the certification services more often than do later Proofs, for which the actual mintage figures have been published.

Background to the Proofs of 1867

We know that early in 1867, the With Rays reverse was used to make an estimated 2,019,000 *circulation strike* Shield nickels. Problems had developed with striking the design, dies broke frequently, and chief coiner A.L. Snowden notified Secretary of the Treasury Hugh McCulloch that as of February 1 the new reverse Without Rays would be used. Thus the 13 rays or stripes disappeared from the reverse, and the design was simplified. The first complete Proof sets, from the cent to the silver dollar, were delivered on February 5. There were some 25 sets in all, followed by 100 more sets on February 18, 200 more on February 25, and a final 100 in June.

As to *Proofs*, the situation has been a numismatic puzzlement for a long time. The information provided here is adapted from Mint data and correspondence provided by R.W. Julian, as modified by modern research by John Dannreuther.[28] In a nutshell, what chief coiner A. Loudon Snowden said he did in early 1867 is contradicted by a careful study of the coins themselves. The scenario unfolded prior to April 2, 1867, when Henry R. Linderman became director. During his tenure, restrikes were made—another element of the story.

Linderman, a very intelligent man, did many noteworthy things, such as work with the remarkably talented John Jay Knox on coinage legislation (including the creation of the highly successful trade dollar), hire George T. Morgan as assistant engraver at the Mint in 1876, and write a fine book, his 1877 *Money and Legal Tender in the United States*. Linderman went on to expand his personal coin collection and line his pockets to an extent unequalled by any other Mint official—which was a remarkable accomplishment, never mind its illegality.

In trying to sort out the nickel coinage of 1867, this comment by John Dannreuther is highly relevant: "The Mint officials even before the infamous Linderman often lied, or more accurately, told only part of the truth."[29] Half-truths are very dangerous, for one often does not know which half to believe. Over the years, quite a few writers and historians have accepted the statements of James R. Snowden, A. Loudon Snowden, Linderman, and others at face value, trusting in the veracity of official government documents. Although I could cite *many* such publications in numismatic literature, a particularly egregious and incredibly naive example is provided by Roy J. Popkin in "Dr. Henry Linderman, Mint Director" (published in *The Numismatist*, June 1959), which included this:

> Henry Richard Linderman, M.D., was a brilliant and conscientious public servant of whom the medical profession may be justly proud. His accomplishments as director of the United States Mint, advisor to Congress on its monetary and coinage laws, creator of the trade dollar and promoter of the doctrine of the gold standard were of paramount importance to the great industrial and commercial expansion of this country after the Civil War. . . .
>
> His contemporaries referred to him as a great and notable American who literally worked himself to death in self-sacrificing service to his country. A bronze medal was struck at the Mint after his death commemorating him as one of the greatest contributors to science and the public good.[30]

Popkin might not have been aware that in June 1878 a committee in Congress preferred charges of misconduct (not involving numismatics) against Linderman, which were denied, but were still being investigated when he died on January 27, 1879 (at the age of 53). Years later, dealer Lyman H. Low prepared an auction catalog listing much of Linderman's "private reserve" from his estate. The government, by that time "having got religion," stepped in and seized many weird patterns, official dies, and other things. A new, revised catalog was made up by Low, and a "cleaner" sale was held, under the imprint of J.W. Scott, on February 28, 1888.

Today, scholars are fairly certain that so-called Class III silver dollars of 1804—great rarities—were made while Linderman was at the Mint. As might be expected, Linderman kept one for himself. Apparently, he gave a cock-and-bull story to his wife about the coin, for on July 1, 1887, widow Emily Linderman swore an affidavit concerning the coin, noting the following:

> The said Dr. Linderman told deponent that he had obtained the 1804 dollar in his collection, that it was an original, that it was of great rarity, there only having been 12 or 14 struck, that it was one of the finest, if not the finest specimen in existence, that he had paid for it in installments, not feeling able to pay for it all at one time.

Such "stuff" adds a lot of humor to numismatic research!

"Forum" on the 1867 With Rays Proof Nickels

Although some have suggested that Snowden refused to make 1867 Proof nickels With Rays, it is unlikely that he would have passed up a profitable opportunity of any kind. The initial distribution of Proof *sets* (complete from the cent to the silver dollar) this year took place on February 5, when the new Without Rays dies were ready. Twenty-five such sets were given out, each likely having a Without Rays nickel. Under this scenario, *no* Proof 1867 With Rays nickels were made at the time for inclusion in sets. However, the absence of written information about *single* Proofs does not suggest that such were not coined. Likely, singles were made in January, but were not openly distributed.

During the preparation of this book, the Proofs of this issue engendered quite a bit of discussion and commentary. John Dannreuther gives this as the realistic scenario:

1867, With Rays. Graded PF-65 Cameo.

> When the order of January 21, 1867, was issued to suspend coinage of With Rays nickels, supposedly no 1867 With Rays Proofs had been struck. Walter Breen concluded that the 25 Proofs reported delivered on February 5, 1867, were of the With Rays type. However, this is uncertain as chief coiner Archibald Loudon Snowden is quoted (per R.W. Julian's archives research) to have "refused to make any Proofs of this type for inclusion in the sets."
>
> However, as recently discovered, there were 1867 With Rays Proofs struck early in the year with an *earlier* state of the same obverse die used for most, if not all, of the 1867 Without Rays Proofs.
>
> These With Rays Proofs struck from this obverse die are *originals*, as die linkage for the shared With Rays reverse (found on all 1867 With Rays Proofs), plus other evidence, proves. Therefore, Breen was probably partially correct with his assessment. Some of the first 25 Proofs struck were the With Rays type! The fact that the common obverse die with the No Rays Proofs of this year is found in its earliest state with 1867 With Rays Proofs is strong evidence for this supposition. If all the 25 Proofs struck on February 5 were of the Without Rays type, all that would prove is that some With Rays Proofs were struck sometime before February 5!
>
> Of course, some 1867 With Rays Proofs may have been struck in January or even December 1866. The original Proof 1867 Rays coins were struck before the majority of the Without Rays Proofs, however.

Dannreuther describes *second* and *third* obverse dies, also dated 1867, that were made in 1867 or shortly thereafter and that were used to strike additional Proofs. This was under the watch of Director Linderman.

To the preceding, Douglas Kurz adds a collecting commentary and overview:

> It is my belief that the original delivery of 25 full Proof sets, cent to dollar, were precisely those containing the early strikings of the Without Rays Proof nickels with the "prototype" handmade reverse die also found on the Judd-507 pattern.
>
> The relative proportion of coins from this die, as compared with the regular 1867 No Rays Proofs, is in the ballpark of 1 to 20, as far as I can tell, which would be about right if only 25 were struck. The T. Harrison Garrett set of 1867 Proofs, bought at auction in December 1878, had a Without Rays nickel from this die, but no With Rays nickel (such being added to the set generations later by his son, John Work Garrett, who obtained the coin from dealer William Hesslein on February 18, 1920).

> Dave Bowers's notes on the Garrett 1867 Proof set indicate that it was purchased some years later, and was not purchased directly from the Mint. In any event, Garrett was not buying coins directly from the Mint at this early date.
>
> John Dannreuther's assertion that some of the With Rays Proofs share the earliest obverse characteristics with these 25 No Rays Proofs, and may have been struck around then, but not for official delivery, is the only way to reconcile R.W. Julian's archival research with Dannreuther's die-state research.
>
> I was so excited to learn of the discovery of the J-507 reverse on the 1867 No Rays Proofs. I believe that these coins, combined with Julian's archival research, prove that the 1867 With Rays Proofs are another clandestine mint delicacy akin to 1885 trade dollars, 1866 No Motto dollars, 1913 nickels, and the like. Of course, looking at those other famous issues, this conclusion does not take anything away from the desirability or market value of the 1867 With Rays Proofs, but it is an interesting conclusion nonetheless.[31]

As a summary of the preceding, it is likely that 1867 With Rays nickels in Proof format were made very early in 1867, but probably distributed individually, and not as part of sets. Whether Proofs of this variety were struck in January or slightly later (after some Without Rays Proofs had been made) is a matter of continuing research by John Dannreuther.

Estimates as to the number of Proof 1867 With Rays nickels minted have varied widely. Mohon and Peters suggest 15 to 25. Walter Breen, in his 1988 *Complete Encyclopedia*, gave information superseding that in his 1977 Proof coins *Encyclopedia*, and suggested that 12 to 15 exist, in two die states (the second highly repolished, indicating later issues or restrikes).

Despite official denials (a.k.a. *lies*) by Mint officials, it was the practice to keep earlier-dated dies on hand, even after all were said to have been destroyed in 1869. It seems that every now and then in the 1870's, there was a demand for earlier Proofs in various popular numismatic series, and restrikes were made privately and sold secretly to satisfy the demand. The coiners at the Mint had no idea that generations later, numismatists would study the die characteristics to learn that in many instances a dated obverse was paired with a restrike with tiny differences not in use until *years* afterward. Appendix A (pattern coins) discusses this further.

Proofs 1868–1883

The Without Rays reverse type was used until the end of the series in 1883. The 1873 Proofs are of the Closed 3 style (sometimes called *Close 3*, since the knobs of the 3 are close together rather than actually touching). Those with the Open 3 were made only as circulation strikes. The 1877 and 1878 nickels were made only in Proof finish, with no related pieces for circulation. Nearly all 1878 Proof nickels have mint luster (sometimes in combination with a Proof surface), and some are fully frosty. Commonly, the reverse will have some grainy areas lacking a full, deep mirror finish. Many Proofs have a sort of mirrorlike but minutely pebbly surface (called an *orange peel* surface when present on gold coins, but less commonly mentioned in listings for nickel coins).

1879, 9 Over 8. Graded PF-67+.

A variety of 1879 Proof is widely described as "1879, 9 Over 8," but I and several consultants to this book believe it is no more than a repunched 1879, not an overdate. Still, it may be so firmly established in the literature that it will continue be described in that manner. On the other hand, sometimes debunked overdates disappear from listings, as with the "1869, 9 Over 8" Indian Head cent, the "1869, 9 Over 8" two-cent piece, and the "1889, 9 Over 8" half dollar, among others. Time will tell.

As noted under 1880 below, in this year (and perhaps for other years as well) the same dies were used to make circulation strikes and Proofs—creating puzzles for a later generation of numismatists to contemplate.

Throughout this era, the quality of Proofs varied—with different degrees of die polish, planchet quality, and other characteristics. Some are deeply struck with wire rims, indicating full-weight planchets that were completely compressed to bring up details of the design. Some other Proofs have lightness in one area or another—the horizontal stripes on the shield and the star centers are the first places to check.

In many instances, the mirror surface was not brought up fully, and patches of non-Proof surface, not lustrous but simply dull metal, can be seen; this feature is most evident on the reverse near the 5. Some Proofs have beveled rims, rather than squared-off rims. When Proof dies were wiped with an oily rag, sometimes threads, hair, or other debris remained, impressions of which were then transferred to the coin, causing lintmarks (tiny recessed lines and squiggles).

5

Shield Nickels 1866–1883: Guide to Collecting

Grading Standards and Interpretations

An important part of collecting Shield nickels is learning the standards by which they are graded. The American Numismatic Association's grading standards are the most widely used—by the leading grading services as well as by others—and are reproduced here (with slight edits) from *The Official American Numismatic Association Grading Standards for United States Coins* (seventh ed., pp. 115–118), which also contains illustrations of each grade. Remember that these and all other grading standards are subject to interpretation.

Official ANA Grading Standards: Shield Nickels 1866–1883

Notes: Shield nickels are occasionally seen weakly struck, and with the horizontal lines joined, even on Uncirculated examples. Many of the early dates are unevenly struck, with weak spots in the details. Brilliant Uncirculated coins are much scarcer than the usual dull or frosty pieces. Surfaces are often marred with small black spots. Coins will not always have the exact stated degree of mint luster, strike, or absence of marks. Overall eye appeal and appearance may also influence the stated grade.

Mint State (MS)

Coin is Uncirculated and shows absolutely no trace of wear.

1868. Graded MS-67.

1875. Graded MS-65.

1873, Closed 3, Doubled-Die Obverse. Graded MS-63.

MS-70. A flawless coin exactly as it was minted, with no trace of wear or injury. Must have full mint luster or attractive light toning.

MS-67. Virtually flawless, but with very minor imperfections.

MS-65. No trace of wear; nearly as perfect as MS-67, except for some small weakness or blemish. Has full mint luster but may be unevenly toned or lightly fingermarked. A few noticeable nicks or marks may be present.

MS-63. A Mint State coin with attractive mint luster, but noticeable detracting contact marks or minor blemishes.

MS-60. A strictly Uncirculated coin with no trace of wear, but with blemishes more obvious than for MS-63. Will lack full mint luster, and surface may be dull or spotted.

About Uncirculated (AU)

Coin shows small traces of wear on the highest points.

1867, Rays. Graded AU-58.

AU-58 (Very Choice). Has some signs of abrasion: tips of leaves; high points of shield. Shallow or weak spots in the relief, particularly in the numeral 5, are usually caused by improper striking and not wear.

AU-55 (Choice). ***Obverse:*** Only a trace of wear shows on the cross. ***Reverse:*** A trace of wear shows on the numeral. SURFACE: Part of the mint luster is still present.

AU-50 (Typical). ***Obverse:*** Traces of wear show on cross and at tips of leaves. ***Reverse:*** Traces of wear show on numeral and stars. SURFACE: Traces of mint luster still show.

Extremely Fine (EF)

Coin shows very light wear on only the highest points.

1867, Rays. Graded EF-40.

EF-45 (Choice). ***Obverse:*** Slight wear shows on the cross and at tips of leaves. There is a trace of wear on the horizontal lines of the shield. ***Reverse:*** High points of the numerals and stars are lightly worn.

EF-40 (Typical). ***Obverse:*** Cross is lightly worn but well defined and bold. Slight wear shows on horizontal lines of the shield. High points of leaves are worn but show all details. ***Reverse:*** Numeral and stars are worn but all details are visible.

Very Fine (VF)

Coin shows light to moderate even wear. All its major features are sharp.

1868. Graded VF-20.

VF-30 (Choice). ***Obverse:*** Leaves show nearly full detail. Vertical lines of shield are worn but sharp and separated. ***Reverse:*** Numeral and stars are worn. Most star-centers show plainly.

VF-20 (Typical). ***Obverse:*** Shield shows considerable flatness, but half of the horizontal lines are clear. Parts of the details still show in leaves. Cross is worn but outlined. ***Reverse:*** Numeral and stars are worn. Star centers show half of details.

Fine

Coin shows moderate to heavy even wear, but its entire design is clear and bold.

1867, Without Rays. Graded F-12.

Fine-12. ***Obverse:*** Some details show in leaves and shield lines. The entire motto is plain but very weak. ***Reverse:*** Some details are visible in stars. Numeral is very smooth but distinct.

Very Good (VG)

Coin is well worn. Design is clear but flat and lacking in detail.

1879. Graded VG-10.

VG-8. ***Obverse:*** Outlines of leaves and cross show, but parts are smooth. Motto is weak but visible. Only a few vertical shield lines show separations. ***Reverse:*** Slight detail shows in stars. The rim is clear. Numeral is worn nearly flat but is completely outlined.

Good

Coin is heavily worn. Design and legend are visible, but faint in spots.

1881. Graded G-4.

Good-4. ***Obverse:*** Entire design is well worn with very little detail remaining. Legend is weak but legible. Rim is worn to tops of letters. ***Reverse:*** Numeral is nearly flat but is outlined. Legend is weak but legible. Rim is worn to tops of letters.

About Good (AG)

Coin's design is only outlined. Parts of date and legend are worn smooth.

1880. Graded AG-3.

AG-3. ***Obverse:*** Design is outlined with nearly all details worn away. Date and motto are partially legible but very weak and merging into rim. ***Reverse:*** Entire design is partially worn away. Rim is merged with letters. Only parts of stars and legend are visible.

Proof (PF)

1882. Graded PF-66.

PF-60 to 70 (Proof). ***Obverse and Reverse*** PF-60, 61, and 62 coins show varying amounts of hairlines in the reverse field in particular, decreasing as the grade increases. Fields may be dull or cloudy on lower-level pieces. At PF-65, hairlines are visible only under magnification and are very light and usually only on the reverse. Above PF-65, hairlines become fewer, and in ultra-high grades are nonexistent, this meaning that the coins have never been subject to wiping or abrasive cleaning. At PF-65 or better, expect excellent aesthetic appeal.

Being a Smart Buyer of Shield Nickels

Overview of Collecting

Shield nickels can be collected in several different ways. Obtaining one of each of the Proof dates from 1866 to 1883 is a possibility (though the 1867 With Rays will be a challenge). Some comments about collecting these coins are given below.

Circulation strikes are the most popular, in the form of date sets—easy enough to gather, except that Proofs must be obtained for the 1877 and 1878 dates, and Proofs are cheaper than high-grade circulation strikes for the years 1879 to 1881. Die varieties can be an especially interesting and challenging pursuit, and extensive comments on this specialty are given shortly.

For general advice on collecting, see chapter 3, "How to Be a Smart Buyer," including the four steps to success. To these steps can be added the information given below, relating to the Shield nickel specialty.

Aspects of Striking

As much as any other denomination in federal coinage, the nickel five-cent piece offers challenges in the quest to find pieces with well-defined design details. Using a 4x or 8x magnifier, examine the coin (or a good catalog or Internet photo of it) closely for signs of weakness. On the *obverse*, check (1) the center of the shield, particularly the tiny horizontal lines in the upper part (all should be crisp and distinct; if they are, the remaining features are likely to be sharp as well); and then (2) the leaves near the top of the shield, the denticles around the border (sometimes mushy or run-together), and all other features.

On the *reverse*, check (1) the centers of the stars (which should be sharp and crisp, not slightly flat); then check (2) the numeral 5, the letters, and the denticles. Howard Spindel adds that "It's very unusual to find a Shield nickel of Reverse Style D with fully struck-up radials on all the stars (which are often seen mushy and puffy on MS-65 coins). For fully struck-up stars, be prepared to wait quite a while."[1]

Finally, check the *rim* on each side. It should be either square at the edge or nicely tapered or rounded. Generally, rims are not much of a problem.

Aspects of Grading

The ANA Grading Standards give basic information. In the real world of the marketplace, interpretations often vary, and sometimes widely. My advice is exactly what you are expecting to read: look at the grade on the holder first, then *look at the coin.*

Coins for the Connoisseur

You do not have to be a connoisseur, but in the Shield nickel series it is enjoyable to follow this route. Neither the publishers of standard reference books, the decision-makers at grading services, nor people in other venues have devised standards for sharpness, so you can buy what I like to call *Full Details (FD)* coins and pay no premium for them! Moreover, unlike with certain Buffalo and (especially) Jefferson nickels, *each and every date* in the Shield nickel series actually exists with Full Details—although for some dates, you will need to do some looking.

Toning is also important to the connoisseur. While nickels can tone deeply in a natural manner, most have not. You should seek brilliant or lightly (and attractively) toned coins—but be mindful that any fully "brilliant" Shield nickel is that way because it has been dipped (expertly and carefully, one would hope). Also keep in mind that many toned Shield nickels, including certified examples, have been given artificial color. Nothing does a better job of concealing friction or dullness than the application, by heat or chemical means, of what is usually sold as "natural" toning!

For circulation strikes, insist on coins with rich luster or, depending upon the die characteristics, a pleasing, partially prooflike character. For Proofs, you want deeply mirrored fields, available for all dates except for 1878, which may be either lustrous (resembling a Mint State coin!) or somewhat mirrorlike. For most mirror-field Proofs, the devices are in cameo contrast—that is, they appear frosty against a dark-appearing mirror background. Cameo contrast can be mild to extreme, and can be present on one side or both sides of the coin. Proofs with high degrees of cameo contrast on both sides are highly prized by the connoisseur. In the Shield series, it is likely that the earliest strikes from a Proof die have the best cameo contrast.

Grading services began applying the terms *cameo* and *deep cameo* (*CAM* and *DCAM* abbreviations) after many Proofs had been certified without this practice. It has been my experience that the cameo and deep cameo designations help coin owners to sell them for higher prices, but that those coins may be no different from Proofs of the same years that do not bear this label.[2] If cameo coins are your forte, some cherrypicking will pay dividends. In many instances, Proof Shield nickels that lack cameo contrast have been cleaned by light polishing, which destroyed some of their original cameo effect.

Avoid any Mint State or Proof coin with a dull or lifeless appearance, which is usually the result of multiple cleanings and retonings. As to circulated coins, examples in grades from Good to About Uncirculated should be light or medium gray, never brilliant, and should have no distracting nicks, scratches, or other marks.

The "I like it" (or eye appeal) test never fails. Once a coin meets your other criteria, be sure it is beautiful to behold. If it is, then when the time comes for you to sell your collection, you can be assured that prospective buyers will feel the same way.

As to market prices, no regular varieties are so rare that in order to acquire them you will have to set a record price at auction, or do without them for a long time. Exceptions do exist, but they are mainly within interesting die varieties (see below) and patterns (see appendix A), plus, perhaps, the 1880 in circulation-strike (not Proof) format.

My recommendation is to learn the approximate market price of each Shield nickel you seek—and when a coin of your selected quality comes along, buy it. Don't be afraid to pay a premium, say 10% or 20% over market, if an opportunity is at hand and the coin is somewhat scarce. In this way, you will own the coin you want, while everyone else is still looking!

Focus on Shield Nickel Specialties

Collecting Circulation Strikes

Collecting a full date sequence of circulation strikes can be a great challenge. Such a display consists of one each of the dates from 1866 to 1883, except 1877 and 1878, the latter two being made only in Proof format. The 1867 Shield nickel comes in two varieties—With Rays (scarcer) and Without Rays. The 1883, 3 Over 2, overdate is a worthwhile addition to such a set.

The rarest single circulation-strike date is the 1880. In Mint State, this is very elusive, although not obviously so, because many readily available Proofs have been sold as "Mint State" over the years. In the next chapter I give some ideas for differentiating Mint State coins from Proofs.

The availability of other dates is generally proportional to their mintages, except that 1883 is plentiful, for many were hoarded for investment purposes.

As circulation strikes are different from Proof strikes, they can be collected separately. Decades ago, most numismatists simply opted to acquire Proofs. Today, specialists strive for separate examples of each for the different dates.

The rarity of Mint State coins is not at all related to the rarity of Proofs. The greatest rarity in a Mint State set is the 1880—one of the more plentiful Proof issues. The rarest of all Proofs, the 1867 With Rays, is scarce in Mint State, but hardly a numismatic landmark.

Collecting Proofs

A full set of Proof Shield nickels consists of one of each date from 1866 to 1883, with three examples of 1867: one With Rays and two Without Rays (the latter representing two reverse die styles).

As a general rule, Proofs from 1866 to 1876 are harder to find in gem (PF-65 or finer) preservation than are the later ones. Cleaned and spotted coins are plentiful. The demand for the 1866 Proof is enhanced by its appeal to numismatists building type sets. Proofs of 1877 vary in quality—those of 1878 (with luster, as noted) are usually seen choice, and those from 1879 through 1883 are easy to find in high levels.

Occasionally, imperfect Proofs with light areas of details, or a mushy appearance, or with lint marks (impressions of pieces of hair, thread, or debris) will be seen, most often for dates in the early 1870's. Other Proofs have patches or areas of the field in which, rather than a mirror surface, there is a grainy texture instead—this being most often seen near the numeral 5 on the reverse. Such characteristics are not mentioned on holders and are seldom noticed in auction or retail descriptions, so you need to be alert. Pass these by, for in each date it is possible to find choice examples.

Introduction to Interesting Varieties

If William Shakespeare were to come to life and consider collecting Shield nickels, he might find that a run of dates would be fine, and that oddities and die varieties are much ado about nothing. And, many others would share his opinion. This is a good

An 1868 Shield nickel with a spectacularly repunched date—one of many curious, indeed bizarre, die oddities in the series (FS-301).

thing in a way, for many varieties are very scarce, but affordable, and a great demand for them would change the equation. *Nowhere else in numismatics does any series offer such a great number of dramatic date repunchings and die doublings.* Howard Spindel suggested this explanation:

> Dies for other series produced far more coins per die, because the planchets they were striking were softer. Even for the nickel three-cent coins, the planchets were thinner and smaller and did not impede metal flow like thick, hard Shield nickel planchets did.
>
> Shield nickel dies wore out at an alarming rate, and the popularity of the coin placed great strain on the Mint to produce dies to keep up with the failures. The haste and carelessness with which these dies had to be produced caused the numerous errors.[3]

The resulting varieties have attracted many people over a long period of time. A "Who's Who" in this specialty would include, alphabetically, Jack Beymer, Walter Breen, Larry Briggs, Thomas K. DeLorey, Bill Fivaz, Edward L. Fletcher Jr., Ken Hill, Douglas Kurz, Cynthia Mohon, Dennis Paulsen, Gloria Peters, Chris Pilliod, Les Leroy Smith, Howard Spindel, J.T. Stanton, and Michael Wescott—this being just a short list![4]

Even among nickel five-cent pieces in general, Shield nickels offer the widest range of spectacular date repunchings, mistakes, and other curiosities. In the pages that follow, I describe some of the highlights, but for total immersion you may want to acquire a copy of two studies: the aforementioned *Cherrypickers' Guide to Rare Die Varieties* and Edward L. Fletcher Jr.'s *The Shield Five Cent Series* (which devotes 219 pages to the subject!). The date 1868, in particular, is a playground for repunching, errors, and the like.

The numismatic world has changed much since September 1949, when very little was known about such things, and even the editor of *The Numismatist* had to call for help:

> Barney Bloom of Rochester, New York, has found a variety of the 1866 nickel 5-cent piece that is evidently a rare, unlisted variety. Apparently the engraver cut the last 6 too far to the right and then recut another when the mistake was discovered.

> As the photograph shows, part of the 6 can be seen plainly to the right of the date. Mr. Bloom, whose address is 160 Rosaling Street, would be interested to learn if other collectors have seen such a variety.

Back to the present day: an overview of some of the more popular categories is given below.

Significant Die Variety Categories

The field of misplaced dates, curiously abbreviated as *MPD* (like the University of Vermont is known as UVM), is a relatively new one. Across the various American series, many dozens have been identified. These typically consist of a small part of a four-digit date logotype impressed into the working die, in the denticles just below the date position. In other instances, a touch of the punch can be seen elsewhere, in the design above the date. The MPD traces are not in the date area and are not errors in date punching.

Although theories vary, here is mine: An engraver seeking to punch a four-digit date logotype into a working die had before him such a die. It was thought to be in soft steel, but exactly how soft was not known, as this aspect varied from die to die. As a little test, a slight tap of the logotype was made somewhere near the date position—often unobtrusively at the rim, slightly into the denticles, to test the hardness. With that done, the engraver moved the punch to the regular position and hit it with a hammer to drive it into the working die in the correct place. Some misplaced dates are located elsewhere, but still close to the date position, such as traces of a 1 in 1867 in the ball below the shield, for at least two dies of 1867.

In the Shield nickel series, a repunched date (also curiously abbreviated, as *RPD*) consists of a coin with a bold, regular four-digit date plus traces of one (usually) or two earlier efforts at punching in the date. Sometimes just a digit or two of the earlier date can be seen. In other instances, as in certain dramatic repunchings of 1866, most of an entire earlier punch can be seen. In some instances in which the numeral sizes of the earlier date do not match those of the later, final date, a four-digit logotype intended for another denomination was used.

Doubled-die coins have a doubling or overlapping of features caused when a working hub was impressed more than once into a working die, but slightly off-register. In the Shield series, most doubled dies are obverses. Generally, a quick (though not foolproof) way to tell if a die is doubled is to examine the little annulet, or raised ring, at the bottom of the pattee cross, where doubling is often most obvious.

The overdate dies of 1883, 3 Over 2, are of course interesting, as are the logotype-punch variations in 1869 and 1873.

The 1870 Shield nickel with an obverse clash from the working die of an *Indian Head cent* is particularly fascinating. It is a shame that it is so rare as to be virtually noncollectible. However, hope springs eternal, and there is always the possibility of finding one that no one else has noticed. The fruit of cherrypicking is one of the greatest appeals of variety hunting.

Other unusual varieties include the "leaf situation" for certain Shield nickels of the earlier years. The second cluster of leaves at the upper right was intended to have

The most dramatic repunched date in the Shield nickel series is FS-302, F-10, sometimes called the 11886666 nickel. The number of different, dramatically obvious repunched-date varieties known for dates in the 1860's and early 1870's is incredible.

This doubled-die obverse is from 1872 and is listed as F-6 (not in the Fivaz-Stanton text). Note the particularly prominent doubling on the annulet.

A dramatically double-punched date on an 1866 Shield nickel, FS-301, F-08. A four-digit punch was first entered too far to the right, and then was corrected. To see such varieties is to love them, and the many varieties available in the Shield nickel series have drawn many collectors like a magnet. This particular coin is from the Sunnywood Collection, one of the more notable cabinets of this specialty.

four leaves, but one was omitted. For many dies, the engraver simply added the missing leaf by hand. On other dies, the missing leaf was ignored. Edward L. Fletcher in particular has studied this aspect, and among collectors, James V. Jones is prominent in this specialty.

Broken and deteriorated letters, especially on the reverse, offer interesting collecting opportunities, but are not considered to be as important as are repunchings or doublings. Different hub and die arrangements on the reverse, called *styles* in the discussion above, can be collected; in some instances, most notably 1868, different reverses can be collected for the same date.

Many Shield nickels show cracks in the obverse and/or reverse dies, this being most evident among the earlier dates. Such coins sell for little or no premium, but can be interesting to own and study. Perhaps it is the sharply struck (Full Details) nickels without cracks that should sell for a premium, but little publicity has been given to such pieces.

At my invitation, noted Shield nickel authority Howard Spindel created the following article, an *enticement* it seems, for the present text. Reading it may be dangerous to your numismatic plans and schedule!

Shield Nickel Varieties

by Howard Spindel

Shield nickel varieties are fascinating and exciting to collect!

One of my first Shield nickels was an 1868 that I purchased from a dealer's junk box for $6. When I took it home and looked at it under good magnification, I didn't understand at all what I was seeing. There were, apparently, two annulets! I took this bizarre coin to my local dealer. He had a copy of the Breen *Encyclopedia* in stock, which showed photos of similar doubled-die obverse Shield nickels. As the song lyrics say, "Just one look is all it took!" I was hooked. I could not believe that the Mint had allowed coins to escape that were so strange looking.

Ed Fletcher's wonderful book about nickel varieties, *The Shield Five Cent Series*, had not yet been published. Aside from the few clues in Breen's *Encyclopedia*, I was very much in the dark about what Shield nickel varieties really were. The Internet was too nascent to be of much help, either. Still, I went to coin shows and tried to find more of these fascinating pieces, with little success. When Ed's book came out, I was absolutely blown away by the incredible numbers of varieties to be had.

As the Internet matured, I gained access not only to a wide range of dealer stock, but also to the few other individuals who collected Shield nickel varieties—most notably Ken Hill. Today there is a growing community of Shield nickel variety collectors, and I have derived at least as much pleasure from interacting with these collectors as I do from collecting. I co-moderate a Yahoo! discussion group on these. We joke that there is "no cure for Shield nickel variety disease."

Why is there no cure? Because pound for pound, Shield nickels offer more to the variety collector than any other U.S. series.

No other specialty in federal coinage comes close to having the depth and breadth of varieties packed into the 18 short years of the Shield nickel. Do you like varieties that you can see without squinting through a 15x glass? Do you want giant doubled dies that make you think you are going cross-eyed? Do you favor repunched dates that are so far off placement that you think the die sinker must have been drunk? Do you seek something really bizarre, like a nickel with a date punch from a dime? You can find all these and more in Shield nickels.

And here's the really exciting secret about Shield nickel varieties: lots of sellers don't look for them. Shield nickels are a cherrypicker's paradise, where you can, with some regularity, claim a rare variety for the price of a common coin. Every day spent looking through Shield nickels is a treasure hunt.

Do you want to collect something that will keep you busy for the rest of your life? No one will ever own all of the Shield nickel varieties. No one will ever own even a complete *subset* of Shield nickel varieties, for example, all of the doubled dies. In fact, new varieties are discovered quite often—you could discover one, too!

Just one look, that's all it will take.

6

Shield Nickels 1866–1883: Analysis by Date

1866

Circulation-Strike Mintage:
14,742,500

Proof Mintage:
800 to 1,200 (estimated)

Key to Collecting: The 1866 Shield nickel is in great demand as the first year of issue and also for inclusion in type sets for the With Rays design. Examples are available in nearly all grade ranges, but quality can be a problem. Most Mint State coins (example illustrated here) have problems of one sort or another, being dull and lifeless (often from overdipping) and/or having weak areas of detail (on at least 90% of the coins examined) and a simple lack of eye appeal. Probably no more than 1 in 10 MS-65 or finer coins is really superb in the eyes of the connoisseur. Most probably, the rarity of this date in the MS-66 grade is due more to overall lack of eye appeal than to actual wear. The good news is that dies of this year abound with interesting repunchings, cracks, and other differences, most of which can be studied and enjoyed with a low-power magnifying glass.

Proofs are readily available and are usually well struck; however, most have been dipped multiple times, giving them lifeless surfaces. Many others have hairlines or are spotted. Cherrypicking is advised, as probably not more than 1 in 5 or 10 will be a "keeper" for a connoisseur. Such Proofs were first sold in the summer of 1866, after many collectors had ordered Proof sets from the Mint. The Mint once offered single Proofs for 10¢ each for those interested.

Circulation Strikes

Characteristics and Appearance: All are from Reverse Style B (illustrated above; Proofs are different, as described below). Details are usually light in some areas, such as the star centers and the horizontal lines in the shield. Luster can range from dull to (not often) very frosty. Most dies show cracks, sometimes very extensive ones—an interesting feature without effect on the market price. At least one die shows extensive crumbling at the denticles at the lower left of the obverse. Striking is usually light in areas. Points to check include the horizontal and vertical shield lines on the obverse and the star centers on the reverse. Not more than 1 coin in 10 has all star-centers sharply defined (although they may be visible). Sharply struck coins with excellent eye appeal are *rare.* Cherrypicking is the order of the day to find one! All are of Reverse Style B, with a *star pointing under the right serif of the E in STATES.*

Mintage and Distribution Notes: Production of the new Shield nickels began on June 11, 1866, and supplies began reaching circulation soon afterward. There seems to have been a wide call for the new coins, this demand continuing through the next several years. No bank or Treasury caches or hoards have ever been reported.

Great problems were experienced with the dies and the hard nickel alloy, and it was unusual for a pair of dies to last for more than 10,000 impressions. "The die usage was so heavy that the engraving department had trouble keeping up with the demand and coinage was actually halted on occasion while waiting for fresh dies."[1]

At the time, there were only a few dozen rare coin dealers, at most, in the United States. Likely, some stocked Proofs, but ignored circulation strikes. The epicenter of the trade was in Philadelphia, and in this and subsequent years, there was a strong interest and lively trade in patterns (see appendix A).

1866: Circulation Strike

GSID	VG-8	F-12	VF-20	EF-40	AU-50	MS-60	MS-63	MS-65	MS-67
2868	$45	$70	$115	$180	$230	$415	$625	$1,700	$36,000

Proof Strikes

Characteristics and Appearance: All seen are well struck, save for a common lightness on certain horizontal shield lines, usually on the right side; however, the separation of the lines is complete.

The obverse die has a tiny, raised center dot, made by a compass point or center punch. It has been suggested that this may have been a handmade die using various elements, but no difference has been located with regard to the positions of the letters, denticles, and the like in relation to each other.

Most Proofs I have seen are sharply detailed. In the past, some circulation strikes with prooflike surfaces have been sold as Proofs. Today, anyone with an elementary awareness of Reverse Style A (with a prominent center dot and with 5 repunched at upper left; used only for Proofs in 1866) and Reverse Style B can determine which is which.

The obverse die is well basined, giving curvature to the field where it meets the border. The reverse is plane (flat), but the field is somewhat wavy, as can be seen if an example is held at a certain angle to the light.

The obverse die was highly repolished late in its career. All known Proofs are from Reverse Style A (see chapter 4) with a *star pointing under the left serif of the final S in STATES.*

Mintage and Distribution Notes: Estimates for Proof mintages (800–1,200) vary widely. Likely, Proofs were restruck in later years as demand for them arose.

1866: Proof Strike

GSID	PF-60	PF-63	PF-64	PF-65	PF-66	PF-67
2889	$1,200	$1,700	$1,950	$2,500	$2,900	$12,500
2890 (Cameo)	1,450	2,000	2,400	3,500	5,500	17,000
2891 (Deep Cameo)	—	—	6,000	8,000	13,000	38,500

Varieties

Repunched Date—Several obverse dies show repunching, with two (Fivaz-Stanton numbers FS-301 and 302, a.k.a. Breen-2461/2462 and Fletcher-8/10) being breathtaking—with virtually the full earlier date being bold and off register to the east by the width of half a numeral and two-thirds of a numeral, respectively. (See the selected bibliography for information on the Fivaz-Stanton, Breen, and Fletcher texts.) These have been known for many years but have achieved publicity only since the 1960's. Few repunchings anywhere in American numismatics are this dramatic.

Repunched Dates: FS-301 and FS-302.

1866, Repunched Date (FS-301): Circulation Strike

GSID	VG-8	F-12	VF-20	EF-40	AU-50	MS-60	MS-63	MS-65	MS-67
376255	$285	$455	$850	$1,100	$1,400	$2,500	$5,000	—	—

1866, Repunched Date (FS-302): Circulation Strike

GSID	VG-8	F-12	VF-20	EF-40	AU-50	MS-60	MS-63	MS-65	MS-67
2887	$285	$455	$850	$1,100	$1,400	$2,500	$5,000	—	—

Missing Leaf—No outside leaf on the second group at right; three leaves instead of four. Edward L. Fletcher describes only three dies with this feature from 25 dies listed, but Howard Spindel (in his computerized *Shield Nickel Viewer*) has found five.

1867, With Rays

Circulation-Strike Mintage:
2,019,000 (estimated)

Proof Mintage:
55 to 80 (estimated)

Key to Collecting: The 1867 With Rays nickel is basically scarce, and it has been recognized as such for a long time. However, in the modern era of emphasis on *condition rarity*, and with relatively few truly choice high-grade examples around, this variety suffers from lack of publicity. Quality is a problem when you find one. As with the 1866, there are usually problems with sharpness, and many coins are dull. Over a long span of years, I have seen only a handful of coins that truly combine a high grading number with sharply struck details and good eye appeal. A choice Mint State 1867 With Rays is, in a word, a *sleeper*. However, coin for coin, the 1867 With Rays has a higher average quality than do the nickels of 1866.

The 1867 With Rays Proof (illustrated above) is a classic rarity. Probably no more than several dozen or so are known; there are some prooflike Mint State coins that have been mistakenly called Proofs. The mintage is unknown. Students of the series have given many opinions, including the statement that no Proofs at all were struck until several years later. John Dannreuther, who has studied the die technicalities, has demonstrated that Proofs were struck on several runs. Per the same authority, an estimated 15 originals were made in 1867, plus perhaps three or more times that many were made on at least five later production sequences.[2] Likely, dealers with close connections to the Mint—John W. Haseltine being the prime example—simply ordered more Proofs as needed for store stock. The depth and breadth of such restriking is just now beginning to be appreciated, with new leading-edge scholarship by Dannreuther and others.

For Proofs, quite a few grading *events* (not necessarily different examples) have been reported by the grading services—numbers that would have been impossible to believe a few decades ago.

Circulation Strikes

Characteristics and Appearance: Usually fairly well struck, better than the typical 1866 of this type. Points to check for weakness include the horizontal lines in the shield and, on the reverse, the centers of the stars. Nicks on areas that are lightly struck are likely from the surface of the original planchet. All circulation strikes have Reverse Style B, as do Proofs.

Mintage and Distribution Notes: The widely published mintage figure for this issue is an estimate by R.W. Julian, per this commentary contributed to the present work:

> The coiner notified Mint Director William Millward that he proposed to change the design on February 1, 1867, but we do not know if this was done on that exact day. As a result the best we can do is estimate the number of Shield nickels with rays struck in 1867 at 2,019,000, the number coined in the month of January. This leaves 28,890,500 as the number of 1867 nickels coined without rays on the reverse. The average for the last 11 months of 1867 is a very creditable 2.6 million pieces

per month, which was the best monthly average (in a given year) until 1906, nearly 40 years later. It also shows the great public demand for the new coin.

1867, With Rays: Circulation Strike

GSID	VG-8	F-12	VF-20	EF-40	AU-50	MS-60	MS-63	MS-65	MS-67
2869	$49	$75	$130	$210	$275	$495	$725	$3,250	$36,000

Proof Strikes

Characteristics and Appearance: The details are usually quite good. Later die states (restrikes) show lightness of some lower-relief details in the dies, due to repolishing. The surfaces of Proofs range from deeply mirrored to somewhat grainy. Although the rims vary from wire to rounded, the outside edge, when viewed edge-on, is always mirrorlike.

All have Reverse Style B (illustrated on page 67). Three obverse dies were used: John Dannreuther's "1867 With Rays Nickel, Proof," revised and updated from time to time on the Collectors Universe website, is an extensive essay on this fascinating rarity, including photographs. While the text is beyond the scope of this book, his conclusions can be summarized as follows: Three obverse dies (I'll call them Dannreuther-1, 2, and 3) were used to make Proofs. These dies were used on multiple occasions.

Dannreuther-1: Left base of 1 over *right* part of denticle; 7 recut; lower shield *clear*; fully "detached" leaf. This die is known in two different states, indicating use on at least two different occasions. The earliest state was used to strike With Rays Proofs on or before February 8, 1867, then Without Rays Proofs, and then more With Rays Proofs. The later state is known only on With Rays Proofs. The later-state coins could have been made in 1867 or at a later time, but before the following.

Dannreuther-2: Left base of 1 over *left* part of denticle; die *polish* in lower part of shield; fully "detached" leaf. Certain characteristics delineated in the Dannreuther text reveal that this die was made in late 1867 or shortly thereafter. Anything was possible with Director Linderman in charge. This die is known in two different states, indicating use on at least two different occasions—the first, likely about 1867 to 1869; the second, about 1873 to 1879.

Dannreuther-3: Left base of 1 over right part of denticle; heavy die polish in lower part of shield; fully "detached" leaf. Also a later striking, likely circa 1873 to 1879. This was a time of extensive restriking, and a related rarity from the era, the famous 1864 L Proof cent, is known with three obverse and two reverse dies!

Mintage and Distribution Notes: John Dannreuther suggests that about 15 originals were made, of which perhaps 10 survive today. Probably 40 to 50 were indeed restruck later, in at least several press runs. It seems that for various regular Proofs in different series, the insiders at the Mint would make restrikes to order, a few at a time, possibly into the early 1870's. No records exist of the practice, and only the die characteristics of the existing coins can help reconstruct what was done. See Dannreuther discussion above, but for a vastly expanded text, check the Dannreuther posting on the Collectors Universe website.

1867, With Rays: Proof Strike

GSID	PF-60	PF-63	PF-64	PF-65	PF-66	PF-67
2892	$21,500	$28,000	$33,500	$36,000	$50,500	—
2896 (Cameo)	—	31,000	38,500	50,500	68,500	—

Varieties

Repunched Date (Nickel over Dime Logotype)—FS-301, F-08. The most dramatic variety shows the final date of 1867 flanked by a 1 to its left and a 7 to its right. Howard Spindel, in the *Shield Nickel Viewer*, confirmed that this is a Small Date (regular for nickels of this year) logotype punched over a Large Date intended for a *Liberty Seated dime*. The telltale overlay is shown at right.[3]

1867, With Rays, Repunched Date (Nickel Over Dime Logotype; FS-301): Circulation Strike

GSID	F-12	VF-20	EF-40	AU-50	MS-60	MS-63	MS-65
376263	$130	$260	$400	$600	$750	$1,000	$7,000

Repunched Date—Several varieties of repunched dates are known. The Fivaz-Stanton and Fletcher texts give descriptions, as does the *Shield Nickel Viewer*. Another interesting variety, FS-303, F-02, seems to have as an underdate an impression from a *smaller-date* logotype with a more delicate 7, but it is usually attributed simply as a repunched date.

1867, With Rays, Repunched Date (FS-303): Circulation Strike

GSID	F-12	VF-20	EF-40	AU-50	MS-60	MS-63	MS-65
376265	$100	$195	$300	$450	$565	$750	$5,250

Misplaced Date—On FS-304, F-01, URS 1, the base of the 1 in 1867 appears outside the ball at lower left. As Fivaz and Stanton note, "To date, this is still a unique example. Hundreds of dedicated Shield nickel enthusiasts are looking for this variety."

1867, Without Rays

Circulation-Strike Mintage:
28,890,500 (estimated)

Proof Mintage:
850 to 1,100 (estimated)

Key to Collecting: This issue has the highest circulation-strike mintage of any Shield nickel (see mintage-estimate notes under the preceding listing). As the first year of the Without Rays design, this coin is in additional demand for inclusion in type sets. These were produced starting in February, the removal of the rays being considered a solution to help reduce the tremendous problems in striking that had taken place the previous year. It was hoped that the life of a pair of dies would exceed 10,000 coins on a regular basis. Indeed, the revision did help, and coins of the new type are generally better struck.

Examples of the 1867 Without Rays nickel are plentiful today in just about any grade desired. Among Mint State coins, most are in the lower ranges, up to MS-64. True gems are rare. Striking is a problem, despite the absence of the rays. Also, the majority of coins are light in one place or another, although generally better detailed than the coins of 1866. Still, if you seek a combination of sharp details, good luster, and good eye appeal, probably not more than 1 in 10 coins will qualify. However, you have an insider's advantage in knowing what to look for—as most buyers are unaware, and certified holders make no mention of anything beyond a number.

Proofs are fairly elusive, and quality can be a problem, more in the way of eye appeal than in sharp details. Proofs exist from two reverse dies, style C (known as the normal reverse) and D (the Pattern Reverse; see pp. 39 and 40 for a detailed discussion). A normal-reverse Proof from the collection of 19th-century Baltimore numismatist T. Harrison Garrett, later in the Sunnywood Collection, is shown above.

Circulation Strikes

Characteristics and Appearance: Most are lightly detailed in one area or another, and many, if not most, show die cracks. The latter is not a negative as far as price goes, but it is a feature that adds interest.

1867, Without Rays: Circulation Strike

GSID	VG-8	F-12	VF-20	EF-40	AU-50	MS-60	MS-63	MS-65	MS-67
2870	$34	$38	$47	$85	$115	$170	$265	$875	$11,000

Proof Strikes

Characteristics and Appearance: Usually seen with deeply mirrored fields, with contrasting devices, and, for coins that have not been overly cleaned, with good eye appeal. Some have lightness at the star centers.

Mintage and Distribution Notes: 750 to 1,100 (estimated). The earliest, and today the rarest, Proofs have the Pattern Reverse (stars point under the upright of E in STATES and at the center of A in AMERICA). These were probably included in the first delivery of 25 full Proof sets of the 1867 year on February 5, although others could have been delivered singly (and no record kept). The obverse die state is very early and slightly different from that seen on the normal Proofs with the normal reverse (stars point under right serif of E in STATES and between A and M in AMERICA).[4] On the Sunnywood/Garrett Pattern Reverse coin, the obverse has a raised graver's line, somewhat resembling a die crack, in the frame of the shield to the left of the horizontal stripes. The base of the 7 in 1867 shows traces of an earlier 7 in the field slightly to the left. On June 5, 1867, the Philadelphia Mint paid photographer M.P. Simons to take pictures of the "reverse of five cents," type of coin not known (regular issue or pattern?).

Proof of 1867 with the Pattern Reverse.

Proof of 1867 with the normal reverse.

1867, Without Rays, Normal Reverse: Proof Strike

GSID	PF-60	PF-63	PF-64	PF-65	PF-66	PF-67
2893	$290	$550	$825	$1,150	$1,900	—
2894 (Cameo)	—	725	950	1,750	2,750	$5,000
2895 (Deep Cameo)	—	—	2,400	8,750	12,500	17,000

1867, Without Rays, Pattern Reverse: Proof Strike

GSID	PF-60	PF-63	PF-64	PF-65	PF-66	PF-67
81149	$2,250	$3,750	$7,500	$10,500	$13,000	—
81150 (Cameo)	—	5,000	8,000	11,000	15,500	—

Varieties

Missing Leaf—No outside leaf on the second group at right; three leaves instead of four. Edward L. Fletcher describes seven dies with this feature, to which Howard Spindel has added two more.

Repunched Date—Several interesting repunched dates beckon, representing dies in which the four-digit logotype was first entered, then entered again in a slightly different position. FS-1102, F-54 has the date repunched to the south southwest and is also a doubled-die obverse (most noticeable at the annulet).

1867, Without Rays, Repunched Date (FS-1102): Circulation Strike

GSID	F-12	VF-20	EF-40	AU-50	MS-60	MS-63	MS-65
379390	$88	$125	$165	$275	$375	$565	$2,000

1868

Circulation-Strike Mintage:
28,817,000

Proof Mintage:
750 to 1,000 (estimated)

Key to Collecting: This is a very plentiful date due to its high mintage. Gem Mint State coins are scarce, however, as few were saved. This high-mintage issue is spiced with many interesting die varieties, a veritable wonderland of delights! Proofs of this year and the next are often especially deeply mirrored.

Circulation Strikes

Characteristics and Appearance: Often with slight areas of light details, especially on the horizontal shield stripes and a few of the star centers. Luster varies but is usually good. Many die pairs were used, causing many variations. Usually seen with the normal reverse (illustrated above), but a few have the Reverse of 1868.

1868: Circulation Strike

GSID	VG-8	F-12	VF-20	EF-40	AU-50	MS-60	MS-63	MS-65	MS-67
2871	$34	$38	$47	$85	$115	$175	$260	$850	$10,000

Proof Strikes

Characteristics and Appearance: Generally well struck. Lightness, if present, is apt to be most noticeable on a few star centers. The field is deeply mirrored on nearly all. Many Proofs have the 68 in 1868 repunched to the south. Normal reverse.

1868: Proof Strike

GSID	PF-60	PF-63	PF-64	PF-65	PF-66	PF-67
2898	$275	$490	$600	$850	$1,600	$3,750
2899 (Cameo)	—	—	650	1,400	2,000	4,400
2900 (Deep Cameo)	—	—	—	—	6,250	—

Varieties

The Mint seems to have gone wild with erratic die punching this year, as there are *many* different repunchings, errors, and the like. The Fivaz-Stanton text devotes 16 pages to this date alone! There are multiple varieties of doubled dies and repunched dates. The CONECA files, maintained by Ken Hill, describe about 60 doubled dies for 1868-dated nickels. FS-102, F-111, is a tripled-die obverse, one of only three in the Shield nickel series.[5] The following are selected favorites of mine among the varieties of this year.

Repunched Date—This year offers a nice selection, the most dramatic being FS-310, F-20, with the first date placed south about 50% off register.

1868, Repunched Date (FS-310): Circulation Strike

GSID	F-12	VF-20	EF-40	AU-50	MS-60	MS-63	MS-65
379397	$70	$100	$130	$220	$300	$450	$1,600

Misplaced Date—FS-312; F-102, Flynn MPD-003. Ample traces of the 1 from a different date punch, much smaller than that used on the 1868 nickel, are seen protruding from the left side of the ball above the date. URS-4.

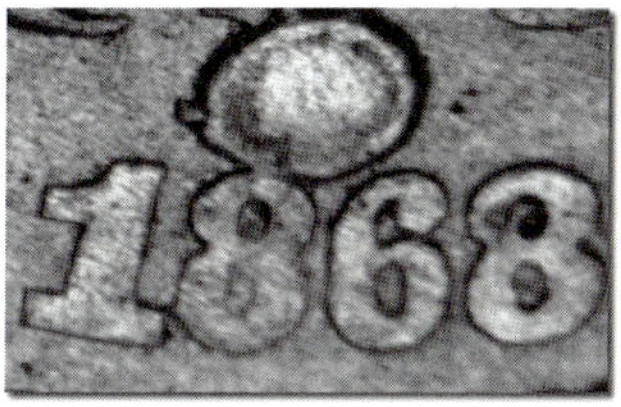

1868, Misplaced Date (FS-312): Circulation Strike

GSID	F-12	VF-20	EF-40	AU-50	MS-60	MS-63	MS-65
379391	$105	$150	$195	$330	$450	$675	$2,400

Scribe Mark—FS-401, F-56. A raised ring or circle line is mostly seen at the shield border. Someone scribed a circle, slightly off-center to the left, on a working die for unknown reasons.[6] The ring is most prominent as an arc above and to the upper left of the shield. As icing on the cake, this is also one of numerous missing-leaf varieties (see below).

1868, Scribe Mark on Obverse (FS-401): Circulation Strike

GSID	F-12	VF-20	EF-40	AU-50	MS-60	MS-63	MS-65
379392	$80	$115	$145	$250	$340	$510	$1,800

Reverse of 1868—Reverse die E was used only this year and only for a limited time. Among 1868 nickels, this scarce style can be quickly identified by stars that point under the left serif of S in STATES and at the interior of M in AMERICA (at the right edge of its left upright). While the Reverse of 1868 is seen much less often than the normal reverse, there are enough around to supply Shield nickel enthusiasts seeking an example.[7] The working hub, with the features in relief, failed at an early date, as certain letters became broken. Working dies made from that working hub display progressive deterioration. Three pages are devoted to the Shield reverse dies of 1868 in the Fivaz-Stanton work, based on the efforts of Dennis Paulsen.

1868, Reverse of 1868 (Reverse Die E): Circulation Strike

GSID	F-12	VF-20	EF-40	AU-50	MS-60	MS-63	MS-65
298945	260	360	455	625	—	—	—

Missing Leaf—No outside leaf on the second group at right; three leaves instead of four. Ed Fletcher lists 14 missing-leaf varieties, to which Ken Hill has added five more. Shown is FS-401, F-56. This is also the above-listed Scribe Mark variety (see for pricing).

1869

Circulation-Strike Mintage:
16,395,000

Proof Mintage:
850 to 1,100 (estimated)

Key to Collecting: The 1869 is plentiful in most grades. In Mint State, most are in the lower range. True gems, sharply detailed and with good eye appeal, are rare. An MS-64 or MS-65 is a good goal for a fine collection, when such pieces are selected with care as to their sharpness and overall quality.

There were two different date logotypes used this year: Narrow Date and Wide Date. These are interesting to collect and can be obtained by a bit of looking, as the varieties are not widely known. Proofs were made in fair quantity and appear on the market with frequency today, although quality can be a problem.

Circulation Strikes

Characteristics and Appearance: Striking is slightly better than on average for the preceding years, but many have some weakness on the horizontal shield lines and star centers. The luster is satiny and sometimes slightly prooflike. As many die pairs were used, no one rule fits all.

1869: Circulation Strike

GSID	VG-8	F-12	VF-20	EF-40	AU-50	MS-60	MS-63	MS-65	MS-67
2872	$34	$38	$47	$85	$115	$155	$280	$775	$6,250

Proof Strikes

Characteristics and Appearance: Striking varies. It is not unusual for one, two, or several stars to be slightly light at their centers, although displaying full separations of the six rhomboids that comprise each star. The field is deeply mirrored on nearly all.

Obverse Style 1a. All have the Wide Date logotype. Normal reverse (multiple dies from master die). Stars on No Rays point under right serif of E in STATES and between A and M in America.

1869: Proof Strike

GSID	PF-60	PF-63	PF-64	PF-65	PF-66	PF-67
2901	$275	$470	$550	$725	$1,000	$4,100
2902 (Cameo)	—	525	625	1,250	3,500	12,000

Varieties

Narrow Date—FS-301, F-01. From the center of the 1 to the center of the 9, the Narrow Date occupies the space of eight denticles, while the Wide Date occupies about nine. The Narrow Date is scarcer and was used only on circulation strikes. All examples have the normal reverse. Certain four-digit date logotypes for the 1869 coinage were supplied to the Mint on October 10, 1868, by local letter-cutter S.E. Adamson.

1869, Narrow Date (FS-301): Circulation Strike

GSID	F-12	VF-20	EF-40	AU-50	MS-60	MS-63	MS-65
377269	$39	$55	$72	$120	$155	$250	$880

Wide Date—FS-1101, F-413. From the center of the 1 to the center of the 9 the Wide Date occupies the space of nine denticles. The Wide Date was used on circulation strikes and Proofs. Circulation strikes are known with Obverse Styles 1a and 1b and with the normal reverse and the Reverse of 1868.

1869, Wide Date (FS-1101): Circulation Strike

GSID	F-12	VF-20	EF-40	AU-50	MS-60	MS-63	MS-65
379393	$56	$80	$105	$175	$225	$360	$1,280

Missing Leaf—No outside leaf on the second group at right; three leaves instead of four. At least six dies have this feature. See the listing for 1868 for a representative illustration.

Other varieties—Several varieties with slightly doubled dies and/or repunched dates are listed by Fivaz-Stanton, Fletcher, and Peters-Mohon. Breen's "1869/8 overdate," B-2480, has been discredited. Coins struck with the combination of Obverse Style 1b and Reverse D (the normal reverse) are rare.

1870

Circulation-Strike Mintage:
4,806,000

Proof Mintage:
850 to 1,100 (estimated)

Key to Collecting: The 1870 Shield nickel is fairly scarce in all grades. When Mint State coins are found, they are apt to be less than MS-65. Gems with sharp details and good eye appeal are in the minority. Proofs have a problem with quality, too, and some searching is needed to find a nice one.

Circulation Strikes

Characteristics and Appearance: Striking is about the same as found with 1869—better than for previous years, but still usually seen with some weakness on the horizontal shield lines and star centers.

1870: Circulation Strike

GSID	VG-8	F-12	VF-20	EF-40	AU-50	MS-60	MS-63	MS-65	MS-67
2873	$40	$65	$85	$110	$155	$245	$455	$1,300	—

Proof Strikes

Characteristics and Appearance: Regular Shield nickel Proof dies of the year, but usually seen with the reverse so highly polished that some of the details of the letters—such as sections from the tops of D, S, S, F, and R in UNITED STATES OF AMERICA, and the bottom of the S in CENTS—are removed. This die was also used on certain patterns. However, some Proofs are from a perfect die without broken letters. Proofs can vary in quality, with flaky or imperfect planchets.

Detail of Proof die showing the D in UNITED and the S in STATES broken at the top.

1870: Proof Strike

GSID	PF-60	PF-63	PF-64	PF-65	PF-66	PF-67
2904	$275	$495	$625	$725	$1,150	—
2905 (Cameo)	—	550	675	775	1,250	$12,000

Varieties

Doubled-Die Obverse—If there is a numismatic equivalent to the *Guide Michelin*, it is the Fivaz-Stanton *Cherrypickers' Guide to Rare Die Varieties.* The authors rate the Interest Factor to determine whether a variety is (to continue the analogy) worth a special trip—this being five stars (points). Then come four stars, perhaps worth a detour. Three-star varieties are mainly of interest to specialists, who are not in the mainstream of the hobby. Two-star varieties seem to be scarcely worthy of notice, but can be interesting. As to one-star varieties, they are not listed. For 1870, Fivaz-Stanton have four 5-star attractions, including FS-103, F-03, which combines a doubled-die obverse (most noticeable on the annulet below the cross) and a slightly repunched date. It is rated as URS-4, meaning an estimated population of 5 to 8 pieces. The *Shield Nickel Viewer*, by Howard Spindel, adds this:

> There are three doubled die reverses for 1870 that are extraordinarily interesting because they combine different hub designs. The FS-05-005.9 [FS-801] is Reverse Style F hubbed over a Reverse Style D. Even more interesting, there are two different doubled-die reverses showing a Reverse Style D hubbed over a Reverse Style F, giving the appearance of an 1870 with a Reverse Style D. Reference books say only that 1870 Reverse Style D is "rumored to exist." Both of the latter varieties are documented in the *Shield Nickel Viewer* (but nowhere else). The FS-05-005.9 [FS-801] is more available than the other two doubled-die reverses.

1870, Doubled-Die Obverse (FS-103): Circulation Strike

GSID	F-12	VF-20	EF-40	AU-50	MS-60	MS-63	MS-65
379394	$300	$400	$500	$750	$1,250	$1,500	$8,750

Clashed Die—FS-301, F-15, Flynn-MPD-001 (as it also has a misplaced date), with the comment that three or four are known, including one in Mint State. An interesting and rare 1870 Shield nickel was discovered by Ken Hill in 1994. In my 1996 book, *A Buyer's and Enthusiast's Guide to Flying Eagle and Indian Cents*, I gave some notice to it and added an illustration. In April 1996, I learned that only one other had come to light since 1994, an example in the inventory of Larry Briggs. Today, the variety remains extremely rare. In 2005, one surfaced on eBay.[8] Ken Hill recently added this: "I have attributed an Abt. G-3 coin, have seen a VF, and have heard from Michael Fey that he found an AU-58."[9] The obverse shows clash-mark impressions of the obverse of an Indian cent die. The face and headdress of Liberty appear clearly and in an inverted position in the background areas between the shield stripes on the nickel. The Indian cent obverse die was in the hammer (or top, movable) part of the setup in the coining press, while the obverse for the Shield nickel was in the anvil (or stake, immobile) position at the bottom.[10] This clashing was probably inadvertent and was caused by mismatched dies in the press during the press setup process (much in the manner that the famous 1857 clashed-die Flying Eagle cents were created).

On the other hand, Thomas K. DeLorey, who has studied two-denomination clashed dies in various series, noted, "I believe that all of the dual-denomination clash mark varieties were deliberate mulings to create novelties."[11] On this 1870 nickel, the 1 in 1870 is lightly quadruple-punched.[12] URS-2.

1870, Clashed Die (FS-301): Circulation Strike

GSID	F-12	VF-20	EF-40	AU-50	MS-60	MS-63	MS-65
379395	$600	$800	$1,000	$1,500	$2,500	$3,000	$17,500

Repunched Date, Misplaced Date—Known as FS-302, Fletcher-01, and Flynn-MPD-001, this misplaced date shows the top of a 0 in the denticles below and to the left of the regular 0 in 1870. Although opinions differ, I believe that most misplaced dates were made by using a numeral punch (not necessarily the one used for the full date) and making a tiny, "test" tap with it, in an unobtrusive spot, to determine the hardness of the die.

1870, Repunched Date (FS-302): Circulation Strike

Doubled-Die Reverse—The reverse of this variety (FS-801, F-14) was first punched by a master die for the normal reverse, then overpunched with a master die for the Reverse of 1868. The illustration shows the star pointing to the M in AMERICA and the rays from each style. This is a very important variety from a technical viewpoint, but few collectors are aware of it.

1870, Doubled-Die Reverse (FS-801): Circulation Strike

1871

Circulation-Strike Mintage:
561,000

Proof Mintage:
850 to 1,100 (estimated)

Key to Collecting: The low mintage figure has made this a key date for a long time. As most collectors who desired an 1871 bought Proofs, very few Mint State coins were saved, and are thus rare today. However, when seen, a gem Mint State example is usually very attractive. Proofs are readily available, but vary somewhat in quality.

Circulation Strikes

Characteristics and Appearance: Generally, fairly well struck. Weak details are sometimes seen at the horizontal lines in the shield. The 1871 date logotype, used on all circulation and Proof dies, has the 71 close.

Mintage and Distribution Notes: Numismatic scholar R.W. Julian told of a highly interesting situation:

> It is an odd fact that the low coinages of the 1870s did not exactly reflect the number of such pieces *issued* by the Mint. At this period of time, the Mint also served as a depository for the government and reissued base coins after they had been properly cleaned. Large numbers of minor coins were received at the Mint and reissued in the 1870s, thus holding down the need for new coins to be struck.[13]

1871: Circulation Strike

GSID	VG-8	F-12	VF-20	EF-40	AU-50	MS-60	MS-63	MS-65	MS-67
2874	$115	$160	$235	$340	$470	$675	$1,000	$2,250	$12,500

Proof Strikes

Characteristics and Appearance: Proofs are generally attractive, but not deeply mirrorlike. The obverse die on some is incompletely polished and shows many striae. Some have irregularities in the horizontal lines within the shield. As at least three die pairs were used to make Proofs, characteristics of striking can vary slightly.

1871: Proof Strike

GSID	PF-60	PF-63	PF-64	PF-65	PF-66	PF-67
2907	$275	$490	$625	$900	$1,200	$5,500
2908 (Cameo)	—	525	675	975	1,300	6,250
2909 (Deep Cameo)	—	—	—	—	7,000	—

1872

Circulation-Strike Mintage:
6,036,000

Proof Mintage:
850 to 1,100 (estimated)

Key to Collecting: The 1872 Shield nickel is available in all grades through gem Mint State, but is somewhat scarce at higher levels. Proofs often lack eye appeal, and care is suggested when buying. Most Proofs have slight doubling of the date numerals.

Circulation Strikes

Characteristics and Appearance: Usually fairly well struck. Mint State coins have satiny (rather than deeply frosty) luster. The Proof die pair with doubled-date obverse was also used to make a few circulation strikes.[14] About 10% of the 1872 nickels are of Obverse Style 1b, with the remaining being of Obverse Style 1c.[15]

1872: Circulation Strike

GSID	VG-8	F-12	VF-20	EF-40	AU-50	MS-60	MS-63	MS-65	MS-67
2875	$60	$100	$120	$130	$155	$220	$275	$1,300	$12,500

Proof Strikes

Characteristics and Appearance: Lintmarks can be a problem on Proofs of this era. Some Proofs have tiny nicks and marks in the shield stripes, the result of the original planchet's not being flattened completely during the striking process. One Proof die has doubling on the obverse (see the illustration above), most obvious at the annulet at the lower tip of the cross and at the meeting of the horizontal and vertical shield lines. Most seen today are from this die. A rare variant from the same die has the alignment in the same direction as the reverse, or medal-wise. "I have seen exactly one of these in years of searching," Howard Spindel reported.[16] As noted above, this die and its mate were also used to make some circulation strikes. Proofs have a mirrored edge (when viewed edge-on), while circulation strikes do not.

1872: Proof Strike

GSID	PF-60	PF-63	PF-64	PF-65	PF-66	PF-67
2910	$275	$490	$625	$675	$925	$3,750
2911 (Cameo)	—	525	675	725	1,000	4,100
2912 (Deep Cameo)	—	—	—	—	5,500	15,500

Varieties

Doubled Die—Many doubled obverse dies are described in the literature, including FS-101 through FS-107; one of these (FS-105, F-05) is tripled.[17] FS-103, (F-124, shown) is strongly doubled, including the upper frame of the shield. One curious die of this year is tagged with this comment by Fivaz and Stanton: "We just love this series, and with the number of new, great varieties that continue to turn up, you should too!" It is truly amazing that only a tiny fraction of the die doublings, repunchings, and so on described by Fivaz-Stanton, Fletcher, and Peters-Mohon were known to numismatists a generation ago.

In total, the CONECA files, maintained by Ken Hill, identify 32 doubled dies for 1872[18] (a number second only to that for the year 1868). These examples are documented in the panorama of photographs in Howard Spindel's *Shield Nickel Viewer* as well.

1872, Doubled-Die Obverse (FS-103): Circulation Strike

GSID	F-12	VF-20	EF-40	AU-50	MS-60	MS-63	MS-65
377272	$180	$240	$600	$420	$565	$720	$3,600

Small Over Large Date—FS-308, F-102. A too-large, four-digit date logotype for a *Liberty Seated dime* was first used, mostly effaced in the die, and the standard (Small Date) 1872 nickel punch was used. Traces of the Large Date remain. This variety was first reported by Ken Hill in the summer 1988 issue of *Nickel News*. URS-4. A similar error (FS-301) exists for the 1867 With Rays.

1872, Repunched Date (Small Over Large Date; FS-308): Circulation Strike

GSID	F-12	VF-20	EF-40	AU-50	MS-60	MS-63	MS-65
377273	$750	$1,000	$1,250	$1,750	$2,350	$3,000	$15,000

1873, Closed 3 and Open 3

CLOSED 3

Circulation-Strike Mintage

2,550,000 (estimated)

Proof Mintage:

1,500 to 2,000 (estimated)

OPEN 3

Circulation-Strike Mintage:

2,000,000 (estimated)

Key to Collecting: Although the mintage of the 1873 Shield nickel is generous, choice and gem Mint State coins are very elusive. When located, the problems of striking and eye appeal arise. In short, finding a nice example of either will be a challenge.

Although Closed 3 and Open 3 varieties exist for circulation strikes, with the Closed 3 being slightly more available, the collecting of both varieties is of limited popularity, except with specialists. Many opt simply to buy a Proof, all of which are of the Closed 3 style. (Opinions differ as to whether the correct term is *Closed 3* or *Close 3*, but *closed* is the more common usage.)[19]

If you have difficulty differentiating Closed 3 from Open 3, particularly on well-worn coins, take heart from this comment by Howard Spindel:

> It can be difficult to distinguish between Close 3 and Open 3 Shield nickels. Variations in how deeply the date logotype was entered by the die sinker into the die created coins than can puzzle collectors today. Shield nickel collectors joke that there are three logotypes for 1873: Close 3, Open 3, and "I Don't Know 3."[20]

A detail of the Closed 3.

A detail of the Open 3.

Mintage and Distribution Notes: Sometimes in numismatics, what starts out as a theory or estimate soon translates into fact. Such is the case with popularly published mintage figures for the circulation strikes of the 1873 Closed 3 and Open 3 nickels. The late Harry X Boosel, who made coins (of all denominations) of 1873 a specialty, published the estimate that for the Closed 3 the figure was 436,050, and for the Open 3 it was nearly 10 times this amount, or 4,113,950. However, my own experience and the population reports published by the grading services contradict this.

What probably happened is that Boosel learned that on January 18, 1873, the chief coiner, A. Loudon Snowden, complained that the 3 in the date logotype looked like an 8 at quick glance. On January 18, 1873, A. Loudon Snowden, chief coiner at the Philadelphia Mint, wrote to James Pollock, director of the Mint, as follows:[21]

Dear Sir,

I desire in a formal manner to direct your attention to the "figures" used in dating dies for the present year.

They are so heavy, and the space between each so very small that upon the small gold and silver and upon the base coins, it is almost impossible to distinguish with the naked eye whether the last figure is an eight or a three. In our ordinary coinage many of the pieces are not brought fully up, and upon such it is impossible to distinguish what is the last figure of the year's date.

I do not think it creditable to the institution that the coinage of the year should be issued bearing this defect in the date. I would recommend that an entire new set of figures, avoiding the defect of those now in use, be prepared at the earliest possible day.

I am Very Truly,
Your Obedient Servant
A. Loudon Snowden, Chief Coiner

Soon, across various denominations, new logotype punches (Open 3) were made, and new dies received this punch. Apparently, Boosel figured that while Shield nickels minted early in 1873 had the Closed 3 logotype, all later ones were struck from Open 3 dies. This is patently incorrect, as is evidenced by the fact that all *Proofs* are of the Closed 3 style, and that the Mint simply kept using the dies already on hand. Likely, for circulation strikes, Closed 3 dies already made were kept in service, until replaced with new dies.

The total circulation-strike mintage was 4,550,000. Circulation strikes of the 1873 Closed 3 are slightly more plentiful than those of the 1873 Open 3. Accordingly, my estimates—and they are simply that, estimates—are 2,550,000 of the 1873 Closed 3 and 2,000,000 of the 1873 Open 3.

Circulation Strikes

Characteristics and Appearance: Often, nickels of both date styles are lightly struck in areas, including the center of the obverse, the date, and certain stars on the reverse. The planchet stock was of mixed quality, and sometimes rough surfaces are seen. As noted above, the search for a high-quality coin of either variety will take some time.

1873, Closed 3: Circulation Strike

GSID	VG-8	F-12	VF-20	EF-40	AU-50	MS-60	MS-63	MS-65	MS-67
2877	$70	$95	$145	$180	$260	$455	$850	$2,300	—

1873, Open 3: Circulation Strike

GSID	VG-8	F-12	VF-20	EF-40	AU-50	MS-60	MS-63	MS-65	MS-67
2876	$49	$65	$80	$100	$190	$310	$650	$1,700	—

Proof Strikes (Closed 3 Only)

Characteristics and Appearance: Most Proofs are well struck and very mirrorlike.

1873, Closed 3: Proof Strike

GSID	PF-60	PF-63	PF-64	PF-65	PF-66	PF-67
2913	$275	$490	$600	$675	$950	$3,000
2914 (Cameo)	—	575	725	800	1,100	5,500

Varieties

Open 3, Large Over Small Date—FS-1301, F-106. A significantly smaller date logotype was punched into the die, and then overpunched with an 1873 Open 3 logotype of the correct size. Discovered by Bill Fivaz in 1987, this variety is best identified by the small 3 visible under and to the left of the final 3. URS-3.

1873, Open 3, Large Over Small Date (FS-1301): Circulation Strike

GSID	F-12	VF-20	EF-40	AU-50	MS-60	MS-63	MS-65
2878	—	—	$7,200	$11,000	$14,500	$16,000	$19,000

1873, Open 3, Doubled-Die Obverse

Circulation-Strike Mintage
Included in 1873, Open 3

FS-05-1101, F-114

FS-05-1102, F-102

FS-05-1103

Key to Collecting: Many interesting doubled-die obverses are known for the 1873 Shield nickel, in both the Closed 3 and Open 3 styles. This listing is for the Open 3 varieties.

On FS-1101, F-113, the doubling is most evident at the annulet. The east/west spread is very unusual; most Shield nickel doubled dies are north/south. URS-4.

On FS-1102, F-102, the obverse doubling is again most evident at the annulet. The date is misplaced, with parts of *several* numbers in the denticles below the 18 in the date. URS-5.

FS-1103 shows extremely strong doubling on the annulet, cross, and leaves. URS-5. This variety is often mistaken for FS-102. They can be distinguished by the date style: Open 3 for FS-1103, Closed 3 for FS-102. Another Closed 3 doubled-die obverse that is worth mentioning is FS-103, F-06, which has probably the widest spread at the annulet in the entire Shield nickel series.

For other interesting 1873 nickel varieties, check Fivaz-Stanton, Fletcher, and Spindel. The values shown here represent the most common doubled-die obverses for 1873, Open 3.

"Overdate" Pretender—Walter Breen reported not one but two different dies with the 1873, 3 Over 2, overdate. However, this has not been recognized by modern scholars. Bill Fivaz, for example, commented, "I've never seen an 1873 that convinced me it was a 3/2."[22]

1873, Open 3, Doubled-Die Obverse: Circulation Strike

GSID	VG-8	F-12	VF-20	EF-40	AU-50	MS-60	MS-63	MS-65	MS-67
326616	$120	$155	$195	$290	$470	$650	$1,100	$3,100	—

Note: Values are for the most commonly found 1873, Open 3 varieties.

1874

Circulation-Strike Mintage:
3,538,000

Proof Mintage:
1,000 to 1,200 (estimated)

Key to Collecting: Shield nickels of this date are available in all grades, but are slightly scarce. Sharpness of strike varies, as do the qualities of luster and eye appeal. Probably not more than 1 in 10 at the MS-63 or higher level is sharp, lustrous, and beautiful. Proofs vary in quality as well.

Circulation Strikes

Characteristics and Appearance: Striking is about average, with some weakness on the horizontal shield lines and, less often, the star centers. Die cracks are common.

1874: Circulation Strike

GSID	VG-8	F-12	VF-20	EF-40	AU-50	MS-60	MS-63	MS-65	MS-67
2879	$55	$90	$110	$130	$145	$230	$325	$1,100	—

Proof Strikes

Characteristics and Appearance: "A good percentage of 1874 proofs have the reverse star at 4 o'clock partially obliterated or flattened due to die grease being in the recess on the die," notes specialist Douglas L. Kurz.[23]

1874: Proof Strike

GSID	PF-60	PF-63	PF-64	PF-65	PF-66	PF-67
2916	$275	$490	$625	$800	$1,000	$3,250
2917 (Cameo)	—	525	725	1,000	1,300	3,750
2918 (Deep Cameo)	—	—	—	—	6,250	—

Varieties

Doubled-Die Obverse—FS-102, F-12. Strongly doubled die, not only at the annulet as usual, but also prominent at IN GOD WE TRUST, this being highly unusual. Edward L. Fletcher Jr. adds this:

> Although doubling has been found in the motto on other Shield varieties, the strength of the doubling (on the motto) on this particular listing is by far the strongest for the entire Shield nickel series and is extremely desirable in all grades. I have only seen three examples of this variety in the last 10 years.[24]

Other doubled-die obverses, with doubling most notable at the annulet, exist for this year.

1874, Doubled-Die Obverse (FS-102): Circulation Strike

GSID	F-12	VF-20	EF-40	AU-50	MS-60	MS-63	MS-65
373963	$260	$320	$500	$680	$1,000	$1,300	$6,000

1875

Circulation-Strike Mintage:
2,097,000

Proof Mintage:
1,000 to 1,250 (estimated)

Key to Collecting: The 1875 Shield nickel is fairly scarce, but enough Mint State and Proof examples come into and out of the market to assure a ready supply for Shield-nickel specialists. Quality varies with both circulation strikes and Proofs, as it seems that some planchets used this year were not of the highest quality. Gem Mint State coins can be very attractive.

Circulation Strikes

Characteristics and Appearance: The striking is usually good. Luster varies from dull to frosty. Quality is elusive for this date, and cherrypicking is advised.

1875: Circulation Strike

GSID	VG-8	F-12	VF-20	EF-40	AU-50	MS-60	MS-63	MS-65	MS-67
2880	$75	$110	$145	$195	$235	$310	$420	$1,300	—

Proof Strikes

Characteristics and Appearance: Proofs vary in reflectivity and quality. Some have graininess (incomplete mirror surface) on the reverse, which is not unusual for other Proofs of this era.

1875: Proof Strike

GSID	PF-60	PF-63	PF-64	PF-65	PF-66	PF-67
2919	$305	$455	$550	$1,000	$1,250	$5,500
2920 (Cameo)	—	500	625	1,150	2,000	7,500

Varieties

Doubled-Die Obverse—FS-101, F-04. Strongly doubled die, most prominent at the annulet. URS-5. Other doubled dies are listed by Fivaz-Stanton and Fletcher.

1875, Doubled-Die Obverse (FS-101): Circulation Strike

GSID	F-12	VF-20	EF-40	AU-50	MS-60	MS-63	MS-65
377274	$170	$220	$270	$375	$470	$615	$2,890

1876

Circulation-Strike Mintage:
2,530,000

Proof Mintage:
1,500 to 2,000 (estimated)

Key to Collecting: The 1876 Shield nickel is of medium scarcity. Mint State coins come on the market with frequency, but not as often as Mint State coins of the more plentiful dates (e.g., the 1860's, 1882, and 1883). The MS-62 to 64 range is typical. A properly graded MS-65 or finer coin, if well struck and with good eye appeal, is a rare find indeed.

Proofs exist in fair quantity, but often lack eye appeal. Some searching is required to find one that is PF-65 or better, deeply mirrorlike in all field areas, and with good eye appeal.

Circulation Strikes

Characteristics and Appearance: As multiple pairs of dies were used, sharpness and other aspects vary. Examples with Full Details (FD) and good luster are hard to find.

1876: Circulation Strike

GSID	VG-8	F-12	VF-20	EF-40	AU-50	MS-60	MS-63	MS-65	MS-67
2881	$65	$100	$145	$195	$215	$285	$360	$950	—

Proof Strikes

Characteristics and Appearance: At least two obverse dies were used. Usually well struck. The quality of mirror surface varies, but deeply mirrored pieces can be found. Some are mirrorlike on the obverse and slightly satiny on the reverse.

1876: Proof Strike

GSID	PF-60	PF-63	PF-64	PF-65	PF-66	PF-67
2922	$275	$455	$625	$725	$850	$2,750
2923 (Cameo)	—	550	675	775	925	3,000
2924 (Deep Cameo)	—	—	—	—	3,750	8,750

Varieties

Tripled-Die Obverse—FS-101, F-04. Strongly tripled die. URS-6.

1876, Tripled-Die Obverse (FS-101): Circulation Strike

GSID	F-12	VF-20	EF-40	AU-50	MS-60	MS-63	MS-65
379396	$400	$575	$750	$1,000	$1,250	$1,625	$6,250

1877

Proof Mintage:
1,250 to 1,500 (estimated)

Key to Collecting: With an estimated Proof mintage of only 1,250 or so, and with no related circulation strikes, the 1877 is far and away the rarest of all regular-issue nickel five-cent pieces from 1866 to the present time. Examples are often seen in the marketplace, this being especially true in recent times, due to the rapid movement of certified coins in and out of collections and investment portfolios.

The low mintage has made this a great attraction for many years. When you find an example, chances are excellent that it will be very attractive, with nice eye appeal. However, the surfaces are apt to be a hybrid of mint luster and mirror Proof.

Mintage and Distribution Notes: The 1877 Shield nickel is the first of two Proof-only dates in the series. Any mintage figure is guesswork (certification data can be useful in making estimates). I estimate the mintage to be on the order of 1,250 to 1,500 pieces. Likely, all were sold as three-piece minor Proof sets, which also included the bronze Indian head cent and the nickel three-cent coin. In addition, the expanded sets with silver coins also included the minors.

R.W. Julian located information in the National Archives to the effect that slightly over 900 Proofs were either included in sets or sold singly. By December 1877, all the Proofs were gone. If more than 900 or so were made, this was done "off the books."[25]

Characteristics and Appearance: At least two obverse dies were used, one with the 8 under the ball and the other with the logotype slightly to the left, with the 8 just about three-quarters under the ball. Usually well struck, although some have slight lightness in the horizontal shield stripes. Surfaces range from mirrorlike, with some graininess or luster, to mirrored. Most are very attractive. David W. Lange commented:

> The 1877 and 1878 nickels were produced only as Proofs, yet specimens that don't fully meet the conventional criteria for Proofs are known. Their fields are not fully brilliant, their rims and edges are not squared, and their strikes are incomplete. Since no nickels were issued for circulation bearing those dates, we must call them Proofs, even when they do not live up to expectations.[26]

1877: Proof Strike Only

GSID	PF-60	PF-63	PF-64	PF-65	PF-66	PF-67
2925	$2,400	$3,000	$3,500	$3,750	$4,500	$7,750
2926 (Cameo)	—	3,300	3,850	4,100	5,000	9,500
2927 (Deep Cameo)	—	—	—	4,400	8,000	11,000

1878

Proof Mintage:
2,350

Key to Collecting: With a mintage of just 2,350 "Proofs" and no circulation strikes, this is one of the rarest issues in the series. Nearly all Proofs are somewhat *lustrous* rather than deeply mirrorlike. It is an interesting debate whether pieces should be called Proofs because they were called that by the Mint and sold as Proofs to collectors, or whether they should be called Uncirculated, for they appear to be in the latter grade. Tradition dictates the Proof classification. The 1878 nickel usually has very attractive eye appeal.

Characteristics and Appearance: The strike is usually excellent on this issue. Many are from unpolished or incompletely polished dies, with mint luster or a combination of satiny luster and semi-prooflike surface. Few are deeply mirrored Proofs.

Walter Breen's Encyclopedia of United States and Colonial Proof Coins (1979) states that a single die pair was used for this coinage, and that the "rare earliest state has shaft of 7 in lower loop of last 8." This information is also found in the 1988 edition of *Breen*. Peters and Mohon (1995) wrote that "Experts do not agree that a genuine 'overdate' of this date exists."

Five obverse dies were made, but most remained unused. On the Internet, "low grade 1873 Close 3 nickels are often presented as impaired Proof 1878 nickels."[27]

Mintage and Distribution Notes: All 1878 Shield nickels were distributed as part of the year's minor Proof sets, which also included the Indian Head cent and the nickel three-cent piece. Some of these were distributed with the silver Proof sets. This is the first year for which the mintage figure is definitely known for a minor Proof set. Perhaps a circulation issue was envisioned, as five obverse dies are known to have been destroyed. R.W. Julian suggests that the large mintage for 1878 Proofs, in comparison to the number made in 1877, was from "demand from speculators, accelerated by the fact that 1877 nickels had been sold out by the end of that year."[28]

1878: Proof Strike Only

GSID	PF-60	PF-63	PF-64	PF-65	PF-66	PF-67
2928	$950	$1,400	$1,400	$1,450	$1,500	$1,750
2929 (Cameo)	—	1,500	1,550	1,600	1,650	1,900
2930 (Deep Cameo)	—	—	—	—	3,750	8,750

1879

Circulation-Strike Mintage:
25,900
Proof Mintage:
3,200

Key to Collecting: The 1879 Shield nickel is very rare in Mint State, but the market value is lower than expected, as Proofs are readily available and, indeed, are plentiful in the context of Proofs of the era. Mint State pieces are somewhat prooflike, rendering historical auction listings unreliable for research purposes. Moreover, one die pair was used to make both Proofs and circulation strikes. In worn grades the 1879 is very elusive, and a key to the series.

Proofs are easy enough to find, and are usually of nice strike and eye appeal. Many have repunching at the 9 and are attributed as "1879, 9 Over 8" by some. In my opinion, however, such coins are from a regular 1879 die with slight repunching.

Circulation Strikes

Characteristics and Appearance: Well struck, with satiny luster and somewhat prooflike, easily confused with Proofs. David W. Lange commented,

> Because of their very low, non-Proof mintages, business-strike nickels of 1879 through 1881 were made from dies that retained much of their initial brilliance. Combined with the fact that the Mint was somewhat careless in its Proof production during this period, the result is that both Proof and non-proof nickels look very much alike![29]

1879: Circulation Strike

GSID	VG-8	F-12	VF-20	EF-40	AU-50	MS-60	MS-63	MS-65	MS-67
2882	$775	$875	$1,000	$1,750	$2,050	$3,250	$4,000	$5,000	$15,500

Proof Strikes

Characteristics and Appearance: Usually well struck, with mirror surfaces and good contrast. Proofs have mirror edges (when viewed edge-on), while circulation strikes do not; this can help differentiate Proofs and circulation strikes of the same die pair. Some Proofs have a doubled date (F-01; see below) and are especially interesting (one in the Walter Childs Collection, sold in 1999, had been kept in the same family since it was ordered from the Mint). Another variety is B-2414, discussed below.

One obverse die, apparently comprising about 40% of the production run of Proofs, has a repunched 9 and is sometimes called an overdate (see below). Two Proof obverse dies are described by Edward L. Fletcher Jr.; one of these was later used to make circulation strikes. Peters and Mohon describe five different obverse dies—the "overdate" plus four with regular date. For dies with the date deeply punched, the numerals are close together, while lighter impressions have wider spacing.

1879: Proof Strike

GSID	PF-60	PF-63	PF-64	PF-65	PF-66	PF-67
2931	$275	$455	$550	$725	$1,050	$2,000
2932 (Cameo)	—	575	775	1,000	1,400	3,000
2933 (Deep Cameo)	—	—	—	—	5,500	—

Varieties

Doubled Date—F-01 (Proof) and 02 (same die used to make circulation strikes; FS-unlisted). Sharply repunched, with the lighter, earlier date slightly west of the final date—most noticeable to the left of the 1 in 1879.

So-Called Overdate "1879, 9 Over 8"—Breen-2414; FS-unlisted. Confirmed only with Proof finish, although Breen (*Encyclopedia*, 1988) mentions two circulation strikes and further mentions that there are "at least two varieties." Overdate status not determined, but likely a regular 1879 with slight repunching. Last digit with repunching within 9, said by Walter Breen to be an overdate, and long cataloged as such by many numismatists. However, in connection with the present study, I have been unable to match the 1878 logotype with the repunching in the 9, and there is no trace of the prominent lower-outside-right bulge of an 8 at the 9 of B-2414. In conversation with a numismatic expert at a leading grading service, Breen agreed wholeheartedly, adding, "but people want to call it an overdate anyway." On the other hand, Thomas K. DeLorey believes it is a true overdate.[30] Howard Spindel comments,

> I can't see anything that makes me want to conclusively state that it's an overdate. There just isn't enough extra metal there to make a solid judgment. The curve of the visible metal in the bottom bowl doesn't really look like the curve of a 9 to me, but I can't state for sure it's the curve of an 8. I don't think there's even enough metal there to do an effective overlay study. My feeling is that it is so visually unimpressive that it doesn't pay to get too worked up over whether it's an overdate or not."[31]

R.W. Julian advised that there is no record of any 1878 obverse dies having been destroyed, although five obverse dies of 1878 had been made.[32] If this is a fact (Mint records occasionally are erroneous), this would strengthen the case for an 1879, 9 Over 8 overdate. Perhaps a high-resolution image overlay—one of these and an 1878 logotype—would resolve the question.

According to Julian, records state that in January 1880, six obverse dies of 1879 were destroyed. Could these have included some dated 1878? Such are the intrigues of Shield nickel research!

1879, 9 Over 8: Proof Strike Only

GSID	PF-60	PF-63	PF-64	PF-65	PF-66	PF-67
2944	$410	$490	$675	$900	$1,400	$2,500
2945 (Cameo)	—	525	750	975	1,500	2,750

1880

Circulation-Strike Mintage:
16,000

Proof Mintage:
3,955

Key to Collecting: The 1880 Shield nickel is a rarity in Mint State and in all circulated grades, but in Proof finish it is one of the more abundant issues in the series. Mint State coins are exceedingly rare, but the number known will never be determined with certainty, for Proof dies were used to make circulation strikes as well. (See the notes below.)

Across all grades, the 1880 is the rarest circulation-strike Shield nickel, even allowing for the many misattributed Proofs listed in that category. There was no need for additional nickels for circulation, and it is likely that Mint Director A. Loudon Snowden ordered a small production simply to avoid creating rarities (as had been done in 1877 and 1878). He also did this for current *silver* denominations (dime, quarter, and half dollar), which were similarly unneeded. R.W. Julian adds this comment, based upon Mint archives: "Snowden specifically asked the Mint Bureau and Treasury for permission to strike limited runs of nickels and three-cent pieces so that collectors of small means, and those needing coins for presents, could obtain them. Applicants were limited to two pieces each, however."[33]

When buying an 1880, likely as not you will acquire a Proof. Most are deeply mirrored and have good eye appeal.

Circulation Strikes

Characteristics and Appearance: For reasons given below, Mint State coins closely parallel Proofs in appearance and are easily confused, even by professional graders.

Mintage and Distribution Notes: In 1880 the nickel five-cent piece was still redundant, due to the flood of long-stored silver coins that had been released into circulation beginning in a significant way on April 20, 1876. The mintage for circulation strikes reached a nadir this year. The 1880 has the lowest circulation-strike mintage for any date in the nickel five-cent series from 1866 to the present day.

1880 Circulation Strikes vs. Proof Strikes

John Dannreuther, Douglas Kurz, Howard Spindel, and I believe that for certain *unquestioned* circulation strikes, the reverse has these characteristics: upper left outside of the first S in STATES repunched, tiny raised "island" in the field below T of the same word (from die pitting), and a tiny line or thorn projecting into the field from the center of a denticle below the space between the T and S of CENTS.[34] This reverse, which we have seen only with a satiny (not Proof) surface, and never with a mirrored edge may be the key to identifying circulation issues. It exists in combination with the obverse used on Breen-2516 (first 8 grazes ball; interior of second 8 with repunching).

Only two obverse dies were produced for 1880, and both were used intermittently for circulation and Proof strikes. However, the use of a reverse die or die state other than that described above (with "island," "thorn," etc.) does not mean a coin is automatically a Proof. If such a coin is found with frosty surfaces and a nonmirrored edge, it, too, may be a circulation strike. The situation has not been completely resolved, but all coins with the die markers just mentioned seem to be circulation strikes.

Many Proofs have a "pebbly" aspect to the field on the reverse (see notes under "Proof Strikes"); it is thought that any coin with this pebbly Proof surface is excluded from the possibility of being a circulation strike.

As to how many Proofs may have been certified as circulation strikes, the study of certification data for related nearby dates has been informative.

1880: Circulation Strike

GSID	VG-8	F-12	VF-20	EF-40	AU-50	MS-60	MS-63	MS-65	MS-67
2883	$3,100	$4,000	$5,250	$8,000	$11,500	$18,000	$36,000	$72,000	—

Proof Strikes

Characteristics and Appearance: Deep mirror surface is the rule, but often with a slightly pebbly characteristic. This is best seen when a coin is held at an angle, reflecting the light into the viewer's eye. This may have been caused by resurfacing a die to remove roughness or rust.[35] Some have slight weakness in the horizontal shield stripes (not that most people would notice). Proofs used special planchets and were struck with a collar that imparted a deep mirror Proof finish to the edge (when viewed edge-on). B-2515 and B-2516 in combination with a *mirrored* reverse die with the perfect first S in STATES, no "island" below the T, and no thorn in the denticles at the lower rim.

1880: Proof Strike

GSID	PF-60	PF-63	PF-64	PF-65	PF-66	PF-67
2934	$275	$455	$550	$600	$725	$1,200
2935 (Cameo)	—	500	625	675	775	1,500
2936 (Deep Cameo)	—	—	—	2,500	3,750	—

1881

Circulation-Strike Mintage:
68,000

Proof Mintage:
3,575

Key to Collecting: The 1881 Shield nickel is remarkable for its scarcity as a circulation strike. Such pieces are so elusive that for many years most collectors have simply opted to acquire the readily available Proofs. It has also been a popular sport to classify Proofs as "Mint State," as the latter bring more money. The exact same thing is true for many of the dates in the nickel three-cent series of this decade. Before you pay a sharp premium for a coin described as Mint State, have an expert check it for you, although even the best of scholars are sometimes uncertain as to the attribution.

Circulation Strikes

Characteristics and Appearance: Pieces offered as circulation strikes tend to closely resemble Proofs, which indeed they may really be. One die that was used to make circulation strikes (traces of repunching near the rim, below the date) is not known to have made Proofs; buying one of these might be insurance if you want a true circulation strike—but keep in mind that as research goes on, accepted "facts" are often discarded. As a prime example, many comments made years ago in *Walter Breen's Complete Encyclopedia of United States and Colonial Coins* are now viewed as incorrect.

Mint records indicate that in January 1882, for circulation-strike nickels of 1881, seven obverse and nine reverse dies were destroyed.[36]

Mintage and Distribution Notes: On November 12, 1881, the Treasury Department's holdings of nickel five-cent pieces reached a low point, and the secretary directed that production in quantity recommence. By that time, many silver coins had been absorbed, and most of the once-competitive silver half dimes had been redeemed and melted.

Absent this call in November, it is likely that there would have been a nominal coinage of circulation strikes, following the path of the 16,000 made for 1880. John Dannreuther notes that years ago a Mint State 1881 nickel was a great rarity, but that in the late 20th century Norm Pullen, a professional numismatist from Maine, came across a remarkable cache of about 50 pieces, all very choice.[37]

1881: Circulation Strike

GSID	VG-8	F-12	VF-20	EF-40	AU-50	MS-60	MS-63	MS-65	MS-67
2884	$390	$470	$525	$675	$850	$1,200	$1,500	$3,250	$7,000

Proof Strikes

Characteristics and Appearance: Some have slight weakness in the horizontal shield stripes (not that most people would notice). Proofs are typically made from an overpolished obverse die, causing the stem on the highest inside berry at right to be incomplete. A deep mirror surface is the rule, although sometimes, there is a grainy non-Proof surface on the reverse near the 5 on various dates of the era. The same characteristic can be observed on certain Proof $3 gold coins of this time.

Peters and Mohon, drawing from Breen, state that one die (of two that were made) was used to make Proofs this year. The outline of the ball is incomplete near the first 8, among other characteristics. However, this die may have been used to make circulation strikes as well. Mint records indicate that in January 1882, for Proof nickels of 1881, two obverse and two reverse dies were destroyed.[38]

1881: Proof Strike

GSID	PF-60	PF-63	PF-64	PF-65	PF-66	PF-67
2937	$275	$455	$550	$600	$725	$1,200
2938 (Cameo)	—	500	625	675	775	1,500
2939 (Deep Cameo)	—	—	—	2,000	3,000	8,750

1882

Circulation-Strike Mintage:
11,472,900

Proof Mintage:
3,100

Key to Collecting: As its high mintage suggests, the 1882 is plentiful in all grades today. Many Mint State coins exist, including into the MS-65 and 66 categories. Most such high-grade pieces are well struck and have excellent eye appeal. Proofs are plentiful as well and are usually of high quality.

Circulation Strikes

Characteristics and Appearance: Slight weakness in the horizontal shield stripes is normal; otherwise, other areas are usually sharp. Many have the 2 in 1882 filled in (some of these have been incorrectly called overdates). Some coins are partially prooflike. Mint records indicate that in January 1883, for circulation-strike nickels of 1882, 507 obverse and 367 reverse dies were destroyed, and 18 reverses were held over for later use.[39]

Mintage and Distribution Notes: The January 1882 issue of *Banker's Magazine* included this:

> Owing to the small amount of five-cent nickel pieces in the Treasury, the Secretary has instructed the Director of the Mint to cause $17,540 in old copper cents and $104,018 in copper nickel cents, now in the Philadelphia Mint, to be recoined into five-cent nickel pieces, and instructions have already been given to carry out the direction. It will be some weeks before the Mint will be ready to begin the recoinage of these pieces, or to receive orders for the five-cent nickel coins from banks and others.

In February, the same magazine followed up with this:

> The coinage of five-cent silver nickels has been resumed by the mint at Philadelphia, and applications for the new coins, accompanied by money or checks, should be made to the superintendent. The cost of transportation of the nickels, in exchange for lawful money, in multiples of $20, will be paid by the mint.

The circulation-strike mintage of 11,472,900 and the destruction of 507 obverse dies after the end of the year indicate an average output of 22,629 coins per die. Although Mint records do not reflect this, some unused obverse dies were kept in service past 1882, and not destroyed, these being the several obverses used to create the 1883, 3 Over 2, overdates. Reverse dies destroyed amounted to 367, with 18 retained for later use.

1882: Circulation Strike

GSID	VG-8	F-12	VF-20	EF-40	AU-50	MS-60	MS-63	MS-65	MS-67
2885	$34	$38	$47	$85	$115	$155	$245	$575	$2,700

Proof Strikes

Characteristics and Appearance: Usually well struck. Deep mirror surface is the rule, although some have a grainy, non-Proof surface on the reverse near the 5. One obverse die has a slight bulge at the denticles below the first 8 in the date. Another has 882 repunched south. Mint records indicate that in January 1883, for Proof nickels of 1882, two obverse dies and one reverse die were destroyed.[40]

1882: Proof Strike

GSID	PF-60	PF-63	PF-64	PF-65	PF-66	PF-67
2940	$275	$455	$550	$600	$725	$1,200
2941 (Cameo)	—	500	625	675	900	1,500
2942 (Deep Cameo)	—	950	1,250	2,000	3,000	8,750

1883

Circulation-Strike Mintage:
1,451,500
(minus 118,975 for
1883, 3 Over 2)

Proof Mintage:
5,419

Key to Collecting: Although the mintage for circulation-strike 1883 Shield nickels is fairly low, this is the most common of all dates in terms of Mint State coins in existence today—even edging out the 1882 with its open-floodgates production of 11,472,900 coins! The explanation is that in early 1883 there was great excitement that Shield nickels of this date would become rare and valuable, in light of their replacement by the new Liberty Head nickels. Many were saved.

Today, most nickels of this date are fairly attractive. This is a very popular year to include in type sets.

Circulation Strikes

Characteristics and Appearance: The digits in the date logotype are very widely spaced on all dies (circulation strike as well as Proof) this year. Usually well struck. Lightness, if present, is apt to be in the horizontal shield stripes. Some are partially prooflike.

1883: Circulation Strike

GSID	VG-8	F-12	VF-20	EF-40	AU-50	MS-60	MS-63	MS-65	MS-67
2886	$34	$38	$47	$85	$115	$155	$245	$575	$2,700

Proof Strikes

Characteristics and Appearance: Usually well struck. A deep mirror surface is the rule, although sometimes with a grainy non-Proof surface on the reverse near the 5.

Mintage and Distribution Notes: The high mintage for this issue is likewise explained by the speculation that 1883 Shield nickels would become very rare. Proof Shield nickels continued to be minted and sold even after the Liberty Head nickels were issued. A. Loudon Snowden was aware of the speculation, and sought and received permission from the Treasury Department to continue making all three types of nickel designs for the rest of the year.[47]

1883: Proof Strike

GSID	PF-60	PF-63	PF-64	PF-65	PF-66	PF-67
2943	$275	$455	$550	$600	$725	$1,200
2984 (Cameo)	—	500	625	675	775	1,500
2985 (Deep Cameo)	—	—	—	—	3,750	—

1883, 3 Over 2

Circulation-Strike Mintage:
118,975 (estimated)

Key to Collecting: There are five known 1883 dies that show traces of an earlier 1882 date.[41] Dies for the 1882 were held over and overpunched with a four-digit 1883 logotype. The varieties, described below, vary in their clarity and, thus, in their appeal to casual collectors of Shield nickels. If you opt to acquire just one, FS-301 is the most dramatic and commands the greatest premium. If you are a dyed-in-the-wool die-variety collector, then all may appeal. The varieties that are not boldly overdated sell for lower premiums.

This variety was a favorite to cherrypick among regular nickels in the 1950's, for it was not widely publicized until the 1960's. A feature in "Collectors' Clearinghouse," *Coin World*, November 14, 1973, provided illustrations of different dies and further advanced the interest. However, consistency of certification attributions did not occur until the 1990's. Accordingly, in the marketplace in the past, the vast majority of 1883, 3 Over 2, overdates were listed as regular issues.

Today, finding a nice 1883, 3 Over 2, is doable, but not easily accomplished. The key is the sharpness of the overdate feature, not the details of the rest of the coin. Any grade from Extremely Fine upward is viewed as very desirable.

Circulation Strikes

Characteristics and Appearance: Usually seen in worn grades. Mint State coins are usually well struck and with a satiny luster. Howard Spindel, who has made a specialty of the overdate, offers this cautionary note:

> Beware of 1882 shield nickels with a filled in blobby 2, as these are very frequently offered as 1883/2. This is possibly the single most misunderstood coin in all U.S. coinage. The 1883 logotype is wider than the 1882 logotype, and the blobby 2 coins are of the narrower logotype.[42]

Mintage and Distribution Notes: The circulation-strike mintage for 1883 Shield nickels was 1,451,500. Sixty-one obverse dies of this date were eventually destroyed; if all were used in striking, this equals 23,795 impressions per obverse die. Four to possibly five or six overdate dies are known today; if, say, five are assumed, this suggests an overdate mintage of 23,795 x 5, or 118,975. Although such figures imply precision, they are hardly precise. Perhaps in the press run, one obverse cracked after 5,000 impressions, and another lasted through 35,000. However, for purposes of estimation I use 118,975 as the mintage figure, and deduct the same amount for the mintage of "perfect date" 1883 Shield nickels next listed.

From Howard Spindel:

> Based on the populations of varieties, I've been able to derive a general rule of thumb that says survival rates for any particular Shield nickel die approximate 1/10 of 1%. The figure will be somewhat higher in later years, such as for the 1883/2, but I believe only 2–3 times higher. These survival estimates do not include coins so worn as to be non-collectable.[43]

Varieties

The 1883, 3 Over 2 varieties are priced collectively at the end of the listing.

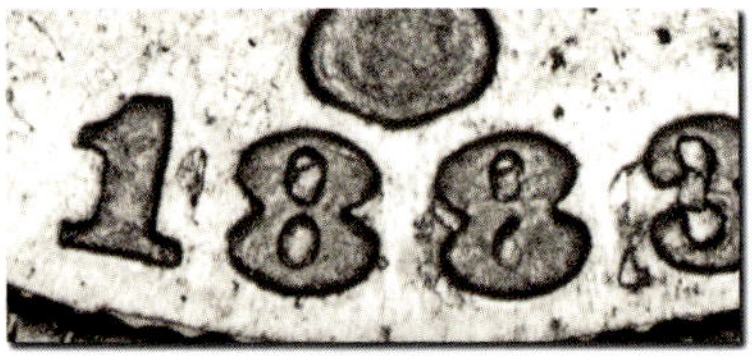

1883, 3 Over 2—FS-301, B-2524, F-08, PM-18V.4. This is the most dramatic of the overdates and is unequivocal. It is also the rarer of the two clearest 1883, 3 Over 2, die varieties.[44] An unused 1882 die was overpunched with a four-digit 1883 date logotype. The left two-thirds of the 2 can be seen at the left edge of the 3. This particular die was known to specialists in the 1950's, and I recall looking for them. However, the overdate was not listed in popular references, and few were aware of its existence. Accordingly, examples could be purchased for the same price as regular 1883 coins. The corollary is that once such a coin was found, customers for it were scarce.

1883, 3 Over 2—FS-302, B-2523, F-09, PM-18V.2. The lower left of the original 2 is clearly seen extending from the lower left of the 3. In my opinion, this is the second most desirable overdate die from the standpoint of clarity. This die eventually shatters, with a large crack mostly above and to the left and right of the date. Once considered to be quite rare, as additional examples have come to light it is now the most often seen of the three varieties listed by Breen. The rarity of certain other dies has not been studied in detail.

1883, 3 Over 2—FS-303, B-2526, F-10, PM-18V.3. To create this die it seems that the 1882 date was partly ground off, then 1883 was punched over it. The 1 of the 1882 and the 1883 were aligned, but the 1882 date is so much narrower than the 1883 that the 2 is between the 8 and the 3. The 2 is discernible, but light, and traces of other, earlier digits can be seen as well. The obverse die later shattered.

1883, 3 Over 2—FS-304, F-08.01. Remnants of a 2 can be seen between the 8 and the 3 in a position similar to that of FS-301. This variety is difficult to see, requiring one to tilt the coin in the light to catch the very low relief of the overdate. As a recent discovery, its availability is still under study. Frequently found in very high grades, reportedly from a roll that surfaced in Southern California sometime within the last few years.

1883, 3 Over 2—FS-305, F-07, URS-3. Traces of something, suggested to be a 2, within the 3, but there is no trace of the lower left of the 2 that would be expected if this were an overdate. The first 8 shows repunching in the upper interior. An early die state shows definite "feet" of the 2 below the 3. Early die states are probably rare, as Howard Spindel has found only one.[45] Late die states, which are unremarkable to look at, seem to be reasonably available.

1883, 3 Over 2—Tentative attribution PM-18V.1. Has what seems to be a very light outline of the base of a 2 between the 8 and the 3, closest to the 8. This may be the same as FS-303.[46] More study is needed.

1866, Repunched Date (FS-301): Circulation Strike

GSID	VG-8	F-12	VF-20	EF-40	AU-50	MS-60	MS-63	MS-65	MS-67
2888	$360	$550	$675	$775	$900	$1,100	$1,500	$3,750	$18,000

Note: Values are for the most commonly found varieties.

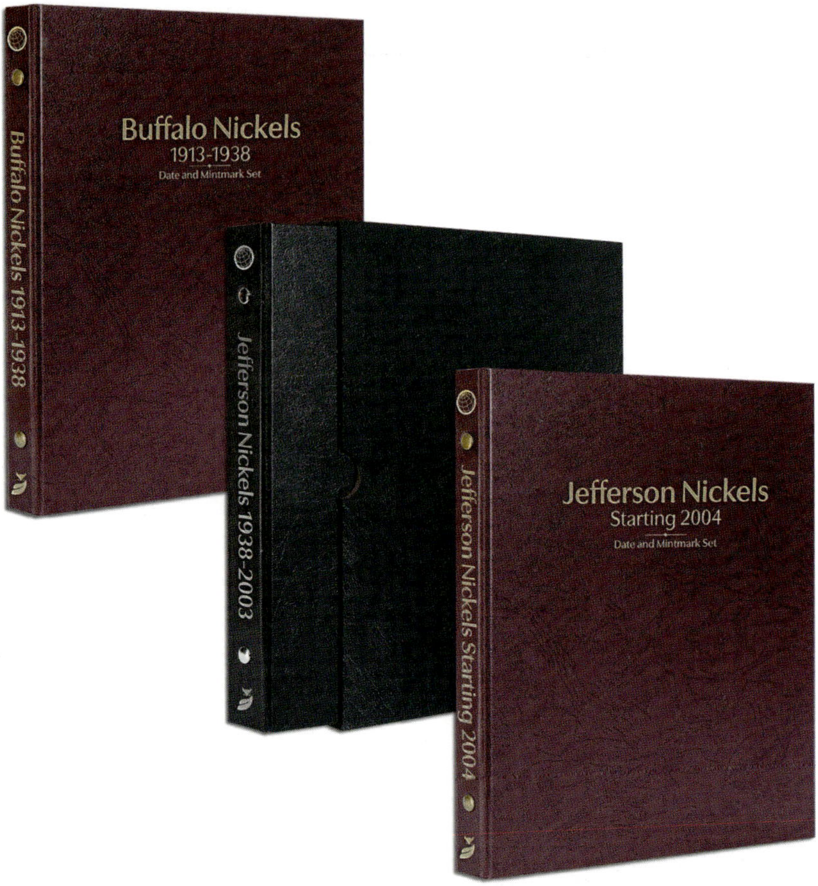
Buffalo Nickels
1913-1938
Date and Mintmark Set
Buffalo Nickels 1913-1938
Jefferson Nickels 1938-2003
Jefferson Nickels
Starting 2004
Date and Mintmark Set
Jefferson Nickels Starting 2004

7

Liberty Head Nickels 1883–1913: History and Background

Setting the Scene

By 1881 the Shield nickel had done its duty (although it continued to be minted for two more years). Launched in 1866 in an era in which there were no silver coins in commerce in the East or Midwest, the nickel circulated widely as the largest American coin of the realm. After April 20, 1876, silver coins (formerly hoarded by the public and, since spring 1862, available only at a premium) once again were plentiful in circulation. The nickel five-cent piece became somewhat redundant, as a flood of old silver half dimes, dimes, quarters, and half dollars reached the marketplace.

In 1877 and 1878 there was no call for new Shield nickels, and production that year was limited only to Proofs for collectors. Then followed 1880 and 1881, with small production figures for the denomination. The *other* nickel-alloy denomination, the three-cent piece, was not in much demand either at that time, and mintages were small. That there were any circulation strikes at all is due to Mint Superintendent A. Loudon Snowden, who thought that small production runs would prevent numismatic rarities from being created.

Archibald Loudon Snowden

In 1879 the superintendent of the Philadelphia Mint was A. Loudon Snowden, who would remain in that post until 1885.[1] Born in Cumberland County, Pennsylvania, Snowden was educated at Jefferson College in Washington, Pennsylvania. Afterward he pursued the study of law, but changed careers on May 7, 1857, when his uncle, Mint Director James Ross Snowden, offered him the position of register at the Philadelphia Mint. His tenure was not continuous. During the Civil War, he headed a volunteer

A. Loudon Snowden, superintendent of the Mint in 1883. Earlier, Snowden had been chief coiner at the Mint.

regiment that he had organized. In 1866 he became chief coiner, serving in that post until 1876, when he was tapped by President Ulysses S. Grant to be postmaster of Philadelphia, starting his duties on January 1, 1877. After joining the Mint, A. Loudon Snowden quickly became one of the insiders and a master at disseminating disinformation, such as a lengthy comment sent to coin dealer and writer E.L. Mason Jr. on December 12, 1871, stating that, of course, no further restrikes had been made, for in 1869 all old dies had been destroyed under his personal supervision as chief coiner.[2]

In December 1878, President Rutherford B. Hayes offered Snowden the directorship of the Mint, with an office in Washington, DC. Snowden did not want to leave Philadelphia, however, and declined the position. After the death of Director Henry R. Linderman, the offer was repeated, and Snowden again declined. Finally, in February 1879 he was given the opportunity to be superintendent of the Philadelphia Mint, a lesser position, but one that did not involve leaving his beloved Philadelphia.

Snowden seems to have been a numismatic Dr. Jekyll and Mr. Hyde—a double identity not unusual among Mint officials of the time, as the same cloak was worn by James Ross Snowden (his uncle), James Pollock, William E. DuBois, and quite a few others. They were caught between, on the one hand, the numismatic market, which beckoned as a source of thousands of dollars in profits from dealers and collectors eager to buy the latest Mint patterns and restrikes; and, on the other hand, the necessity for an outward appearance of decorum. Generally, Mint directors and superintendents maintained friendly and seemingly straightforward relations with numismatists, and occasionally helped them by supplying information on Mint policies. On March 18, 1879, A. Loudon Snowden joined the American Numismatic and Archaeological Society as an honorary member (probably ex officio rather than for any real interest in coin collecting).

Now and again Snowden got a bit of "good press," as when dealer S.K. Harzfeld included a note (excerpted here) in his January 24 to 25, 1881, sale catalog. At a time when many collectors and dealers were complaining of favorable treatment given to insiders with connections to the Mint, Harzfeld wrote, "Superintendent Snowden shows an earnest effort to suppress the abuses and acts of favoritism I complained of, and to assist the legitimate efforts of legitimate coin dealers." Snowden, seemingly a champion of numismatic correctness, was also noticed under "Numismatic Gossip," in *Numisma* (November 1883): "A Philadelphian lately informed us that under the stringent rules adopted by Col. Snowden, the efficient superintendent of the Philadelphia Mint, it is now impossible for coin speculators to obtain, through private influence, specimens of the pattern coins issued."

The preceding may be informative more by omission than by content, for it seems to imply that up to that time (autumn 1883), "private influence" could be used to obtain pattern rarities—as, indeed, it could. This was a free-for-all era for insider profits, with Philadelphia dealer John W. Haseltine being one of the main outlets for Mint officials to market their goods. S. Hudson Chapman (a dealer in Philadelphia at the time, and not an insider) later referred to the "Snowden-Thatcher [?] gang 1874–1880" as makers of rare pattern restrikes bearing dates back to the 1830's.[3]

As to making current coins (not patterns) available for face value, it seems that this was a popular offer, and certain dealers and collectors acquired quantities. Because of this, silver dimes, quarters, and half dollars of the low-mintage dates 1879 and later exist today in fair quantities in Mint State. (However, no record has been located of any similar offering of Uncirculated 1879, 1880, or 1881 Shield nickels, also with low mintages.) Many fancy pieces and secretly made rarities were also produced on Director Snowden's watch, including the 1879 Coiled Hair and 1880 Flowing Hair and Coiled Hair $4 gold Stellas, and the 1884 and 1885 trade dollars.

Snowden resigned his commission in January 1885.

The Market Problem for Nickel Metal

By 1881 it seemed that the market for nickel metal as a 25% alloy in the production of three- and five-cent pieces was in a death spiral. Joseph Wharton, nickel-manufacturing magnate, who had loomed large in the creation of the three-cent coin in 1865 and the Shield nickel in 1866, was deeply concerned. He, too, was a man of contradictions. On one hand, he was viewed as a public benefactor, as in the 1881 funding and establishment of the Wharton School of Finance and Economy at the University of Pennsylvania. On the other hand, he was a political infighter, using his connections to advantage for his business. Such was not particularly unusual for the era. Sometimes it was almost impossible to separate the interests of industry and politics, railroads being the most egregious example.

For a long time, Wharton had supplied metal to the Mint for these coins through his American Nickel Works in Camden, New Jersey. In 1877, as nickel use was starting its precipitous slump, he published a booklet, *Memorandum Concerning Small Money and Nickel Alloy Coinage, with Illustrations and Descriptions of Existing Alloy Coins.*

Then, in 1881, Wharton pursued a new plan. Bronze Indian Head cents were being struck in record numbers, but, unfortunately, they contained no nickel. The solution? Try to persuade the Mint to make cents using nickel alloy!

This was done, and in the same year Superintendent A. Loudon Snowden directed Chief Engraver Charles E. Barber to prepare designs for a series of small (one-, three-, and five-cent) denominations, all to be in an alloy of 75% copper and 25% nickel. The designs were to be consistent, creating a uniformity in step with the duplicate motifs used on Liberty Seated silver coinage, the Liberty Head gold coins, and the Indian Princess $1 and $3 pieces.

Charles E. Barber

Charles Edward Barber was born in London on November 16, 1840, the son of William and Anna May (Coultart) Barber. Charles came to America with his family in 1852, settling in Boston; later, Charles moved to Providence, Rhode Island. In 1865 his father gained a position as an assistant engraver at the Mint. In January 1869, when his father was named chief engraver (succeeding James B. Longacre), Charles was hired as an assistant,

Chief Engraver Charles E. Barber (left) with Assistant Engraver George T. Morgan, photographed at the Mint, circa 1895–1900.

although he had little experience in engraving dies. His salary as of 1877 was $4 per day.

In the meantime, the workmanship of Chief Engraver William Barber had been viewed as subpar.[4] In 1875, Mint Director Henry R. Linderman sought the services of a local artist, Hermann Faber, to create a "classic head of Liberty," a "heraldic eagle with olive branches or arrows in talons," and other motifs, seemingly due to dissatisfaction with William Barber's work.[5] In 1876, Linderman brought George T. Morgan from England to serve as "special engraver" (not "assistant" at first, although he was later called that), reporting directly to Linderman in Washington, not to Superintendent James Pollock at the Philadelphia Mint. In Linderman's eyes, this put Morgan on a par with the chief engraver. Indeed, Linderman invited Morgan to come to Washington to visit him at any time, a courtesy never extended either to Chief Engraver Barber or Superintendent Pollock.

In 1877 Morgan distinguished himself by creating illustrious motifs for patterns, mostly half dollars, that even today are admired for their beauty. In Mint correspondence the director lauded Morgan's talents without mention of Assistant Engraver Charles E. Barber. In fact, on April 20, 1878, Linderman proposed to Superintendent James Pollock that Barber be sent to the distant San Francisco Mint, in a position as a mechanic—in effect, an exile, although with slightly better pay.

> If Mr. Charles Barber understood thoroughly the hardening of dies, I incline to the opinion that it would be in the interest of the government to have him go to the San Francisco Mint and remain there. It would also give him an opportunity for doing better pecuniarily than where he is now.[6]

Linderman died on January 27, 1879, ending an era. By that time his reputation had been tarnished by a congressional investigation launched in June 1878 and that was still unresolved.

In February 1879, Horatio C. Burchard was appointed director of the Mint. Morgan was no longer the fair-haired favorite, and other people came into play. On August 31, 1879, the senior Barber died in Philadelphia, the result of an affliction brought on by severe chills h sustained while bathing at the New Jersey shore. The heir apparent in the chief engravership was son Charles, whose talents were viewed as modest at best.

What went on behind the scenes in autumn 1879 can only be guessed at, but certainly, there was a lot of politicking. Still, matters remained unsettled—George T. Morgan obviously had great artistic skills, but Charles E. Barber was better connected with Mint officers. Likely, the facts that Morgan was not an American citizen and that he was viewed as a protégé of the late Director Linderman worked against his candidacy.

Moreover, certain Mint officials viewed him as an outsider. Finally, in early 1880, after an unusually long delay, a new chief engraver was appointed, and it was Barber. Morgan stayed on and was designated an assistant engraver. No doubt, had Linderman lived, Morgan would have gained the post.

The first coins Charles Barber worked on were before his appointment, and consisted of the reverses of goloid metric patterns (1879) and *both* sides of the 1879 Flowing Hair and 1879 Coiled Hair $4 Stellas, although the obverse of the Coiled Hair is popularly attributed to Morgan.[7]

In the July 1883 issue of the *American Journal of Numismatics*, Patterson Dubois, Mint spokesperson, furnished these glowing comments:

> [Barber] was appointed as assistant in 1869, and became the official head by promotion in 1880, to fill the vacancy caused by his father's death. The appointment was not unmerited.
>
> Mr. Barber's latest card to the public is the new five-cent piece—a successful venture in very low relief. But his handiwork is more or less visible in all the principal medals executed since 1869. Since his appointment as chief engraver, the work of his department has been enormously increased by the number of medal dies demanded for the War Department and from other government sources. The medal dies made last year [1882] number twenty-eight. Mr. Barber's best work is seen in the medals of Snowden, Garfield, President Arthur, Indian Peace, Army-Marksmanship, and Great Seal. He is particularly happy in "catching a likeness." The head of Superintendent Snowden is a rare specimen of medallic portraiture. Messrs. [William] Key and [George T.] Morgan are the engraver's assistants.

On January 21, 1885, Barber wrote to A. Loudon Snowden, giving his opinion (completely erroneous) that certain federal coin hubs had been used to make Moffat & Company $5 pieces in San Francisco years earlier:

> Sir,
>
> The dies sent for my inspection are evidently original dies from which hubs have been taken to make coining dies. We have one of these coins in the Cabinet . . . with the name Moffat & Co. in the place of the word Liberty, and examples of many others, both as coins and rubbings. All of these pieces having been issued by the different assay offices of California.

In fact, the 1849 and 1850 $5 coins of Moffat & Co. had been struck from dies by Albert Küner. The motifs were copied from federal designs, but the workmanship is different.

Barber's tenure proved to be very troubled, beset with sharp criticism of his coin designs (not that of the Liberty Head nickel that is the focus of the present book, but the designs of his Liberty Head silver coins of 1892, along with other work).

In 1905 the government sent Barber on a tour of European mints to study the procedures in use there. Upon his return to Philadelphia, he implemented many changes that resulted in the Mint Medal Department's becoming one of the world's finest facilities.[8]

Barber's Design Techniques

In May 1895 *The Numismatist* told of certain processes used by the chief engraver in preparing coin designs:

> Though various materials may be employed, Barber uses a wax composition for designing coins. He takes a quantity of an extremely pure quality of beeswax, with which he mixes a small proportion of resinous gum and a little of the finest vermilion. The mixture, after being melted and stirred so as to make it homogenous, is poured into cold water. When cool, it is thoroughly kneaded like so much dough.
>
> Having thus made ready for business, the designer draws on a slate a circle a foot in diameter. This is the outline of the coin model, which is made on a large scale for convenience. The circular space is then covered with a layer of the wax mixture, perhaps three quarters of an inch in thickness, and on this surface the design in relief is made with delicate modeling tools of boxwood. The method is much the same as that employed for modeling in clay, but the material is finer and smoother. If hair is to be represented a brush of fine bristles is something employed, while the over-long thumbnail of the operator serves occasionally as a supplementary instrument, being a sensitive organ of touch.
>
> From the finished wax model is made an electrotype, and from the latter is produced the die for the coin by a simple process. A machine is used which operates on the principle of the "pantograph" employed in drawing. While a blunt point is guided by hand over every curve and intricacy of the wax medallion, another point, tipped with a diamond, revolves rapidly and cuts away the surface of the steel disk, which is just the size of the future coin. Thus an exact reproduction is obtained of the original model, but in it every course detail of the wax medallion becomes fine and delicate. This is the cameo—that is, a bas-relief. The die, of course, must be in intaglio. To get the intaglio from the cameo is easy enough. The cameo, which is of hard steel, is squeezed against a disk of soft steel under enormous pressure. The soft steel disk, having received a perfect impression, has only to be tempered, and it is then ready to serve as a die.

The preceding describes the creation of design motifs, such as a Liberty Head or wreath. Stars and letters were added by the use of hand punches and were not part of the original modeling and transfer-lathe processes.

The Liberty Head Coins

In 1881 the plan for the uniform coinage of pattern one-, three-, and five-cent pieces called for the cent to be 16 mm in diameter and to weigh 1.5 grams; for the three-cent coin to measure 19 mm and weigh 3 grams; and for the five-cent coin to be 22 mm and weigh 5 grams. The use of grams (metric system) rather than grains had been employed at the Mint since 1866—the weight of the new nickel had been set at 5 grams, followed by the weight adjustments of dimes, quarters, and half dollars in 1873 (with arrows added to the date to indicate the change). For example, the half dollar had been 192 grains, and after the Coinage Act of 1873 was 12.5 grams (192.9 grains). Metric-system patterns in various denominations, especially dollars, had been all the rage at the Mint from 1878 to 1880. The famous $4 gold Stellas of 1879 and 1880 have metric inscriptions.

Rising to the challenge admirably, Chief Engraver Barber created the Liberty Head design, later to become standard on the nickel. In 1881 it was used on the three minor coins, each of which had the inscription UNITED STATES OF AMERICA around the obverse, and the date below. The reverses were of uniform design as well, displaying a new-style wreath of corn and cotton (nicely pleasing both the North and the South) enclosing the denomination I, III, or V. The five-cent pattern was made in two variations, one unique today and in the Smithsonian Institution, with the motto IN GOD WE TRUST tucked at the top border in tiny letters.[9] Today, this suite of pattern coins falls under Judd numbers 1665 to 1764a. Examples of the one-, three-, and five-cent patterns in copper-nickel alloy seem to have been made in fairly large numbers for a pattern coin, and are encountered with some frequency today.

A Classic Motif

Art historian and numismatist Cornelius Vermeule reviewed this motif in his 1971 book, *Numismatic Art in America, Aesthetics of the United States Coinage:*

> The diademed and wreathed head of Liberty on the obverse was modeled almost verbatim from a Greco-Roman head of Juno or a major personification such as Concordia, a marble cult-statue for some shrine in Rome or the provinces.

There seems to be no particular record of what specific image Barber used. Sometimes in numismatic circles the lady on the nickel is referred to as Diana (the huntress, who would seem unlikely as an inspiration), seldom if ever Juno, and never as one of the *Concordia* goddesses. *Liberty* and *Liberty Head* are standard terms and seem best suited in concordance with the emerging patterns of assistant engraver George T. Morgan at the time. The facial features are not much different from those used by Morgan on his pattern half dollars of 1877 and on the silver dollar of 1878.

More Pattern Nickels

In 1882, Dame Fortune smiled on James Wharton and his American Nickel Works. The Mint increased its production of regular nickel five-cent coins (of the Shield design then in use) to a record 11,472,000 pieces—a sharp contrast to the paltry 68,000 of 1881. The idea of making cents and three-cent pieces of Barber's new Liberty Head design was dropped, but the pursuit of a new nickel motif continued. The Liberty Head nickel was found to be acceptable, and it formed the mainstay of an extensive production of pattern five-cent pieces in 1882. Obverse varieties with the Liberty Head portrait include, first, a die with UNITED STATES OF AMERICA around the border (as used in 1881); second, a die with IN GOD WE TRUST at the top border and stars to each side; and third, a die with stars surrounding, the last as later adopted for the regular issue. On all, the date 1882 is below the portrait.

The reverses of the patterns all displayed the denomination as "V" within a wreath of cotton and corn, some without any lettering; others with IN GOD WE TRUST or E PLURIBUS UNUM at the top border; and one with a smaller wreath, a V at the center, and around the border, UNITED STATES OF AMERICA / E PLURIBUS UNUM. The last is the style later adopted.

None had the word CENTS as part of the motif. This was not deemed necessary, as for many years the Roman numeral III, without an accompanying CENTS, had proved sufficient to identify the silver three-cent pieces (1851–1873) and nickel three-cent pieces (first made in 1865 and still being produced in the early 1880's).

The diameter of the coins was different from that used on the Shield nickels, with the old width being 13/16 inch (or 20.6 mm), and the new being 5/6 inch (or 21.2 mm). A. Loudon Snowden, earlier the chief coiner, had been superintendent of the Philadelphia Mint since 1879 and supervised much of the experimentation.

Finally, Director Snowden settled on a Liberty Head design with UNITED STATES OF AMERICA around the obverse border, and, on the reverse, a V within a wreath, and E PLURIBUS UNUM above. What happened next, in the words of historian R.W. Julian, was this:

> In mid-December 1882 Snowden sent 25 examples of the proposed nickel to the Treasury and waited for their usual approval. He was in for a rude shock because Treasury Secretary Charles J. Folger was something of an oddity for those days: he actually read the relevant coinage laws to make certain that everything was done properly. Folger found that the new design was clearly illegal and could not be accepted.
>
> The 1873 coinage law, in particular, required that LIBERTY appear on the obverse, which was done properly on the pattern, but that UNITED STATES OF AMERICA had to be on the reverse, no exceptions. Folger consulted with President Chester Arthur and both men agreed that the pattern coin was unacceptable. They also decided, however, that the liberty head and wreath were well done and should be retained.[10]

Snowden suggested that an exception could be made, but Folger said this was not going to happen so long as he was in charge. Accordingly, the design was revised to comply with Secretary Folger's wishes. Early in 1883 the new motif combined an 1882-dated obverse displaying Liberty Head and stars with the reverse showing UNITED STATES OF AMERICA / E PLURIBUS UNUM around the border. Today, these are known as Judd-1690. Examples were sent to the Treasury Department and were approved quickly. Apparently, some found their way into the hands of congressmen or others and were mishandled—for today, impaired examples of J-1690 are seen more often than are lightly worn examples of any other five-cent pattern of the era.

Details of the Liberty Head Design

Overview

The same Liberty Head obverse hubs and masters (see chapter 4 for information on the making of hubs and masters) were used on all Liberty Head nickels from 1883 to 1913.

During the course of the series, three different reverse styles were used, as described below, with Reverse Style C existing in original and modified form (Reverse Style Ca).

In July 2005 I published information about Reverse Style A, its use being unknown to Gloria Peters and Cynthia Mohon in their excellent *Complete Guide to Shield and Liberty Head Nickels*. As to whether a collector demand develops for it remains to be seen. Circulation strikes and Proofs of 1901 are known with both Reverse Style C and its slightly modified version, Reverse Style Ca, with no special premium for either. In other series, such as Barber silver coins and Morgan dollars, there were slight adjustments of the dies at the turn of the 20th century, but collector interest has been scant and has been limited to dedicated specialists.

The dates seem to have been punched into the working dies by the use of a four-digit logotype through 1912, while for certain other series, the date had been included in the master die by that time. The adding of dates separately is reflected by the existence of nickels with slight repunching of the date numerals as late as 1912, as described in the Peters and Mohon text. Although some later nickels (1908 is an example) have significant variations as to date position, and dates on 1911 nickels vary only slightly, the coins examined for 1912 show all dates in about the same location with regard to the denticles below and the neck truncation above. Perhaps some sort of a guide or positioning jig was used.

Obverse Style 1

Obverse Style 1 (multiple dies from master die): Liberty Head at the center, facing left, with 13 stars around, date below. Denticles are at border. The word LIBERTY is on the coronet, with wheat and cotton bolls above, seemingly inspired by the 1878 Morgan silver dollar.

Reverse Style A

Reverse Style A, Without CENTS (handmade die): The leaves above the top of each side of the V are much closer to the V than on Reverse Style B. The arrangement of lettering is slightly different with regard to the wreath—for example, the upright of the R in AMERICA, if extended downward, would intersect the sharp end of a leaf point below, whereas on Reverse Style B the upright of the R is to the right of the point.

This die was made for use on patterns of 1882, most notably Judd-1690; slightly relapped so as to remove the repunching on the S, it was used to strike certain *1883* pattern nickels (e.g., J-1714). The un-relapped die was used on a minority of 1883 regular-issue Proofs; whether the relapped die was used to coin regular Proofs with the standard 1883 obverse is not known.

Reverse Style B

Reverse Style B, Without CENTS (multiple dies from master die): The leaves above the top of each side of the

V are farther from the top of the V than on Reverse Style A. The upright of R in AMERICA, if extended downward, is to the right of the point of a leaf. The star points under the right serif of the E in STATES. This die was used on most (but not all) 1883 regular-issue Proofs and on all circulation strikes.

Reverse Style C

Reverse Style C, With CENTS (multiple dies from master die): This is the standard style used for the With CENTS coinage. This reverse has the leaf "high" above the top of the left side of the V; the letters AM in AMERICA touch at their bases. This die was used on all circulation strikes and Proofs through 1900 and some of 1901. Examining 1902-dated nickels for use of this die might yield results.

Reverse Style Ca

Reverse Style Ca, With CENTS (multiple dies from master die): Modified from the preceding, but with no change in the basic layout of letters, etc. This reverse has the leaf "low" above the top of the left side of the V; the letters AM in AMERICA do not touch at their bases. This die was used on some circulation strikes and Proofs of 1901, and exclusively on all later dates.

The 1883 Debut of the Liberty Head Nickel

Production Begins

On January 30, 1883, the first new Liberty Head nickels were struck. By that time, 1,451,500 Shield nickels had been made with the 1883 date. This caused a flurry of speculation in Proof 1883 *Shield* nickels, as dealers, collectors, and investors thought they would prove to be very rare. In fact, record quantities of Proofs were made.

Joseph Wharton was not completely satisfied. He continued to maintain that it certainly would be nice to have more than just 25% nickel in the alloy of the coin. In response to Wharton, in 1883 Superintendent A. Loudon Snowden directed Chief Engraver Charles Barber to make some more patterns. These were made, including one inscribed PURE NICKEL (a dream come true for Wharton!); one with 75 N. 25 C.; one with 50 N. 50 C. (or half and half); and one with 33 N. 67 C.

Although the Mint would not admit it in 1883, nickel had caused problems for a long time, starting with the difficulty of striking copper-nickel (88%-12%) with cents in 1857, one of the reasons for switching to bronze for cents in 1864.

The patterns of 1883, which are discussed along with other pattern nickel five-cent pieces in appendix A, yielded no new results, and the old alloy of 75% copper and 25% nickel was continued in the denomination.

Into Circulation

On January 8, 1883, Mint Superintendent Snowden authorized that the new design be used. Production commenced soon thereafter, and on February 1 the first pieces were placed into circulation.[11]

The *Portsmouth* (New Hampshire) *Daily Evening Times*, February 2, ran this item:

> **The New Five-Cent Piece**
>
> The coining of five-cent pieces of a new design has begun at the Philadelphia Mint, after a design by [*sic*] Col. A.L. Snowden of the above-named mint. It is said the Treasury Department was not satisfied with the present five-cent coin, and obtained authority from the last session of Congress to make a new one. The size of the new piece is a trifle larger than the old, and is of the same weight and alloy, the proportions being one-quarter nickel and three-quarters copper. No more of the old piece is to be coined. . . .
>
> By way of excuse for changing the style of the five-cent piece, it is said that the old one was near the three-cent piece in size—as though the one might be mistaken for the other. If this be all the reason for the change, the existence of the new piece has but a flimsy excuse. It is the ten-cent piece that is oftener confounded with the three, there being but a little difference either in size or thickness, while a blind man could by a touch distinguish the thicker five-cent piece from the three or ten. Another piece gives more trouble than either. The 20-cent piece is very often taken for the quarter-dollar. One or other of these should be withdrawn; and perhaps the 20-cent should be retained as more in accordance with our decimal system of money.[12]

At that time, the *American Journal of Numismatics* (*AJN*) was the premier periodical devoted to the coin hobby, having been published since May 1866. The April 1883 issue included these mentions of the new coin:

> MINT COINS FOR 1883: At the opening of each year demands are made at the Mint by coin collectors, numismatic societies, and others, for Proof coins, or sets representative of a year's coinage. To meet this demand, special coins are struck as is well known, and sold at rates proportional to the extra labor involved. These sets are in gold, silver, nickel and copper. The regular Proof set of gold coins is sold for \$43; the silver and minor \$4.05, and exclusive of the trade dollar \$3.05. The minor coins, embracing the old and new 5-cent coin, the 3-cent piece, and the bronze penny, are sold at 18 cents the set. . . .
>
> The stamping of the new 5-cent coin has increased the interest among collectors, and many requests are made for the set containing the old and new half-dime piece. Large orders have been received from the Northwestern states, Mississippi Valley, and the Pacific Coast, where there are few small coins, for the new 5-cent piece. This demand has been greatly increased by the descriptions of the new coin so widely printed.
>
> The Mint supplies this coin in amounts of \$5 each, and the parties to whom the coins are sent pay for the expressage, but if sent in sums of \$20, the expressage is paid by the Mint itself. We have noticed boys peddling this new coin along the

streets at 20 cents each, the price varying with the demand. Some impressions are found struck from a broken die. It is reported that all of this issue are to be recalled by order of Secretary Folger,[13] and the dies altered by adding the word CENTS.

Oops!

By the time the Mint took this step, however, more than five million of the "error" nickels had been placed into circulation.[14] The interest of numismatists was aroused immediately, especially when both the *AJN* and the popular press stated that these pieces were to be recalled. How exciting!

The new "V nickel," as it came to be called, was nearly the same diameter as a $5 gold piece. The name of whoever first thought to reed the edge (by filing or using a tool-shop milling machine) and gold-plate these coins is lost to history. However, a bright yellow, gold-appearing coin with a bold V was readily accepted as a $5 half eagle—even if examined closely, it might appear just to be a new half-eagle design.

It was related that the scam ran something like this: A gold-plated nickel, posing as a $5 gold coin, would be tendered for the purchase of an item (e.g., a newspaper or a cigar) priced from one to five cents. The clerk, glancing quickly at the "five-dollar" coin, would put it in the cash drawer and give the purchaser the appropriate change—$4.95 or a few cents more.

When arrested, the passer of these pieces simply claimed that no statement had been made that the coin was a $5 gold piece. He or she had simply given it without comment to a clerk, who'd then *assumed* it was a $5 coin.

This caper attracted the attention of various writers, who in time related that a man named Josh (often given the surname Tatum) was convicted in Boston (or Philadelphia or New York) of exchanging these gilded pieces, giving rise to the saying "You're joshing me," used when someone attempts a minor deception. Never mind that *josh* was already a part of American slang at that time! This is one numismatic tale that refuses to go away, and every once in a while it reappears in print.[15]

Shenanigans

The Treasury Department was not about to let such a fraud pervade the United States. In 1883, $5 was a respectable amount of money. Some factory workers made little more than that *per week*. In the West in particular, nickel five-cent pieces were not circulating—but half eagles were plentiful, so there was even less chance that someone would recognize such a piece as a nickel.[16] The Secret Service branch of the department set to work, and operatives (as agents were called) were soon hot on the trail of suspected fraudsters, who, when caught, faced a year in prison at hard labor.[17]

A Boon for the Hobby

Word spread that the Treasury Department would soon be calling in all of its "mistakes." It seemed logical that these nickels would soon become very rare and valuable. Citizens began looking through their pocket change. Among those looking was young Farran Zerbe, a newsboy in Tyrone, Pennsylvania. Years later, in autumn 1908 (upon his reelection as president of the American Numismatic Association), Zerbe recalled, "You all know of the numismatists' nightmare, the nickels without CENTS. I have a sentimental regard for this all too numerous and troublesome piece. It commanded my interest in our subject. That was in 1883, 25 years ago."[18]

This peculiar variety of 1883 Liberty Head nickel acted as a little salesman for the coin hobby to many others, as well. Doubtless, hundreds or even thousands of new faces were attracted to the hobby as a result. This was an early-day equivalent to the nationwide groundswell in numismatic interest that began in 1999, when the first five varieties in the 50-coin "statehood reverse" Washington quarter series were launched, followed in 2004 with new varieties of Jefferson nickels in the Westward Journey Nickel Series.

Meanwhile, in Numismatics

Collecting coins was already popular by early 1883, and the cognoscenti perused the pages of the *AJN* and enjoyed the auction catalogs of W. Elliot Woodward, John W. Haseltine, Edward D. Cogan and his up-and-coming son George, and others. It was a rare numismatist, however, who enjoyed *only* coins. Typically, those involved in the numismatic hobby also collected autographs, stamps, or other specialties.

Similarly, rare-coin dealers handled such other things as well. The Chapman brothers—S. Hudson and Henry—called themselves "antiquaries," and their letterhead advised that they were "Importers of and dealers in ancient Greek and Roman coins, engraved gems, bronzes, pottery, and antiquities, foreign coins and medals; dealers in American coins and medals, and especially of fine and rare specimens, numismatic books, Indian pottery and stone implements, patent cabinet."

In a more popular vein, a dozen or more periodicals catering to coin hobbyists and general collectors flourished in the mid-1880's. Some were driven by the new interest in the nickel; others focused on stamps (a hobby even more popular than coins at the time) but also contained occasional numismatic tidbits.

In the latter category was the *Granite State Philatelist*, launched in 1881 by John M. Hubbard of Lake Village, New Hampshire. The masthead proclaimed that the periodical was "Devoted to Stamps, Coins and Curiosities." This newspaper contained occasional items on rare coins, including a feature on the 1883 Liberty Head nickel published shortly after the five-cent piece appeared in circulation.

In September 1886 a new publication, the *Curiosity World*, made its bow under the ownership of Hubbard and the editorship of H.J. Miron. The printer was apparently the same person who published the *Lake Village Times*. Miron's lead article, "The Coins of the United States," was included in the *Times* as well. Perhaps some of them became numismatists in due course.

Measuring 13 by 19 inches, the *Curiosity World* was issued on newsprint. The periodical was "devoted to stamps, coins, Indian relics, birds' eggs, autographs, postmarks, tags, etc." The "tags" specialty referred to tin and cardboard tobacco tags (once collected widely, such tags are scarcely heard of today). Miron's lead article, which occupied nearly the entire front page, indicated that the *Curiosity World* placed particular editorial emphasis on coins. Interestingly, most of the advertisers in the first issue were stamp dealers, probably past acquaintances of Hubbard.

In the lower right corner of the first page of the first issue, John M. Hubbard commented as follows:

> Probably everyone in the United States knows that there are many coins in circulation that are worth much more than their face value, but they wouldn't know them if they should meet them in the middle of the street.
>
> We have issued a Premium Coin List containing 94 illustrations, and giving our buying prices for *every U.S. coin worth over face value*. Every one who handles money should possess a copy. Price 10¢ or three for 25¢, post free, address John M. Hubbard, publisher, Lake Village, N.H.

Not one to do things halfway, Hubbard announced with bravado that "the October issue of the *Curiosity World* will be 5,000 copies," followed by 2,500 in November (the reason for the diminution was not given), then back up to 5,000 in December. The subscription rate was 25¢ per year, with free sample copies available singly to potential readers. Advertising was solicited at the rate of 10¢ per line for four insertions, $1 per inch for one insertion, and $3 per inch for four insertions.

The October 1886 number (vol. 1, issue 2) of the *Curiosity World* continued with H.J. Miron's "The Coins of the United States" article, which discussed silver dollars from 1794 through 1804, with a fairly lengthy commentary on the last-named rarity. Sharing the front page was another article by Miron, "Birds, Eggs, Nests."

Capturing the prevailing fad of the era, an illustration was given of the 1883 Liberty Head nickel, accompanied by this copy:

> The government has been calling in the V nickels of 1883 without CENTS, ever since their coinage was stopped. They are melted and coined into the common nickels.
>
> We have a few of the variety without CENTS, like the above cuts, which we are willing to sell at 15¢ each. Every one who does not have a specimen should procure one at once as in a short time they will cost much more.
>
> *John M. Hubbard, Lake Village, NH.*

In the meantime, the 1883 Liberty Head nickel had become a stock-in-trade item for rare coin dealers such as E.L. Mason Jr., who had been promoting them for a long time. The August 1884 issue of *Mason's Monthly Illustrated Coin Collector's Magazine* made this offer:

> We are in receipt of a few of these now rapidly disappearing nickel five-cent pieces, and can fill a few orders at $7 per hundred, or 10 cents each. Proofs 20 cents each.

The Rest of the Story

What happened to the 1883 Liberty Head nickels? The story that the Mint would recall them prompted just about everyone to look for examples, with the result that millions were saved—probably a generous proportion of the entire production. The result was that in later years, the 1883 without CENTS nickel was recognized as the single most common date in the 19th-century nickel five-cent piece series, despite many dates' having substantially higher mintages.

There were so many such coins in the hands of collectors and dealers they had virtually no premium value 40 years later. In April 1929, Henry Chapman, billing himself as "America's Leading Numismatic Dealer," offered for sale such pieces in "Very Good to Fine" grade, for 6¢ apiece!

Time vindicates most numismatic purchase decisions, and the case of the 1883 nickel was no exception. In the 1930's, when coin collecting became one of America's most popular hobbies—spurred on by the publication of Wayte Raymond's *Standard Catalogue of United States Coins* (1934) and his "National" coin albums—the price of the coin rose. And continued to rise. Today, a lightly worn piece is worth a few dollars, and a gem Mint State coin commands a three-figure price. Hubbard was right: they were worth buying. But the profits went to the grandchildren of those who bought such coins from dealers for 15¢ each in the 1880's.

In the meantime, the story of the gold-plated nickels made great fodder for articles in coin papers, often with speculation as to whether Josh Tatum was a real character or a figment of some long-forgotten person's imagination. Two aficionados of the scenario, Richard G. Young and Wade J. Wilkin, have been corresponding with me about these for a long time, and in 2004 published a study, *Racketeer Nickel and Its Many Mysteries*, which may be the last word on this subject.

Continuing Chronicle of the Liberty Head Nickel

Adding CENTS

The CENTS-less nickels would not do, and pattern reverse dies were made to incorporate the missing word. One of these patterns, Judd-1717, had CENTS on a scroll on top of the V. Finally, the reverse was rearranged: E PLURIBUS UNUM, formerly at the bottom, was moved to above the V, and CENTS was returned to its previous location. On March 13, 1883, examples were sent to Secretary of the Treasury Charles J. Folger.

Approval was quick, after which the Mint had to prepare master dies and working dies. Production of the new design began about March 22, but without any special announcements or ceremonies.[19]

The Mid-1880's

In late winter and early spring 1884, there was a chill in the financial market. Stocks fell on the New York Stock Exchange, and in the East there were many business failures. This was not a panic but a temporary setback. For the time, there were enough minor coins in circulation. Accordingly, mintages of cents and nickels dropped sharply that year, followed by even lower production in 1885. The need for nickels remained slow until September 1886, when quantities were again made, but still resulting in a low mintage overall.

At the Mint in 1884 and 1885, rarities continued to be struck privately for the account of privileged employees and officials. These included silver trade dollars of those years, full Proof sets struck in aluminum, from the cent to the $20 piece, and other items that would be enticing to later generations of numismatists. In the same year, there were transitions at the Mint. Colonel Oliver C. Bosbyshell, who created his share of numismatic delicacies, resigned as chief coiner and was replaced on February 1, 1885, by William S. Steel, assistant coiner.[20] Bosbyshell returned in 1889 as superintendent, and remained in that post until 1894, but no numismatic horseplay has been attributed to him in that later period.

On July 1, 1885, A. Loudon Snowden was succeeded by the appointment of Daniel M. Fox. On the same date, Horatio C. Burchard was replaced as Mint director by James P. Kimball. This seems to have ended the era of making restrikes and rarities—including pattern coins that were neither necessary nor logical—for private sale. From 1886 to the present day, relatively few patterns ever escaped the Mint. Legal and moral considerations aside, numismatists can be thankful for all of the chicanery going on at the Philadelphia Mint from 1859 to 1885, as productions from this era account for more than 90% of the pattern coins known to exist today.

The Act of August 4, 1886, called for worn minor coins at the Mint, if fit for circulation, to be "cleaned and reissued." This eventually involved 1,264,249 coins and helped to alleviate a shortage.[21] The cleaning of coins and, especially, of paper money, was done many times by the Treasury Department in the late 19th and early 20th centuries.

The 1890's

The Coinage Act of September 26, 1890, officially discontinued the nickel three-cent piece, gold dollar, and $3 gold coin, although production of each had been halted in 1889. The nickel three-cent coin had been competitive with the nickel five-cent piece in the early days, but by the 1880's the larger denomination had almost entirely replaced it.

The same Coinage Act had a provision that designs for circulating denominations were not to be changed until they had been in use for 25 years. This would have an impact on later designs in the five-cent series.

The Panic of 1893 affected all of America, not just Wall Street. Particularly hard hit were the prairie states, where, during the boom times of the 1880's, cities had sprung up like mushrooms in the night. There were many bank failures in Kansas, Iowa, and other districts, which in turn affected eastern banks and businesses that had loaned money to the entrepreneurs. This resulted in a reduced need for coins, and production of both cents and nickels slumped in 1894. Still, there was much interest in undeveloped land in the region. On September 16, 1893, the government opened six million acres of land to homesteaders, setting off a rush. The land had been bought from the Cherokees. For years, hunting bison—including shooting the beasts from the comfort of passenger railroad cars and leaving the carcasses to rot—had been a grand sport on the prairie. Native Americans, too, had their difficulties with expansion. All of these events and circumstances were chronicled by Theodore Roosevelt, later to become president, in a four-volume set of books, *The Winning of the West.* Today, *stealing* would probably replace *winning*, but sentiments were different then.

In 1893 it was estimated that only 1,100 bison survived, in contrast to the countless millions of years earlier. Had it not been for the establishment of Yellowstone National

Park in 1872, it is likely that the beasts would have been exterminated by this time. Remaining bison and traveling "Wild West" shows evoked nostalgia for the creatures and may have been responsible in part for their use on American money, most famously on the "Buffalo" nickels of 1913.

Each year, the Mint purchased nickel for coinage from outside suppliers. Also on a continuing basis, older coins with nickel content were melted and converted into five-cent pieces. The *Annual Report for the Fiscal Year Ended June 30, 1899*, noted that minor coins of the face value of $190,667.25 were received and melted for recoinage during the year. Among these were copper-nickel cents with a face value of $1,808.38, nickel three-cent pieces totaling $1,572.75, and nickel five-cent pieces totaling $175,170. Certain of this metal was reprocessed to make new Liberty Head nickels. Probably the more than 3.5 million nickels ($175,170 face value) melted consisted of worn pieces of the Shield type plus damaged and mutilated coins of all dates sent in by the Treasury Department. No record was ever kept of the specific dates redeemed, although such would be interesting to read today.

In this fiscal year we also have this entry: "Cost of pure nickel added to nickel one-cent metal [copper-nickel cents] to convert it into nickel five-cent alloy for recoinage into the nickel five-cent coin, $75.16," and, "cost of bronze to add to nickel three-cent metal for recoinage into nickel five-cent coins, $30.02." The reason for the last is unexplained, as nickel three-cent pieces used the same alloy as nickel five-cent pieces.

Unprecedented Demand for Nickels

Increasing prosperity by the turn of the century, as well as the strong call for cents and nickels to use in vending machines, amusement devices, and general commerce prompted the director of the Mint to include this in his *Annual Report for the Fiscal Year Ended June 30, 1900*:

The Philadelphia Mint typically purchased nickel alloy strip or, often, coinage blanks, from outside suppliers, such as Benedict & Burnham, a metal manufacturer in Waterbury, Connecticut, shown here in the early 20th century.

Section 3528, Revised Statutes of the United States, provides that "for the purchase of metal for the minor coinage, a sum not exceeding $50,000 in lawful money of the United States shall be transferred by the Secretary of the Treasury to the credit of the superintendent of the Mint at Philadelphia, at which establishment only, until otherwise provided by law, such coinage shall be carried on."

For the last four years this fund has been inadequate to enable the Mint to supply promptly the demands for minor coins at certain seasons of the year, especially from September 1 to January 1. In fact, for the last two years the demand has continued with more or less activity throughout the entire year. When this fund was created by act of February 28, 1873, the demand for minor coins was inconsiderable as compared with the present (which in the year 1900 has been unprecedented), and the fund was then ample for the purchase of the metal required to manufacture the 1-cent bronze and 5-cent nickel pieces in sufficient quantities to supply all demands.

Within the past two years the price of metals entering into the manufacture of minor coinage has advanced and necessitates a larger sum of money than heretofore to purchase the same weight of metal, in addition to which increased coinage requires a greater amount of metal with which to meet same. The minor-coinage metal fund should be increased to $250,000 as a maximum, and it is respectfully recommended that Congress be again requested to provide for an increase of this fund to that sum.

The Mint continued to realize profit from the production of minor coins (the seignorage representing the difference between the cost of metal and coinage and the face value of the pieces). Thus, from the perspective of the Mint and the Treasury Department, the more nickel five-cent pieces made, the better. However, now and again there had been gluts of minor coins in circulation, or they had become redundant (as in the late 1870's, when long-hoarded silver coins were released), and mintages of nickels were reduced.

The third Philadelphia Mint went into operation in October 1901.

The Mint Cabinet at the Philadelphia Mint in the early 20th century. On display were coins and other items that had been gathered ever since the collection was established in 1838. The exhibit included Proof sets for most years since 1821, including all Shield nickels from 1866 onward.

The Early 20th Century

In 1900 and 1901 there was some tweaking of hub dies for certain denominations, resulting in small adjustments to relief and certain details. In the Liberty Head nickel series a new reverse hub was made, with some very slight differences from the older one, most obviously a lengthening of the leaves above the top of each side of the V.

In October 1901 the third Philadelphia Mint building was occupied, and much new equipment was installed. In the Medal Department, a new person must have been put in charge of making Proof coin dies, for the next round of production, in 1902, was with the portraits of Liberty polished in the dies, rather than in frosty or cameo contrast.

In October 1907 a panic swept New York City, resulting from the failure of the Knickerbocker Trust Company and initiating the collapse of the venerable Mercantile National Bank. This precipitated a run on banks, a tightening of funds held by brokers, and general financial distress. The immediate cause of all of this was F. Augustus Heinze, a copper magnate from Montana, who that summer had taken control of the Mercantile National Bank and had used its funds to speculate in copper. The "corner" failed, creditors called on the bank for funds, and a domino effect ensued. This happened late in the year and may have been a minor contributing cause to the low mintage figure of just 1,745 Proof nickels, as some collectors may have felt the economic pinch.

Branch-Mint Coinage in 1912

By the late 19th century the director of the Mint was making repeated pleas to permit branch-mint coinage. In the *Annual Report of the Director of the Mint for the Fiscal Year Ending June 30, 1900*, he writes:

> Under the provision of section 3528 of the Revised Statutes of the United States, the manufacture of all the minor coins is restricted to the mint at Philadelphia. At the time this provision was enacted the demand for such coins was confined principally to the eastern, middle, and western states, east of the Missouri River, but in recent years there has been a very heavy increase, which has extended not only to the section named, but to the southwestern states and the Pacific Coast as well, and has become so great that at times much difficulty has been experienced at the Philadelphia mint to furnish at all times an adequate supply, which can not be done, except by working overtime.
>
> Much relief would be afforded if the mints at San Francisco and New Orleans were authorized to manufacture 1-cent bronze and 5-cent nickel pieces, and the demand for the southwestern and Pacific coast states and territories could be supplied much more economically than at present.

Despite similar comments in later *Mint Reports*, nothing was done about coining nickels at the branch mints until 1912, by which time the New Orleans Mint had been closed for coinage since 1909 and was out of consideration. In that year, Liberty Head nickels were made at Denver and San Francisco.

The Denver Mint was constructed beginning in 1904 and struck its first coins in 1906, these being in silver and gold. It was not until 1911 that the first cents were made there; nickels followed in 1912.

The San Francisco Mint struck its first nickels in the waning days of 1912, after which the denomination was produced nearly continuously. The facilities, located in the second building to be called the San Francisco Mint, had gone into operation in 1874. The impressive structure had earned the nickname the *Granite Lady*. During the earthquake and fire of April 1906, the Granite Lady was the only building in its district to survive.

Sunset

The 1912 Liberty Head nickel, with its full panorama of production at all three mints, could have been the beginning of an extensive series of mintmarks (as happened with other denominations). This was not the case, though, and in early 1913 the motif was replaced by the Indian Head or Buffalo nickel designed by James Earle Fraser.

December 1912 was the official termination of the series, but, unofficially, a few were made with the date 1913, these forming the subject of much interest today. The story will be found in chapter 9.

8

Liberty Head Nickels 1883–1913: Guide to Collecting

Grading Standards and Interpretations

As with Shield nickels, an important part of collecting Liberty Head nickels is learning the standards by which they are graded. The American Numismatic Association's grading standards are the most widely used—by the leading grading services as well as by others—and are reproduced here (with slight edits) from *The Official American Numismatic Association Grading Standards for United States Coins* (seventh ed., pp. 118–121), which also contains illustrations of each grade. Remember that these and all other grading standards are subject to interpretation.

Official ANA Grading Standards: Liberty Head Nickels 1883 to 1913

Notes: Liberty Head nickels are subject to laminations and rough planchets. Carbon spots are typical, as are lint marks on the Proofs. Not all Proofs of this series are of the same brilliance. Some dates in the 1880's and 1890's merely have a frosty appearance, but can be identified as Proofs by their sharp edges. Nickels dated 1912-D and 1912-S, and those of the 1883 No CENTS variety, are often weakly struck. Because the obverse design is in higher relief than the reverse design, all dates appear to be more worn on the reverse in low grades. Very few circulation-strike coins have Full Details throughout the design. Kernels on the left ear of corn are nearly always weakly struck, regardless of condition. Coins will not always have the exact stated amount of mint luster, sharpness of strike, or absence of marks. Overall eye appeal and appearance may also influence the stated grade.

Mint State (MS)

Coin is Uncirculated and shows absolutely no trace of wear.

1902. Graded MS-67.

1894. Graded MS-65.

MS-70. A flawless coin exactly as it was minted, with no trace of wear or injury. Must have full mint luster, which may range from brilliant to frosty.

MS-67. Virtually flawless but with minor imperfections.

MS-65. No trace of wear; nearly as perfect as MS-67, except for some small weakness or blemish. Has full mint luster, but may be unevenly toned, frosty, or lightly fingermarked. A few minor nicks or marks may be present.

MS-63. A Mint State coin with attractive mint luster, but noticeable detracting contact marks or minor blemishes.

MS-60. A strictly Uncirculated coin with no trace of wear, but with blemishes more obvious than for MS-63. May lack full mint luster, and surface may be dull or spotted.

About Uncirculated (AU)

Coin shows small traces of wear on the highest points.

1885. Graded AU-58.

AU-58 (Very Choice). Has some signs of abrasion: high points of hair left of ear and at forehead; corn ears at bottom of wreath.

AU-55 (Choice). ***Obverse:*** Only a trace of wear shows on the highest points of hair left of ear. ***Reverse:*** A trace of wear shows on corn ears. SURFACE: Some mint luster is still present.

AU-50 (Typical). ***Obverse:*** Traces of wear show on hair left of ear and at forehead. ***Reverse:*** Traces of wear show on the wreath and corn ears. SURFACE: Trace of mint luster is still present.

Extremely Fine (EF)

Coin shows very light wear on only the highest points.

1885. Graded EF-40.

EF-45 (Choice). ***Obverse:*** Slight wear shows on high points of hair from forehead to the ear. ***Reverse:*** High points of wreath are lightly worn. Many lines in corn are clearly defined. SURFACE: Traces of mint luster may still show.

EF-40. ***Obverse:*** Wear shows on hair from forehead to ear, on the cheek, and on curls. ***Reverse:*** High points of wreath are worn, but each line is clearly defined. Corn shows some wear.

Very Fine (VF)

Coin shows light to moderate even wear. All its major features are sharp.

1888. Graded VF-20.

VF-30 (Choice). ***Obverse:*** Three-quarters of hair details show. The coronet has full, bold lettering. ***Reverse:*** Leaves are worn but most of the ribs are visible. Some of the lines in the corn are clear, unless weakly struck.

VF-20 (Typical). ***Obverse:*** More than half of the details still show in hair and curls. Head is worn but bold. Every letter on coronet is plainly visible. ***Reverse:*** Leaves are worn but some of the ribs are visible. Most details in the wreath are clear, unless weakly struck.

Fine

Coin shows moderate to heavy even wear, but its entire design is clear and bold.

1885. Graded F-15.

Fine-12. ***Obverse:*** Some details show in curls and hair at top of head. All letters of LIBERTY are visible. ***Reverse:*** Some details are visible in wreath. Letters in the motto are worn but clear.

Very Good (VG)

Coin is well worn Design is clear but flat and lacking in detail.

1885. Graded VG-8.

VG-8. ***Obverse:*** Bottom edge of coronet and most hair details are worn smooth. Some letters in LIBERTY are clear. Rim is complete. ***Reverse:*** Wreath shows only bold outline. Some letters in the motto are very weak. Rim is complete.

Good

Coin is heavily worn. Design and legend are visible, but faint in spots.

1885. Graded G-6.

Good-4. ***Obverse:*** Entire design is well worn with very little detail remaining. Stars and date are weak but visible. ***Reverse:*** Wreath is worn flat and not completely outlined. Legend and motto are worn nearly smooth. Rim is incomplete in spots.

About Good (AG)

Coin's design is only outlined. Parts of date and legend are worn smooth.

1885. Graded AG-3.

AG-3. ***Obverse:*** Head is outlined with nearly all details worn away. Date is legible but very weak and merging into rim. ***Reverse:*** Entire design is partially worn away.

Proof (PF)

1883, With CENTS. Graded PF-66 Deep Cameo.

PF-60 to 70 (Proof). ***Obverse and Reverse:*** PF-60, 61, and 62 coins show varying amounts of hairlines in the field, decreasing as the grade increases. Fields may be dull or cloudy on lower-level pieces. At PF-65, hairlines are visible only under magnification and are very light; the cheek of Liberty does not show any abrasion or "album slide marks." Above PF-65, hairlines become fewer, and in ultra-high grades are nonexistent, this meaning that the coins have never been subject to wiping or abrasive cleaning. At PF-65 or better, expect excellent aesthetic appeal. Blotched, deeply toned, or recolored coins can be found at most Proof levels from PF-60 through 65 or even 66, and should be avoided. Watch for artificially toned lower-grade Proofs colored to mask the true nature of the fields.

Being a Smart Buyer of Liberty Head Nickels

Liberty Head nickels—while not exactly a piece of cake—are easier for you to buy as a connoisseur than are any other of the major types. The recipe is fairly simple: just add the ingredients of patience and common sense to an awareness of market values.

Evaluating Striking Sharpness

Collectors have paid very little attention to the quality of sharpness on Liberty Head nickels, with almost no mention of this subject in auction catalogs or value guides, on certified coin holders, or anywhere else. And yet, sharpness can vary, and sometimes widely, although not as dramatically as for Indian/Buffalo nickels, 1913 to 1938. Accordingly, with the knowledge given here, *you* can seek sharply struck coins while most collectors and dealers are unaware of such differences! Among the four major types of nickels (Shield, Liberty Head, Buffalo, and Jefferson), the Liberty Head coins are the easiest to evaluate. Still, it is a challenge to find nice pieces.

During the course of research for this book, I reviewed thousands of images of nickels, including many posted in Internet offerings. For a long time, I have been aware that sharpness can vary, but I was not cognizant of the degree to which grading numbers

A sharply struck Mint State 1889 Liberty Head nickel. Notice that on the obverse the stars are full, including the centers. The hair above Liberty's forehead shows individual strands. The denticles are sharp. On the reverse, the ribbon bow and areas to the left and right, including the corn ear to the left, are sharply defined.

A weakly struck Mint State 1889 Liberty Head nickel. Notice that on the obverse most of the stars are lightly struck at the centers, and the last three stars on the right are flat. The hair above Liberty's forehead is a blob and shows no strands. On the reverse, the leaves and ear of corn to the left of the bow are flat.

overwhelm everything else. One of the rarities among Mint State issues is the 1885. I came across an instance in which a flatly struck 1885 (with some stars flat at the centers and with the reverse flat to the left of the bow), graded MS-66, was valued at nearly three times the price of an MS-65 with needle-sharp details. I was astounded! If you want to share in this amazement, do this yourself—examine the key points mentioned below (either on the coins or in images of them on the Internet).

For *you* as a buyer, this translates into very good news. The marketplace seems to be blissfully unaware of quality in this series. For a Liberty Head nickel to be struck sharply, the metal had to flow into the deepest recesses of the dies. That happened only when the dies were spaced precisely the correct distance apart. In addition, the planchets had to be annealed properly, to soften them for coinage (after which the coinage process hardened the metal). Circulation strikes were not made with care. Accordingly, probably no more than 25% of Mint State Liberty Head nickels have Full Details.

In contrast, Proofs were usually struck from carefully spaced dies and properly annealed planchets, and thus most have Full Details.

In the following paragraphs I give you guidelines as to what to look for in a *circulation-strike* coin.

Sharpness of Obverse Details

Generally, when lightness is seen on Liberty Head nickels, it is at the star centers and hair details on the obverse and/or on the reverse wreath, especially on the ear of corn, and on the leaf pair on the inside of the wreath immediately to the left of the ribbon bow.

Sometimes several or even most of the 13 stars are flat at the centers. More often, the six diamond- or rhomboid-shaped elements that comprise each star can be seen, with lines to the center of the star, but with some flatness. Sometimes two or three stars have slight lightness on the star details, while the others are sharp. The topmost star, the one immediately to the left of the coronet point, is sometimes weak, while all other stars are sharp. Look at the stars first, for they can be viewed quickly. If all are sharp, then go to the next step.

The hair details of Liberty were never bold to begin with. Even so, the various tresses or groups of hair strands are all separated on sharp strikes. When lightness occurs, as it often does, it is usually in the area between the forehead and the coronet. This is also the spot in highest relief on the coin and deepest in the die.

If you find a coin with sharp stars and with the hair tresses delineated, then look at the rest of the coin, which will probably be just fine. These other details include the denticles, the digits in the date, and the fine points of the coronet and above it.

Sharpness of Reverse Details

For a quick take on the reverse, look at the ear of corn on the inside of the wreath, immediately to the left of the ribbon bow. If there is weakness on the reverse, it is apt to be here, rendering the corn and the husk leaf as a blob without details, or sometimes as only partially struck. On *sharp* coins, the kernels in the ear will all be separated.

Some reverses are *very flat*, usually at the ribbon bow and knot to the left, including the corn-ear area and even beyond, and to the right of the ribbon knot, but not a great distance.

When the dies were in the press, the hair above the forehead of Liberty was opposite the corn and husk. If the metal did not completely fill the recesses of both sides, there were weaknesses in one or both of these areas. Generally, the ear of corn can be evaluated in a wink, while it takes a magnifying glass and a few seconds to check the hair.

If the ear of coin has all of its kernels, chances are that the rest of the reverse will be sharp. However, do a routine check—of the leaves in the wreath, the letters, and the denticles.

Surface Quality

Check the fields on both sides. Sometimes one side or both show metal flow or pebbly, stippled fields, rather than flat surfaces with frosty luster. Such coins were struck from "tired dies," or dies that had parts of their surfaces worn away. In other instances, coins from tired dies can be lustrous, with sort of a "greasy" aspect, but with details blurry and with irregular fields. Coins from tired dies can be sharply struck or even have Full Details, but be washed out and lifeless. Some experience is needed to evaluate this aspect, which is most often encountered in the high-mintage dates from the late 1890's onward.

Planchet laminations in the form of chips or flakes out of the surface, leaving recesses, are very common in this series. In other instances, there are cracks or bulges (from air occlusions), even on Proofs.

Summary of Striking

As you can see, the strike quality of a simple Liberty Head nickel, in a holder marked MS-63, MS-65, or some other number, can vary widely. For convenience in nomenclature, I have devised the following four categories. Differentiating the first three categories will be a matter of opinion, but I believe you'll quickly grasp the intended concept.

Weak Details. On the obverse, four or more stars will be incomplete or even flat at their centers. The hair above the forehead will be mainly a blob, with little separation. The ribbon knot will be flat, as will an area to the left, including and past the ear of corn. To the right, there will be flatness as well, but not extending as far. In addition, there may be weakness of denticles or other areas. One or both fields can be pebbly or show flow lines.

If I were forming a collection, I would not buy coins in this category.

Typical Details. One to several stars will have some slight lightness, but each of the six elements will be fully outlined. The hair above the forehead will be weak, but some of the horizontal strands will be visible. The ear of corn to the left of the ribbon bow will be a blob, without the individual kernels visible. The fields can be slightly grainy or with some metal-flow lines, but generally attractive. Sometimes just one side (usually the obverse) has grainy fields. The luster may be a bit dull or lifeless.

The majority of Liberty Head nickels fall into this category, although some dates are better struck than others.

Sharp Details. On the obverse, the denticles and all elements of each star will be sharp. The hair above the forehead will not be completely delineated, but will show separation in areas. On the reverse, the ear of corn may be a blob or just show a few kernels, but everything else will be sharp. The coin will have been struck from fairly fresh dies on both sides, without pebbly surfaces or metal flow. The coin will have good luster, ranging from satiny to frosty.

Generally, this indicates a very nice Liberty Head nickel, one most collectors would be proud to own. The 1912-S never comes sharper than this.

Full Details. On the obverse, the stars, hair details, and all else will be sharp. On the reverse, all of the kernels will be visible in the ear of coin, and all other details will be sharp. The fields should be smooth, not grainy or pebbly, and with luster ranging from satiny to frosty.

Coins like this are in the minority for circulation-strike examples of most dates, and *should* be worth a good premium. Some *Proofs*, supposed to have been made with care, cannot qualify as Full Details coins. Right now 99% of the buyers of Liberty Head nickels are not aware of this category.

Eye Appeal

If you are a connoisseur, you will want circulation-strike coins with Sharp Details or, better yet, Full Details. However, that is not the end of the challenge. Beyond that, a coin must have good eye appeal. The good news is that, in general, Liberty Head nickels have better eye appeal than do the Shield nickels that precede the series or the Buffalo nickels that follow it.

Art is in the eye of the beholder, and, because of this, rules can only be approximate. If I were buying Liberty Head nickels, I would want coins that are lightly toned or brilliant. I would avoid dull gray, brown, and lusterless coins. Nickel tones in a different manner from silver, and Liberty Head nickels can be a light gold or often a lilac or blue. Exceptionally few Liberty Head (or Shield) nickels display original "rainbow" toning, with tightly defined concentric circles in the succession of gold, green, blue, magenta, red, and orange.[1] Such toning can be very attractive if delicate.

Dark, vividly iridescent, or stained coins should be avoided. Without a doubt, experience and the wide consideration of many coins is key to discerning coins that display naturally and attractively toned surfaces from those that may have been artificially colored.

Finding Quality Proofs

Proof coins are much easier to find in high quality than are circulation strikes. Nearly all display Sharp Details or Full Details. There are exceptions, and some Proofs have flat stars and/or light areas on the reverse, but not many. If I were assembling a set of Proof Liberty Head nickels, I would aspire to acquire Full Details on all coins.

As to eye appeal, use the same guidelines given above. Spotting and staining are more common on Proofs than on circulation strikes—avoid such coins. Also, avoid coins that are toned deep brown or gray, are mottled, or are vividly toned. Often these coins are simply low-grade Proofs that were once cleaned and are really in grades of PF-60 to 63, and are hairlined, but have heavy toning artificially applied to mask the hairlines. Lint marks can be a problem, as can planchet flakes and laminations.

Today there are all sorts of vividly toned Mint State and Proof Liberty Head nickels, often deep blue with reds, and so on, often certified in high grades. Years ago, few such coins were in collections. I can conclude only that the vast majority of these are "better coins through chemistry," so to speak.

To find high-quality Proofs from the standpoint of eye appeal, you will probably have to consider pieces graded PF-64 or higher. All Proofs from 1902 onward for the next several years are of low contrast, and the portraits on them were polished in the die. For certain dates, all are this way, although some have been certified as "cameo." To me, *cameo* means frosty contrast; in any case, the term has been applied very inconsistently on Liberty Head nickel Proofs. Generally, such a designation means a higher price, although the coin is seldom any different from one that does not bear a cameo designation. *Always buy the coin, not the label on the holder.*

Consider Proof Liberty Head nickels one by one. Any that are fully brilliant are that way by having been dipped. That is okay, but don't dip them more, for repeated dipping dulls the surface. "Original" toning is nearly always light in hue and is often bluish in tint, sometimes with a bit of yellow or gold.

Locating nice Proofs is much easier than finding nice circulation strikes. Nonetheless, I can envision that even with an appropriate checkbook balance, you should allow yourself a year to finish collecting a full set from 1883 to 1912.

In their excellent 1995 study, *The Complete Guide to Shield and Liberty Head Nickels*, Gloria Peters and Cynthia Mohon note that for the 1905 Proof nickel, the population reports listed 38 coins graded as PF-65, but just one as PF-66. As the present book is being written, a decade later, the corresponding figures are 190 PF-65 coins and 85 in PF-66, perhaps indicating that grade-flation and loosening of grading interpretations has marvelously increased the rarity ratio from 38 to 1 to the present 2 to 1. However, that is not all: now we even have 31 coins graded as PF-67. My take is that some of these PF-67 coins used to be PF-65. What do you think?

Further, of the 206 coins that have been graded from PF-65 to PF-67, many of these listings represent the same pieces' being resubmitted to the grading service in hopes of gaining a higher, more valuable grade, and others represent crossovers—coins that have been in and out of more than one grading service.

The Right Price

Most Liberty Head nickels have market prices that can be looked up in *Monthly Greysheet* or other listings. From guide to guide, there may be differences—not dramatic ones, but still worth noting. For example, one guide might say a certain coin is worth $300 in MS-63, $400 in MS-64, and $600 in MS-65, while another will list the same coin in MS-63 at $275, MS-64 at $380, and MS-65 at $560.

In the marketplace, the selling prices for coins certified by the leading services are apt to hover around such listings. A coin listed at $560 or $600 in MS-65 might be priced at (or might sell at auction for) $540 or $660—not precisely what was listed, but not dramatically far off the mark. You will not find a certified MS-65 available for $450, and if one is listed at $900 it may be overpriced.

Here is what I recommend as strategy when buying circulation strikes: review price lists and determine what grade level you would like to acquire. If you are on a budget, perhaps EF-40 to MS-60 will be the goal. If you have a generous amount to spend, I would start at MS-64 and look at coins certified from there up to MS-66, cherrypicking for quality. As holders ignore sharpness (marvelous for *you!*), cherrypick by choosing pieces with Full Details if possible; select with regard to eye appeal, something also not mentioned on the holders.

Perhaps at the outset, for the first half of your collection, you should stay around the market price listings, say within 25% on the high side. If you find an MS-65 coin that is in a guide at $600, and the seller wants, say, $750; if it is sharp and has good eye appeal, it is probably worth buying. A year into the game, if you come across a coin you've been seeking but have had no opportunity to buy, loosen up your purse strings and pay a 50% premium if you have to. However, while you should be *prepared* to pay a premium price for magnificent sharpness and eye appeal, often you will not need to—unless the coin is marked with a high grade. Even if you have a lot of money to spend, in my opinion, there is no sense paying a long price for coins graded MS-67 or higher, when, at present, many great gems are available in holders marked MS-65 and 66. Also, remember that a coin listed as MS-67 or 68 may be a poor strike, or may be so heavily toned that its true nature cannot be learned, or may be struck from tired dies and have a pebbly surface.

If you are computer oriented, look at a lot of Liberty Head nickels on the Internet and pick out the different details and characteristics on many of the images. Such depictions are best for determining sharpness of strike. Overall quality may be impossible to discern, as photographers can adjust the pictures they take, and images that have been scanned have the luster diminished or altered. Accordingly, for buyers such pictures are not a substitute for in-person inspection.

Take your time. Savor the experience. Spend a year or two (or three) in the completion of a quality Mint State set. As noted, the assembly of a set of Proofs will take less time.

Interesting Varieties

Liberty Head nickels offer slim pickings, as they say, for variety hunters—at least in comparison to the extensive and sometimes fantastic panorama of oddities in the Shield nickel series. However, there are many doubled dies and repunched dates, not dramatic, but easily enough seen under low magnification. A few misplaced dates exist as well. No doubt more varieties remain to be discovered.

Cherrypickers' Guide to Rare Die Varieties lists 14 varieties among 1883 to 1913 Liberty Head nickels, taking just 9 pages to do so, in comparison to the 16 pages it devotes to Shield nickels of the single year 1868. (Still, this is a marked increase from the single Liberty Head nickel it listed in the first edition, in 1990.)

The Complete Guide to Shield and Liberty Head Nickels takes the reader into deep territory with more than 70 varieties described, accompanied by dozens of close-up illustrations. *Treasure Hunting Liberty Head Nickels* (second edition, 2005, by Kevin Flynn and Bill Van Note) lists and illustrates even more and is the source for selected close-up illustrations among the date listings in the present text.

The marketplace has taken little notice of Liberty Head nickel varieties, with the result that you can find nearly all of them at regular prices simply by cherrypicking.

9

Liberty Head Nickels 1883–1913: Analysis by Date and Mintmark

1883, Without CENTS

Circulation-Strike Mintage:
5,474,000

Proof Mintage:
5,219 (but estimated as 9,219)

Key to Collecting: This historical and fascinating variety was saved in quantity at the time of issue. Today, examples are common in all Mint State grade levels. Striking sharpness can vary considerably. Many have die cracks and other interesting features. There are enough around for just about everyone interested. Such a coin is a fascinating addition to any collection, for few issues have more remarkable stories. Several youngsters who later become prominent professional numismatists, Farran Zerbe and Arthur M. Kagin among them, became interested in coin collecting after obtaining one of these curious nickels.

Circulation Strikes

Characteristics and Appearance: The dies were not widely studied until the 1960's. Of the 630 obverse dies used to coin both types of 1883 Liberty Head nickel, an estimated 200 or more were used exclusively for this issue. Some 242 reverse dies, all of Reverse Style B, are known to have been made. So many die pairs were used that no one rule can fit all. The striking of details ranges from weak to sharp, but is usually above average, with full stars and with decent details on the reverse, but with some lightness on the corn. The luster is usually satiny, sometimes slightly prooflike, but not often deeply frosty. Die cracks are very common on this issue; some are so extensive it seems surprising that the dies held together. This letter from Herman K. Crofoot, published in the July 1956 issue of *The Numismatist*, reflects this:

> In starting over a quantity of 1883 No CENTS five-cent pieces I find one with a die break joining the UN of UNITED with the rim of the coin, first I have seen. I would like very much to hear from anyone who has a similar die break so that I may compile a list of them.

Of those 630 obverse dies, probably not all were used. If all *were* employed for the combined coinage of 21,500,000 for both types, that would indicate a life of about 34,000 impressions per die. Most dies were probably retired due to cracking, not wear.

Mintage and Distribution Notes: As discussed in the narrative above, this issue was eagerly snapped up by the public and was saved in quantity.

1883, Without CENTS: Circulation Strike

GSID	VG-8	F-12	VF-20	EF-40	AU-50	MS-60	MS-63	MS-65	MS-67
2947	$8.00	$9.50	$11	$15	$20	$55	$95	$260	$2,500

PROOF STRIKES

Characteristics and Appearance: Proofs are usually well struck and with good contrast.

Mintage and Distribution Notes: Reverse Style A (with repunched S in PLURIBUS; rare) and Reverse Style B (usually seen). By March 31, Proof production amounted to 3,519 coins, reflecting the tremendous demand for this curious variety. By June 30, an additional 1,700 were delivered. This accounts for the figure of 5,219 commonly quoted, as here. R.W. Julian, in "Notes on U.S. Proof Coinage" (1966), cites 2,850 *With CENTS* Proofs delivered on June 26, with 1,000 more on October 11, and a further 2,993 by December 31. These figures are somewhat confusing as they indicate a great demand for the With CENTS, a sentiment that seems unlikely and is questioned by Breen in his Proof coins encyclopedia. It would seem reasonable to me that *much* of the With CENTS mintage quantity should be moved to the Without CENTS, an action that seems to be verified by market appearances and certification data. Likely, collector demand for Without CENTS Proofs lasted throughout the year, and orders for such coins were filled. Breen states that at least seven Proof obverse dies were used, indicating a large coinage. This includes varieties with the 1 close to the neck and distant from the denticles, another with the 1 close to the denticles, and several with the digit about centered. In any event, for a time in 1883 the Mint continued to strike and sell all three designs of nickels of the year, the Shield and both types of the Liberty Head.[1]

1883, Without CENTS: Proof Strike

GSID	PF-60	PF-63	PF-64	PF-65	PF-66	PF-67
2980	$260	$310	$430	$625	$800	$1,750
2982 (Cameo)	—	415	525	675	900	2,500
2983 (Deep Cameo)	—	—	1,500	1,900	2,500	12,000

Varieties

Repunched Date—FS-1301. As described in the Fivaz-Stanton book, *Cherrypickers' Guide to Rare Die Varieties*, the lower left serif of the 1 in the date extends outward from the lower left side of the first 8. URS-4.

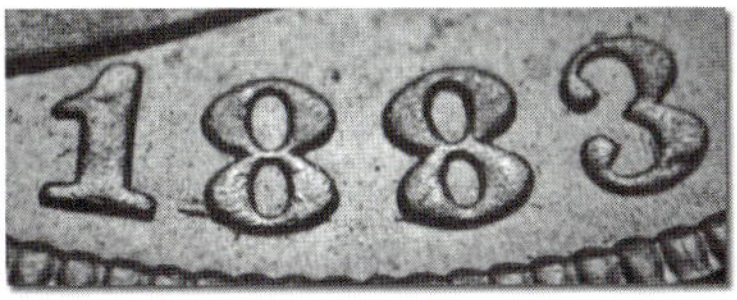

1883, Without CENTS, Repunched Date (FS-1301): Circulation Strike

GSID	VG-8	F-12	VF-20	EF-40	AU-50	MS-60	MS-63	MS-65	MS-67
346843	—	—	40.00	70.00	100.00	195.00	325.00	—	—

1883, With CENTS

Circulation-Strike Mintage:
16,026,000

Proof Mintage:
6,783 (but estimated as 2,783)

Key to Collecting: Despite its circulation-strike mintage of about triple the Without CENTS figure, the With CENTS is much scarcer in Mint State. Very few were saved at the time of issue, and there was little public interest in the correction of the design.

Examples today are fairly elusive in a combination of high grade, sharp details, and nice eye appeal. Proofs are readily collectible.

Circulation Strikes

Characteristics and Appearance: Striking varies, as might be expected from the large mintage quantity. Die cracks are often seen. Luster is usually lightly frosty. Most dies seem to have been retired due to cracking. As a result, strikings from tired dies are not often seen for this or other early dates.

1883, With CENTS: Circulation Strike

GSID	VG-8	F-12	VF-20	EF-40	AU-50	MS-60	MS-63	MS-65	MS-67
2948	$31	$40	$55	$90	$120	$160	$215	$525	$3,750

Proof Strikes

Characteristics and Appearance: Proofs are usually well struck. Lint marks and planchet flakes are sometimes seen, and such coins should be avoided.

Mintage and Distribution Notes: Although conventional wisdom puts it at 6,783, my estimate is 2,783. It is likely that the popularly published figure of 6,783 is significantly exaggerated, as verified by market appearances and certification service data. For further explanation see commentary under Without CENTS Proofs.

1883, With CENTS: Proof Strike

GSID	PF-60	PF-63	PF-64	PF-65	PF-66	PF-67
2981	$230	$310	$405	$500	$750	$1,750
2986 (Cameo)	—	345	445	575	925	4,750
2987 (Deep Cameo)	—	—	1,550	2,500	3,250	11,000

1884

Circulation-Strike Mintage:
11,270,000

Proof Mintage:
3,942

Key to Collecting: The 1884 is a plentiful date and is available in almost any grade desired. Among Mint State coins, most are lower than MS-65. Gems are truly scarce, especially if sharply struck and with good eye appeal. Proofs are usually attractive and well struck.

Circulation Strikes

Characteristics and Appearance: Striking varies, but examples with Full Details can be found with some searching. Luster is usually frosty. Die cracks are not seen as often as for 1884, but are common. Such cracks often lend interest. There were 167 obverse dies made this year, which equals 67,000 impressions per die, if all were used. Such information may be of more theoretical than practical interest, as wide swings in impressions per die probably indicate that for some years, many dies were never used. However, the trend is upward for die use—as data for later years reflect.

1884: Circulation Strike

GSID	VG-8	F-12	VF-20	EF-40	AU-50	MS-60	MS-63	MS-65	MS-67
2949	$35	$40	$60	$90	$135	$195	$300	$1,150	$8,750

Proof Strikes

Characteristics and Appearance: Deeply mirrored fields are the rule. Most Proofs are well struck, but check the hair details on the obverse and the ear of corn to the left of the ribbon bow on the reverse.

One die has the 1 in 1884 dramatically double punched, most evident at the base; the top of the 1 pierces the neck truncation of Liberty. At least two other obverse dies were used as well.

1884: Proof Strike

GSID	PF-60	PF-63	PF-64	PF-65	PF-66	PF-67
2988	$230	$310	$425	$525	$800	$1,250
2989 (Cameo)	—	345	445	575	850	2,500
2990 (Deep Cameo)	—	—	1,000	2,000	3,100	12,000

Varieties

Repunched Date—Proof die with repunched 1 (shown). Variety FS-301, seen on circulation strikes, has several date numerals repunched, most prominently the 1, which has a doubled base. URS-7.

1884, Repunched Date (FS-301): Circulation Strike

GSID	VG-8	F-12	VF-20	EF-40	AU-50	MS-60	MS-63	MS-65	MS-67
346845	—	—	$65	$100	$135	$200	$335	$1,500	—

1885

Circulation-Strike Mintage:
1,472,700

Proof Mintage:
3,790

Key to Collecting: Among regular-issue Liberty Head nickels, the 1885 is *the* key date—the date that everyone sought when collecting nickels from circulation became popular, beginning with Wayte Raymond's "National" albums, Whitman boards, and other convenient holders that became available in the 1930's. In that long-ago era, nickels of this design were plentiful in the channels of commerce, but those of 1885 were elusive due to their low mintage. Even so, many thousands were fished out of pocket change and elsewhere, most of these being well worn, down to grades that we call Good and Very Good today.

The numismatic community ignored the freshly minted circulation strikes of 1885. Those who collected by dates simply bought Proofs. Because of this, the survival of Mint State coins was a matter of rare chance, while the 3,790 Proofs were sold at a premium and were prized by their recipients.

Today, the 1885 nickel remains scarce in worn grades, rare in Mint State, but generally available in Proof format. The emphasis years ago on key dates has been eclipsed in recent decades by focus on the grade alone. Remarkably, today a Proof 1885 can be acquired at only a modest advance over a date that is more plentiful (in terms of overall mintage—Proofs plus circulation strikes). This is a change from the comment by Peters and Mohon in 1995, "Date pressure, due to the rarity of the business strike, keeps the price of Proofs at an unrealistic level for its rarity."

A sharply struck gem Mint State 1885 nickel is a great find for the knowing connoisseur. Some Mint State coins, even certified as MS-65 or 66, have several obverse stars flat. In the meantime, Proofs handily fill the need of most buyers who seek high-grade examples of this prized date. The market price for Proofs seems to be taking a nap.

Circulation Strikes

Characteristics and Appearance: Striking varies but is usually quite good, though some have several obverse stars flat at their centers. Some early strikes from fresh dies show parallel striae. The mint luster on some Uncirculated coins is satiny and attractive, while on others it is lifeless. Some have slightly prooflike surfaces. These are more available than those with deep, frosty luster.

Mint records indicate that in January 1886, for circulation-strike nickels of 1885, 29 obverse and 23 reverse dies were destroyed.[2] If 29 obverse dies were actually used, this equates to an average of about 51,000 impressions per die. This was probably about the upper range of optimal use for the time, without creating surface problems.

Mintage and Distribution Notes: This represented the nadir of demand for the nickel five-cent piece during the early era of Liberty Head coinage. The slump, resulting from a nationwide economic chill, lasted until autumn 1886. Historian Neil Carothers commented,

> Progress in metallurgy and mint processes eliminated the difficulties in coining nickel, and the attractive color and fine wearing qualities of the alloy made it a popular coinage material. After 1885 the mints had difficulty in keeping up with the demand. The street railway, the cheap cigar, the "notions counter," sale of toys, candies, gum, cigarettes, and soda waters requiring payments of 5, 10, or 15 cents very rapidly increased.[3]

1885: Circulation Strike

GSID	VG-8	F-12	VF-20	EF-40	AU-50	MS-60	MS-63	MS-65	MS-67
2950	$625	$775	$1,150	$1,250	$1,500	$2,400	$4,100	$7,500	$24,000

Proof Strikes

Characteristics and Appearance: Quality of striking varies, and some show weakness. Most, however, are fairly sharp. *The Numismatist*, April 1951, included a letter from Robert Scott, of Aurora, Illinois, noting that his "1885 Liberty Nickel in brilliant Proof condition . . . has a sizeable die break on the obverse side through the hair and out to the edge of the coin, at about 2:00 as for position."

Mintage and Distribution Notes: Most examples show the 1 in the date very close to Liberty's neck; fewer show the 1 distinctly separated with an area of Proof field. The 1885 nickel is justly advertised as a rare *date* in an overall context, but among Proofs it is one of the more plentiful coins in the series. Mint records indicate that in January 1886, for Proof nickels of 1885, one obverse and one reverse die were destroyed.[4]

1885: Proof Strike

GSID	PF-60	PF-63	PF-64	PF-65	PF-66	PF-67
2991	$950	$1,200	$1,250	$1,300	$1,500	$2,000
2992 (Cameo)	—	1,250	1,300	1,600	2,000	3,100
2993 (Deep Cameo)	—	—	1,750	2,400	3,250	8,000

1886

Circulation-Strike Mintage:
3,326,000

Proof Mintage:
4,290

Key to Collecting: The 1886 nickel is generally ranked as the second-rarest Liberty Head nickel in the early series, with 1885 first. However, in Mint State, particularly at the gem level, the 1886 nickel eclipses the 1885 in rarity. High-grade (Very Fine to Mint State) examples are elusive across the board, as little numismatic notice was paid to the date until the 1930's, by which time most had become well worn. Finding a sharply struck gem would be an accomplishment indeed! Mark Hooten adds this comment:

> As with its 1885 "key companion," many collectors who typically seek out Mint State pieces will settle for a choice AU (About Uncirculated) piece. Often times, the AU grades house coins that possess better detail than many or most of their "Uncirculated" counterparts, making those grades a true bargain.[5]

Paralleling the situation for 1885, most of the demand for high-grade nickels with the 1886 date is supplied by Proofs, which were made in a fair quantity.

Circulation Strikes

Characteristics and Appearance: The striking is usually quite good. Some nickels are prooflike, but not mirrorlike enough to be mistaken for Proofs. The date logotype used on all dies (circulation strikes and Proofs) has the 1 too high in relation to the curved baseline of the following three digits, this being characteristic of other years in the 1886 to 1889 era. There were 101 obverse dies made. If all of them were used, each die would have made 33,000 impressions—a low figure that probably indicates many of the dies were never used (since dies were sometimes retired before they were overly worn, the number isn't impossible).

1886: Circulation Strike

GSID	VG-8	F-12	VF-20	EF-40	AU-50	MS-60	MS-63	MS-65	MS-67
2951	$235	$365	$450	$650	$800	$1,300	$2,200	$4,250	$33,000

Proof Strikes

Characteristics and Appearance: Most are well struck with Full Details, but a few have lightness on the highest parts of the hair. On the reverse, the ear of corn to the left of the ribbon bow also shows lightness.

Mintage and Distribution Notes: At least three obverse dies were used, one with the second 8 repunched, another with the last two digits slightly repunched. The making of multiple Proof dies for short production runs is unexplained, but is perhaps best exemplified by the use of at least five obverse dies in 1895 to coin just 880 examples.

1886: Proof Strike

GSID	PF-60	PF-63	PF-64	PF-65	PF-66	PF-67
2994	$495	$575	$625	$900	$1,150	$2,400
2995 (Cameo)	—	675	775	1,000	2,250	5,500
2996 (Deep Cameo)	—	—	1,250	2,000	3,750	8,750

Varieties

Repunched Date—FS-301. Slightly repunched, date most noticeable at the top of the 6.

1886, Repunched Date (FS-301): Circulation Strike

GSID	VG-8	F-12	VF-20	EF-40	AU-50	MS-60	MS-63	MS-65	MS-67
346846	—	—	$475	$675	$850	$1,375	$2,250	$4,350	—

1887

Circulation-Strike Mintage:
15,260,652

Proof Mintage:
2,960

Key to Collecting: The 1887 nickel is easy to find in just about any grade desired, from About Good to Mint State. However, quality can be a problem for coins in higher levels, and discrimination is needed. Many Mint State coins have granular surfaces from dies that remained in service too long. Although the mintage quantity for Proofs was on the low side for this era, today they come on the market with regularity and are usually well struck and attractive.

Circulation Strikes

Characteristics and Appearance: Luster and surface quality vary from frosty to dull. Coins with certain details lightly struck are the rule, not the exception. Flashy gems are rare. The date logotype used on all dies (circulation strikes and Proofs) has the 1 too high in relation to the curved baseline of the following three digits, this being characteristic of other years in the 1886 to 1889 era. There were 143 obverse dies made for this year, equating to 107,000 impressions per die, if all were used. Ready-made planchets were obtained from the American Nickel Works in Camden, New Jersey. More than a million worn nickels were cleaned and reissued.

1887: Circulation Strike

GSID	VG-8	F-12	VF-20	EF-40	AU-50	MS-60	MS-63	MS-65	MS-67
2952	$20	$32	$45	$80	$100	$155	$285	$775	$7,500

Proof Strikes

Characteristics and Appearance: Usually well struck with Full Details. Sometimes with slightly rounded (rather than sharp) rim edges.

Mintage and Distribution Notes: At least two obverse dies were used.

1887: Proof Strike

GSID	PF-60	PF-63	PF-64	PF-65	PF-66	PF-67
2997	$230	$310	$405	$500	$750	$2,500
2998 (Cameo)	—	395	500	650	1,900	7,500

1888

Circulation-Strike Mintage:
10,715,901

Proof Mintage:
4,582

Key to Collecting: Although the 1888 is not generally considered to be a scarce date, at the choice and gem Mint State levels quality can be a big problem. Finding a sharply struck coin with rich luster and good eye appeal is not easy to do.

Proofs are plentiful enough, but many have problems, such as planchet roughness and dull surfaces.

Circulation Strikes

Characteristics and Appearance: Striking varies in sharpness. Luster is often unsatisfactory as a result of overly long use of the dies. The date logotype used on all dies (circulation strikes and Proofs) has the 1 too high in relation to the curved baseline of the following three digits, this being characteristic of other years in the 1886 to 1889 era. There were 86 obverse dies made for this year, equating to 125,000 impressions per die, if all were used, which may have approximated actuality. When dies were used for long stretches, a deterioration of quality resulted.

1888: Circulation Strike

GSID	VG-8	F-12	VF-20	EF-40	AU-50	MS-60	MS-63	MS-65	MS-67
2953	$45	$70	$130	$175	$235	$310	$390	$950	$7,500

Proof Strikes

Characteristics and Appearance: Often somewhat dull and unattractive. Walter Breen suggests that the metal alloy was not standard, perhaps with a different crystalline structure that did not take a mirror surface well. Many 1889 Proofs are similar. Some have lightness on the ear of corn to the left of the ribbon bow on the reverse.

Mintage and Distribution Notes: At least two or three obverse dies were used.

1888: Proof Strike

GSID	PF-60	PF-63	PF-64	PF-65	PF-66	PF-67
3000	$230	$310	$405	$500	$850	$2,250
3001 (Cameo)	—	345	445	950	1,800	4,400

1889

Circulation-Strike Mintage:
15,878,025

Proof Mintage:
3,336

Key to Collecting: The 1889 nickel is plentiful in most grades up to and including Mint State. However, once again quality can be a challenge. The good news here, and for other years, is that most buyers don't notice sharpness of strike or eye appeal, leaving the choice pieces for you! Proofs vary in quality, but the mintage was large enough that you will find a choice example without difficulty.

Circulation Strikes

Characteristics and Appearance: Sharpness and luster vary, but choice pieces with good eye appeal are definitely scarce. The date logotype used on all dies (circulation strikes and Proofs) has the 1 too high in relation to the curved baseline of the following three digits, this being characteristic of other years in the 1886 to 1889 era. There were 134 obverse dies made for this year, equating to 118,000 impressions per die, if all were used—compare this to earlier issues. The increase in impressions per die created many coins with surfaces showing metal flow or pebbly characteristics. Light striking of certain areas is common for this year.

1889: Circulation Strike

GSID	VG-8	F-12	VF-20	EF-40	AU-50	MS-60	MS-63	MS-65	MS-67
2954	$16	$32	$55	$90	$130	$180	$245	$625	$11,000

Proof Strikes

Characteristics and Appearance: Proofs are usually well struck with Full Details. Surfaces sometimes are dull, grainy, and lifeless, as with 1888 Proofs. Others have satiny, somewhat lustrous surfaces reminiscent of a gem Mint State coin.

1889: Proof Strike

GSID	PF-60	PF-63	PF-64	PF-65	PF-66	PF-67
3003	$230	$310	$405	$500	$750	$2,500
3004 (Cameo)	—	—	3,750	6,250	9,500	17,000

1890

Circulation-Strike Mintage:
16,256,532

Proof Mintage:
2,740

Key to Collecting: The 1890 nickel should be plentiful in choice and gem Mint State, but it is not. There are two reasons for this. First, at this time the nation was having economic hiccups from overexpansion in the prairie states, and the coin market was in the doldrums. Many of the rarities in the auction offering of the Lorin G. Parmelee sale this year failed to find buyers. Second, as if the market problems were not enough, many coins were lightly struck. Peters and Mohon wrote in 1995, "If a fully struck gem is found, buy it!"

Proofs are elusive, but when found they are apt to be nicer in quality than those of the preceding two years.

Circulation Strikes

Characteristics and Appearance: Striking is often subpar, with lightness on the stars or on the corn ear. Luster can be dull. This date is a challenge for the connoisseur. There were 132 obverse dies made.

1890: Circulation Strike

GSID	VG-8	F-12	VF-20	EF-40	AU-50	MS-60	MS-63	MS-65	MS-67
2955	$16	$27	$40	$70	$115	$160	$230	$675	$11,000

Proof Strikes

Characteristics and Appearance: Proofs are usually well struck with Full Details. Planchet flakes and chips are common on these and other Proofs of the era, as are lint marks.

1890: Proof Strike

GSID	PF-60	PF-63	PF-64	PF-65	PF-66	PF-67
3006	$230	$310	$405	$500	$750	$3,750
3007 (Cameo)	—	345	445	575	850	8,750
3008 (Deep Cameo)	—	—	3,000	6,250	15,500	—

1891

Circulation-Strike Mintage:
16,832,000

Proof Mintage:
2,350

Key to Collecting: Echoing the situation for the 1890 nickels, those dated 1891 are much scarcer in high grades than their mintage might suggest. Add to that the light striking and dull luster of many of the pieces, and a challenge is presented.

Proofs are somewhat scarce, as the mintage was low and the coin market continued in a slump.

Circulation Strikes

Characteristics and Appearance: The details vary, but many have lightness on the hair of Liberty and, on the reverse, the ear of corn to the left of the ribbon bow. Others have weakness on several stars as well. There were 69 obverse dies made.

In today's world of the Internet, certified coins, and fast-paced transactions, scarce issues are much more easily found than they were years ago. In the 1960's, dealer Abe Kosoff told me that he had spent several *years* looking for an Uncirculated 1891 Liberty Head nickel for a customer. His client insisted on an Uncirculated piece; a Proof wouldn't do. Finally, he located an example. Equipped with this knowledge, I set about looking for 1891 Uncirculated nickels on my own, and while the issue seemed to be scarce, I was able to buy several over a period of years—but today, with some inquiries sent here and there, I could probably buy several within a *week*.

1891: Circulation Strike

GSID	VG-8	F-12	VF-20	EF-40	AU-50	MS-60	MS-63	MS-65	MS-67
2956	$8	$22	$38	$60	$120	$150	$210	$550	$12,000

Proof Strikes

Characteristics and Appearance: Proofs are usually well struck with Full Details, but are sometimes slightly light on the corn ear to the left of the ribbon bow.

1891: Proof Strike

GSID	PF-60	PF-63	PF-64	PF-65	PF-66	PF-67
3009	$230	$310	$405	$500	$750	$3,750
3010 (Cameo)	—	380	490	775	1,100	5,000
3011 (Deep Cameo)	—	—	1,150	1,750	2,200	8,500

1892

Circulation-Strike Mintage:
11,696,897

Proof Mintage:
2,745

Key to Collecting: The 1892 nickel follows in the footsteps of its immediate predecessors and is difficult to find with the combination of sharp strike, frosty luster, and good eye appeal. Most people active in the market are unaware of this, giving you an advantage. Proofs are on the scarce side and can have problems, but enough nice ones are around that you will not have to wait long to get a coin that is just right.

Circulation Strikes

Characteristics and Appearance: Striking varies, with most having lightness in one place or another. Check the usual star centers and ear of corn to the left of the ribbon bow. A total of 89 obverse dies were made.

1882: Circulation Strike

GSID	VG-8	F-12	VF-20	EF-40	AU-50	MS-60	MS-63	MS-65	MS-67
2957	$8	$22	$40	$70	$120	$160	$245	$850	$26,500

Proof Strikes

Characteristics and Appearance: Striking varies, and some Proofs have lightness at several stars and the hair of Liberty on the obverse, and, on the reverse, the ear of corn to the left of the ribbon bow. Cherrypicking is advised!

1892: Proof Strike

GSID	PF-60	PF-63	PF-64	PF-65	PF-66	PF-67
3012	$230	$310	$405	$525	$800	$3,100
3013 (Cameo)	—	345	445	575	850	3,500
3014 (Deep Cameo)	—	900	1,000	1,900	5,000	—

1893

Circulation-Strike Mintage:
13,368,000

Proof Mintage:
2,195

Key to Collecting: The 1893 nickel is another challenge for you, with the combination of sharp strike, good luster, and outstanding eye appeal being elusive. In America this was a year of economic depression, the effects of which would linger for the next several years. Proofs are scarce, but usually are attractive when found.

Circulation Strikes

Characteristics and Appearance: Striking varies, and some have flat stars and, on the reverse, flatness near the ribbon bow. Avoid these. Luster ranges from subpar to attractive. As many die pairs were used, no single rule fits all coins. A total of 70 obverse dies were made.

1893: Circulation Strike

GSID	VG-8	F-12	VF-20	EF-40	AU-50	MS-60	MS-63	MS-65	MS-67
2958	$8	$22	$38	$60	$110	$150	$215	$650	$14,500

Proof Strikes

Characteristics and Appearance: Usually well struck with Full Details, but planchet flakes and lintmarks can be a problem.

Mintage and Distribution Notes: At least three obverse dies were used, with the date (as measured by the 1) high and close to neck, at the center, or close to the denticles. As Proofs are nearly always collected by date and not by die varieties, such differences are interesting but academic. Again, it is curious that multiple dies were needed for what amounted to the lowest production run up to this time for the Liberty Head nickel series.

1893: Proof Strike

GSID	PF-60	PF-63	PF-64	PF-65	PF-66	PF-67
3015	$230	$310	$405	$500	$750	$1,550
3016 (Cameo)	—	345	445	575	1,150	3,250
3017 (Deep Cameo)	—	—	1,000	1,550	2,000	8,000

1894

Circulation-Strike Mintage:
5,410,500

Proof Mintage:
2,632

Key to Collecting: The mintage of nickel five-cent pieces fell sharply this year, the aftermath of what some have called the Panic of 1893. Times were difficult, and many banks and other businesses failed. The coin market continued its slump as well, although George F. Heath and other proponents of the recently formed (in 1891) American Numismatic Association were endeavoring to stir up a lot of interest.

Mint State coins are scarce, and no-problem gems are rare. Many Proofs have problems, such as planchet flakes and lint marks.

Circulation Strikes

Characteristics and Appearance: Most are lightly struck in one area or another. Luster varies, but is usually satisfactory. There were 41 obverse dies made.

1894: Circulation Strike

GSID	VG-8	F-12	VF-20	EF-40	AU-50	MS-60	MS-63	MS-65	MS-67
2959	$31	$100	$160	$255	$325	$430	$575	$1,450	$10,500

Proof Strikes

Characteristics and Appearance: Usually well struck and with mirrored fields. However, planchet flakes, lint marks, and other defects rear their heads, with the result that really choice coins are in the minority.

Mintage and Distribution Notes: These coins were struck from at least two obverse dies, one with a repunched 4 in the date.

1894: Proof Strike

GSID	PF-60	PF-63	PF-64	PF-65	PF-66	PF-67
3018	$230	$310	$405	$500	$750	$1,750
3019 (Cameo)	—	420	525	725	925	4,400

1895

Circulation-Strike Mintage:
9,977,822

Proof Mintage:
2,062

Key to Collecting: Once again, problem-free choice and gem nickels are a challenge, and relatively few of the 1895 date pass the test. Fortunately, enough are around that you will have no problem finding one; however, you may have to inspect a half dozen or more before locating an example that is just right. Proofs are usually quite nice, with deeply mirrored fields.

A word of caution is in order concerning the population reports of grading services. For this and many other years of the late 19th and early 20th centuries, values are modest for circulation strikes and Proofs below the 63 or 64 designation. Because of this, relatively few have been submitted, giving them the undeserved appearance of scarcity and rarity when such reports are studied. Actually, most nickels of this era are very common in grades from MS-60 through 63.

Circulation Strikes

Characteristics and Appearance: Sharpness can be a problem, as can luster and eye appeal. There were 47 obverse dies made.

1895: Circulation Strike

GSID	VG-8	F-12	VF-20	EF-40	AU-50	MS-60	MS-63	MS-65	MS-67
2960	$6.75	$17.50	$40	$70	$120	$170	$290	$1,000	$22,000

Proof Strikes

Characteristics and Appearance: Proofs are on the scarce side, but when found are apt to have fewer problems than for the several immediately preceding dates.

1895: Proof Strike

GSID	PF-60	PF-63	PF-64	PF-65	PF-66	PF-67
3021	$230	$310	$405	$500	$750	$3,750
3022 (Cameo)	—	345	445	775	3,100	12,000
3023 (Deep Cameo)	—		—	5,000	9,500	17,000

1896

Circulation-Strike Mintage:
8,841,048

Proof Mintage:
1,862

Key to Collecting: The mintage of nickels was relatively small in 1896, creating a key date. The nation had not yet calmed down from the Panic of 1893, and fewer coins were saved as souvenirs than might have been the case otherwise. For the first time in the Liberty Head series, the Proof mintage figure slipped below the 2,000 mark.

Today, sharply struck Mint State coins in higher grades are very elusive—making this one of the top keys in the series. Proofs are scarce, but when found they are apt to be choice.

Circulation Strikes

Characteristics and Appearance: Most are lightly struck in one area or another, and luster can be a problem as well. A total of 56 obverse dies were made.

1896: Circulation Strike

GSID	VG-8	F-12	VF-20	EF-40	AU-50	MS-60	MS-63	MS-65	MS-67
2961	$22	$40	$70	$130	$170	$220	$365	$1,100	$11,000

Proof Strikes

Characteristics and Appearance: Quality varies. At least one obverse die was heavily repolished; Proofs struck from this die have some stars with flat centers and show prominent lint marks from debris.

1896: Proof Strike

GSID	PF-60	PF-63	PF-64	PF-65	PF-66	PF-67
3024	$230	$310	$405	$500	$750	$3,450
3025 (Cameo)	—	345	470	725	2,400	5,500
3026 (Deep Cameo)	—	1,250	1,750	3,100	7,500	13,000

1897

Circulation-Strike Mintage:
20,426,797

Proof Mintage:
1,938

Key to Collecting: From this year forward Liberty Head nickels are generally readily available in high circulated grades through MS-65 or even MS-66. While many show weakness or were made from dies that were worn, enough exist that nice examples can be found. The availability of Proofs trends downward, reaching a low spot in 1907, and remaining fairly low thereafter, except for 1909.

Circulation Strikes

Characteristics and Appearance: Many show areas of weakness and/or granular fields. Take the time to find a nice one. In all, 99 obverse dies were made.

Mintage and Distribution Notes: Treasury rules for the distribution of certain coins in effect in this era were as follows:

> Five-cent nickel and one-cent bronze pieces will be furnished in the order of application from the United States Mint at Philadelphia, Pa. to points reached by the United States and connecting express companies, free of transportation charges, in sums of $20, or multiples thereof, except New York, Boston, Baltimore, Philadelphia, Cincinnati, Chicago, St. Louis, New Orleans, and San Francisco, upon receipt and collection by the superintendent of that mint of a draft on New York or Philadelphia payable to his order.[6]

1897: Circulation Strike

GSID	VG-8	F-12	VF-20	EF-40	AU-50	MS-60	MS-63	MS-65	MS-67
2962	$3.70	$8	$20	$47	$80	$110	$190	$750	$11,000

Proof Strikes

Characteristics and Appearance: Portrait satiny, not deeply frosty. Usually well struck with Full Details, but sometimes with light striking on the corn ear to the left of the ribbon bow.

1897: Proof Strike

GSID	PF-60	PF-63	PF-64	PF-65	PF-66	PF-67
3027	$230	$310	$405	$500	$750	$1,200
3028 (Cameo)	—	345	445	575	850	1,800
3029 (Deep Cameo)	—	—	1,500	2,250	3,000	9,000

1898

Circulation-Strike Mintage:
12,530,292

Proof Mintage:
1,795

Key to Collecting: Probably no more than one in four Mint State coins combines decent sharpness with rich luster. Happily, the supply of 1898 nickels is sufficiently large that a nice one can be found in due course. Proofs are rather scarce and are usually less than PF-65 in numerical rating. When found, examples are apt to be choice. I reiterate that population data are of limited use as coins thought to be below MS-63 or 64 are not often submitted, due to the high cost of grading compared to the market value of the pieces.

Circulation Strikes

Characteristics and Appearance: Striking varies in sharpness, and luster varies as well. This date is fairly plentiful, and a choice example can be found. A total of 91 obverse dies were made.

This seems to be the last year that the Treasury Department cleaned and reissued large quantities of worn nickels of earlier dates.

1898: Circulation Strike

GSID	VG-8	F-12	VF-20	EF-40	AU-50	MS-60	MS-63	MS-65	MS-67
2963	$3.70	$8.00	$17.50	$60	$95	$150	$230	$650	$8,000

Proof Strikes

Characteristics and Appearance: Usually well struck and of nice appearance.

Mintage and Distribution Notes: Breen describes three obverse dies, one with slightly repunched date, another with final 8 especially bold (probably from the uneven punching of the four-digit logotype into the working die).

1898: Proof Strike

GSID	PF-60	PF-63	PF-64	PF-65	PF-66	PF-67
3030	$230	$310	$405	$500	$750	$1,450
3031 (Cameo)	—	345	525	575	850	3,750
3032 (Deep Cameo)	—	—	1,250	1,900	3,100	11,000

1899

Circulation-Strike Mintage:
26,027,000

Proof Mintage:
2,031

Key to Collecting: The 1899 nickel is plentiful in just about any grade desired. Most pieces, however, were struck without care, and often from worn dies, placing quality coins in the minority. Proofs are scarce in comparison to those dating from the heady dates of the numismatic hobby in the 1880's.

Circulation Strikes

Characteristics and Appearance: The same story: this is a plentiful date, but the majority of coins will not please the connoisseur. Take your time. In all, 119 obverse dies were used.

1899: Circulation Strike

GSID	VG-8	F-12	VF-20	EF-40	AU-50	MS-60	MS-63	MS-65	MS-67
2964	$2.20	$4.10	$9.50	$32	$60	$110	$180	$500	$4,000

Proof Strikes

Characteristics and Appearance: Proofs are usually well struck and attractive.

1899: Proof Strike

GSID	PF-60	PF-63	PF-64	PF-65	PF-66	PF-67
3033	$230	$310	$405	$500	$750	$1,500
3034 (Cameo)	—	345	445	775	3,100	5,500

Varieties

Repunched Date—Within the bottom of the last 9, there is a curved remnant or artifact, positioned too low to be an earlier 8, although Walter Breen calls it such and attaches no. 2564 to it in his 1988 *Encyclopedia*. Kenneth E. Bressett, editor of the *Guide Book*, dismisses it as simply a repunched 1899, as do I and the NGC and PCGS grading services. In their excellent work, *Complete Guide to Shield and Liberty Head Nickels*, Gloria Peters and Cynthia Mohon are skeptical: "It even looks as if it could be a 9 first punched very low. . . ." However, ANACS has certified some as overdates, following the Breen listing. Fivaz-Stanton list it as FS-301, "repunched date," with a note that it was formerly designated an overdate. Flynn lists it as 1899 RPD-005.

1899, Repunched Date (FS-301): Circulation Strike

GSID	VG-8	F-12	VF-20	EF-40	AU-50	MS-60	MS-63	MS-65	MS-67
346854	—	—	$35	$75	$125	$175	$225	$750	—

1900

Circulation-Strike Mintage:
27,253,733

Proof Mintage:
2,262

Key to Collecting: In this year the Mint continued in overdrive, with all the demand to use nickels for goods, services, and amusement. The story of quality continues to be unpleasant: most were made in a careless manner and often show light striking, granular fields, or other problems. In particular, granular and pebbly fields are unappealing to specialists, but this characteristic is hardly ever mentioned in print and is not noted on certified holders, so most buyers are unaware of the difference.

Proofs are somewhat scarce, as the mintage suggests, but are usually attractive when found.

Circulation Strikes

Characteristics and Appearance: Striking ranges from Full Details to pieces with flat stars and reverse details. Some are from grainy-surfaced dies that should have been retired. Cherrypicking is the order of the day if you are at all particular. There were 125 obverse dies made.

1900: Circulation Strike

GSID	VG-8	F-12	VF-20	EF-40	AU-50	MS-60	MS-63	MS-65	MS-67
2965	$2.20	$4.10	$9.50	$32	$60	$95	$160	$500	$4,500

Proof Strikes

Characteristics and Appearance: Striking varies, and some were sloppily made—with weakness at the stars and in the hair of Liberty (obverse), and at the ear of corn to the left of the ribbon bow (reverse).

1900: Proof Strike

GSID	PF-60	PF-63	PF-64	PF-65	PF-66	PF-67
3036	$230	$310	$405	$500	$750	$1,200
3037 (Cameo)	—	345	445	575	850	1,800

1901

Circulation-Strike Mintage:
26,478,228

Proof Mintage:
1,985

Key to Collecting: The 1901 is a very common date and can be bought quick as a wink, unless you are particular and desire a sharp strike with rich luster. At that point you will be confronted with a challenge. Since the total population is large, you will find one eventually.

Proofs are fairly scarce and are usually of high quality.

Circulation Strikes

Characteristics and Appearance: Usually seen with light striking in areas and/or poor luster. Choice coins are fairly difficult to locate. There were 93 obverse dies used, yielding about 285,000 impressions average per die if all were used. Quality suffered!

1901: Circulation Strike

GSID	VG-8	F-12	VF-20	EF-40	AU-50	MS-60	MS-63	MS-65	MS-67
2966	$2.20	$4.10	$9.50	$32	$60	$95	$175	$500	$7,500

Proof Strikes

Characteristics and Appearance: The fields are sometimes slightly grainy—that is, with subtle luster, rather than deeply mirrorlike. The portrait is low contrast (not deeply matte or frosty).

1901: Proof Strike

GSID	PF-60	PF-63	PF-64	PF-65	PF-66	PF-67
3039	$230	$310	$405	$500	$750	$1,200
3040 (Cameo)	—	345	445	575	850	2,000
3041 (Deep Cameo)	—	—	1,200	2,000	3,750	12,000

1902

Circulation-Strike Mintage:
31,487,581

Proof Mintage:
2,018

Key to Collecting: The 1902 Liberty Head nickel is most often seen well worn. This is also true of other dates of the era. Mint State coins are plentiful, but Full Details can be quite elusive. At present, most buyers do not pay attention to quality, so you have a distinct advantage if you use your knowledge. Proofs are scarce, but are usually attractive when found.

Circulation Strikes

Characteristics and Appearance: Striking of details ranges from sharp to poor. Some are from tired dies. Many planchets are rough or otherwise subpar. A total of 114 obverse dies were used.

1902: Circulation Strike

GSID	VG-8	F-12	VF-20	EF-40	AU-50	MS-60	MS-63	MS-65	MS-67
2967	$2.20	$4.10	$9.50	$32	$60	$95	$160	$525	$6,250

Proof Strikes

Characteristics and Appearance: The portrait is in low contrast, reflecting changes at the Mint, which had just recently moved into a new building. The obverse die is deeply basined. At this point, "cameo" pieces were no longer available, a situation that would last for several years. Regardless of this fact, collectors and dealers continue to label coins as *cameo contrast* in order to boost sales to uninformed buyers, or perhaps because the graders do not examine the coins carefully.

1902: Proof Strike

GSID	PF-60	PF-63	PF-64	PF-65	PF-66	PF-67
3042	$230	$310	$405	$500	$750	$1,500
3043 (Cameo)	—	345	445	575	1,250	4,050

1903

Circulation-Strike Mintage:
28,004,930

Proof Mintage:
1,790

Key to Collecting: The 1903 is another common date, obtainable in any grade desired, through gem. Despite this, quality is elusive, and relatively few Mint State coins in the marketplace will appeal to the discriminating buyer. Proofs are scarce, but when seen are usually attractive. A few Proofs have the reverse die misaligned.

Circulation Strikes

Characteristics and Appearance: Most have some areas of light striking, but sharp coins can be found. The luster is usually quite good. Many die pairs were made, creating numerous variables. A total of 116 obverse dies were made.

1903: Circulation Strike

GSID	VG-8	F-12	VF-20	EF-40	AU-50	MS-60	MS-63	MS-65	MS-67
2968	$2.20	$4.10	$9.50	$32	$60	$95	$160	$470	$4,000

Proof Strikes

Characteristics and Appearance: Proofs are usually well struck. Low-contrast portrait and devices, following the revised procedure (starting in 1902) for making Proof dies.

Mintage and Distribution Notes: The portrait of Liberty is lightly polished in the die, as in 1902. The date is very low, with the 1 close to the denticles and distant from the neck. Some small part of this mintage, probably a particular press run, was accomplished with the obverse and reverse dies aligned in the same direction, rather than 180 degrees apart. I discovered this variety in 1961, if I recall correctly. I do remember the occasion: a trip on a snowy day with Jim Ruddy to visit Ambrose Brown, a numismatist of Penn Yan, New York, who had offered his collection for sale. Included was a set of Liberty nickels with Proof finish, in a small Raymond "National" page. Upon looking at the back of the page I noticed that, as expected, all of the reverses were upside down, except for one that must have been placed in the holder incorrectly. I flipped back and saw that the corresponding obverse was actually right-side up, and that the dies had been misaligned. Ever since then I've kept an eye out for these special finds, which seem to be at least five or six times rarer than a regular issue.

1903: Proof Strike

GSID	PF-60	PF-63	PF-64	PF-65	PF-66	PF-67
3045	$230	$310	$405	$500	$750	$1,200
3046 (Cameo)		345	445	575	850	1,800
3047 (Deep Cameo)	—	—	—	4,400	9,500	14,500

1904

Circulation-Strike Mintage:
21,403,167

Proof Mintage:
1,817

Key to Collecting: The 1904 nickel is similar to the 1903—common enough, but sharply struck coins with good luster are in the minority. Proofs are somewhat scarce, but most are attractive.

Circulation Strikes

Characteristics and Appearance: Vary widely. Sharply struck, lustrous coins are elusive.

1904: Circulation Strike

GSID	VG-8	F-12	VF-20	EF-40	AU-50	MS-60	MS-63	MS-65	MS-67
2969	$2.20	$4.10	$9.50	$32	$60	$95	$160	$470	$5,000

Proof Strikes

Characteristics and Appearance: The contrast continues to be low, as the portrait and devices are not frosted. Proofs are scarce. Most are attractive. Again, there is the caveat that lower-grade Proofs are usually not certified, giving a false impression of rarity.

1904: Proof Strike

GSID	PF-60	PF-63	PF-64	PF-65	PF-66	PF-67
3048	$230	$310	$405	$500	$750	$2,100
3049 (Cameo)	—	—	—	2,200	3,100	7,500

1905

Circulation-Strike Mintage:
29,825,124

Proof Mintage:
2,152

Key to Collecting: The 1905 nickel is another common date, one that is readily available in Mint State. Many are well struck, and most have decent luster. Proofs are somewhat scarce, this being true of most other Proofs of the era.

Circulation Strikes

Characteristics and Appearance: Striking and luster vary, but finding a choice example will present no problem.

1905: Circulation Strike

GSID	VG-8	F-12	VF-20	EF-40	AU-50	MS-60	MS-63	MS-65	MS-67
2970	$2.20	$4.10	$9.50	$32	$60	$95	$160	$470	$4,000

Proof Strikes

Characteristics and Appearance: Proofs have deeply mirrored fields and are usually well struck and attractive.

1905: Proof Strike

GSID	PF-60	PF-63	PF-64	PF-65	PF-66	PF-67
3051	$230	$310	$405	$500	$750	$1,300
3052 (Cameo)	—	345	445	575	1,200	5,500

1906

Circulation-Strike Mintage:
38,612,000

Proof Mintage:
1,725

Key to Collecting: The 1906 nickel was produced in quantity, with little attention paid to quality. Cherrypicking is needed to find one with sharp details. Proofs are scarce but are usually of high quality.

Circulation Strikes

Characteristics and Appearance: Sharpness varies, but most have some weakness. The luster is usually quite good.

1906: Circulation Strike

GSID	VG-8	F-12	VF-20	EF-40	AU-50	MS-60	MS-63	MS-65	MS-67
2971	$2.20	$4.10	$9.50	$32	$60	$95	$160	$470	—

Proof Strikes

Characteristics and Appearance: Proofs are usually well struck with deeply mirrored fields.

1906: Proof Strike

GSID	PF-60	PF-63	PF-64	PF-65	PF-66	PF-67
3054	$230	$310	$405	$500	$750	$1,300
3055 (Cameo)	—	430	525	725	1,000	3,250
3056 (Deep Cameo)	—	—	—	2,750	5,500	—

1907

Circulation-Strike Mintage:
39,213,325

Proof Mintage:
1,475

Key to Collecting: The 1907 nickel is a study in contrasts—common in circulated grades, and plentiful (relatively speaking) in Mint State. This year was marked by the Panic of 1907, which happened in the autumn. The saving rate of new nickels as souvenirs seems to have been lower than usual. Probably not related to the national economic situation, Proofs, most of which had been ordered early in the year, registered the lowest mintage of the entire Liberty Head series. Quality of striking and appearance can vary widely among 1907 nickels in both circulation strikes and Proofs.

Circulation Strikes

Characteristics and Appearance: Most have nice luster, but striking can vary.

1907: Circulation Strike

GSID	VG-8	F-12	VF-20	EF-40	AU-50	MS-60	MS-63	MS-65	MS-67
2972	$2.20	$4.10	$9.50	$32	$60	$95	$160	$625	$14,000

Proof Strikes

Characteristics and Appearance: Striking varies due to multiple press runs, although the overall mintage was small. Sometimes these coins lack detail on the ear of corn to the left of the ribbon bow, causing it to be flat. Date low on die. Microscopic raised area at denticle to left of outermost point of the third star.

Mintage and Distribution Notes: Lowest Proof production figure in the regular Liberty Head nickel series.

1907: Proof Strike

GSID	PF-60	PF-63	PF-64	PF-65	PF-66	PF-67
70787	$230	$310	$405	$500	$750	$1,200
3057 (Cameo)	—	345	525	575	850	3,100

1908

Circulation-Strike Mintage:
22,684,557

Proof Mintage:
1,620

Key to Collecting: This is another common-date Liberty Head nickel. However, most are in grades below MS-65. A sharply struck gem with good eye appeal is scarce. Proofs are among the most elusive in the series, but are usually of nice quality.

Circulation Strikes

Characteristics and Appearance: Sharpness and surface quality can vary widely, but choice examples can be found without much effort.

1908: Circulation Strike

GSID	VG-8	F-12	VF-20	EF-40	AU-50	MS-60	MS-63	MS-65	MS-67
2973	$2.20	$4.10	$9.50	$32	$60	$95	$160	$550	$11,000

Proof Strikes

Characteristics and Appearance: 1908 Proofs are among the rarest in the series. When found, they are usually attractive. Pristine, undipped Proofs of this era often have delicate, bluish toning, probably from the tissue-paper wrappers in which they were housed when sold by the Mint.

1908: Proof Strike

GSID	PF-60	PF-63	PF-64	PF-65	PF-66	PF-67
3059	$230	$310	$405	$500	$750	$1,200
3060 (Cameo)	—	—	—	650	1,150	2,750

1909

Circulation-Strike Mintage:
11,583,763

Proof Mintage:
4,763

Key to Collecting: The 1909 Liberty Head nickel is a study in contrasts. The circulation-strike mintage of 11,583,763 is the lowest of any Philadelphia Mint issue after 1896. Today, the 1909 is the hardest to find of the later dates in gem Mint State. Interestingly, just the opposite is true of Proofs: this is the most plentiful single Proof issue of its type. Proofs can vary in quality.

Circulation Strikes

Characteristics and Appearance: Quality varies, but most high-grade coins have good visual appeal. Striking sharpness ranges from average to Full Details. Finding an all-around high-quality coin can be a challenge.

1909: Circulation Strike

GSID	VG-8	F-12	VF-20	EF-40	AU-50	MS-60	MS-63	MS-65	MS-67
2974	$2.20	$4.10	$9.50	$32	$60	$95	$160	$550	$10,000

Proof Strikes

Characteristics and Appearance: Frosty cameo portrait and devices. Often lightly struck, with some stars showing lightness at the centers (although with separation of elements) and with a weak corn ear and nearby areas on the reverse to the left of the ribbon bow. Many Proofs of this year were made in haste.

Mintage and Distribution Notes: Public interest in minor coins, driven by the new Lincoln cent, accounts for the large mintage. Orders for cent and nickel Proofs were especially large, with the nickels likely being spent (or else not all distributed). Proofs are much scarcer than their mintage suggests.

1909: Proof Strike

GSID	PF-60	PF-63	PF-64	PF-65	PF-66	PF-67
3062	$230	$310	$405	$500	$750	$1,200
3063 (Cameo)	—	345	445	575	850	1,800
3064 (Deep Cameo)	—	900	1,000	1,550	2,000	8,000

1910

Circulation-Strike Mintage:
30,166,948

Proof Mintage:
2,405

Key to Collecting: The 1910 nickel is easily available in Mint State, although many have areas of light striking and/or granular surfaces. Seek quality, as it will always pay dividends in the long run. Proofs are somewhat scarce and are usually very beautiful.

Circulation Strikes

Characteristics and Appearance: Sharpness ranges from flat, such as on some of the stars and on the corn ear at lower left reverse, to sharp. Luster and surface quality vary as well.

1910: Circulation Strike

GSID	VG-8	F-12	VF-20	EF-40	AU-50	MS-60	MS-63	MS-65	MS-67
2975	$2.20	$4.10	$9.50	$32	$60	$95	$160	$480	$5,000

Proof Strikes

Characteristics and Appearance: Usually deeply mirrored and very attractive. The 1 in the date has ample space separating it from the neck and the denticles. Proofs are usually found well struck, but sometimes light on the ear of corn to the left of the ribbon bow. The Proof surface is somewhat grainy—with a bit of luster. The fields are flat (having little in the way of curvature or basining).

1910: Proof Strike

GSID	PF-60	PF-63	PF-64	PF-65	PF-66	PF-67
3065	$230	$310	$405	$500	$750	$1,400
3066 (Cameo)	—	345	445	575	850	2,250
3067 (Deep Cameo)	—	1,150	1,600	2,200	3,750	8,000

1911

Circulation-Strike Mintage:
39,557,639

Proof Mintage:
1,733

Key to Collecting: This issue has the highest circulation-strike mintage of any Liberty Head nickel. Sharpness, luster, and other aspects of desirability vary, but there are many coins to choose from in the marketplace. Proofs are somewhat scarce and are usually very attractive.

Circulation Strikes

Characteristics and Appearance: Striking and luster vary, due to worn dies, spacing in the press, and other considerations.

Mintage and Distribution Notes: *Mehl's Numismatic Monthly*, March 1911, included this: "The Mint at Philadelphia is working twenty-four hours a day to turn out token money, pennies and nickels, and can not keep pace with the demand for them."

1911: Circulation Strike

GSID	VG-8	F-12	VF-20	EF-40	AU-50	MS-60	MS-63	MS-65	MS-67
2976	$2.20	$4.10	$9.50	$32	$60	$95	$160	$470	$7,500

Proof Strikes

Characteristics and Appearance: Usually well struck with Full Details. Cameo portrait contrast on some, at long last (see remarks under 1902). The nickel alloy was not well mixed, causing streaking in the rolled-out strips from which planchets were cut. Toned nickels of this date often have streaks as a result. The fields are quite flat (not basined).

1911: Proof Strike

GSID	PF-60	PF-63	PF-64	PF-65	PF-66	PF-67
3068	$230	$310	$405	$500	$750	$1,200
3069 (Cameo)	—	345	445	575	850	2,800
3070 (Deep Cameo)	—	—	—	3,100	5,000	—

1912

Circulation-Strike Mintage:
26,234,569

Proof Mintage:
2,145

Key to Collecting: Circulation strikes are very plentiful, including at gem (MS-65) and, less often, even higher grades. However, many are struck from overused dies and show granular fields. Quality can be a challenge.

Proofs are generally of high quality, with good eye appeal.

Circulation Strikes

Characteristics and Appearance: Striking and luster vary, due to the large number of die pairs used. Planchet laminations and flakes can be a problem. Coins with frosty luster and with sharply struck details are in the minority, but enough of this date are around that in time a suitable coin can be found. A total of 160 obverse dies were made.

1912: Circulation Strike

GSID	VG-8	F-12	VF-20	EF-40	AU-50	MS-60	MS-63	MS-65	MS-67
2977	$2.20	$4.10	$9.50	$32	$60	$95	$160	$470	—

Proof Strikes

Characteristics and Appearance: The fields are very flat (not with significant basining or curvature). Proofs are usually very attractive, and when seen they are typically in higher grades.

1912: Proof Strike

GSID	PF-60	PF-63	PF-64	PF-65	PF-66	PF-67
3071	$230	$310	$405	$500	$750	$2,000
3072 (Cameo)	—	345	445	575	850	5,500
3073 (Deep Cameo)	—	—	—	4,400	7,500	—

1912-D

Circulation-Strike Mintage:
8,474,000

Key to Collecting: This is the first Denver Mint nickel. Examples in worn grades are usually Good to Very Good. Extremely Fine and About Uncirculated coins are quite scarce. In Mint State the 1912-D is much rarer than the mintage figure might suggest, especially when compared to the 1912-S (mintage 238,000, or 1/36 that of 1912-D). For a long time I have suggested this, but the high published mintage figure has kept the price down. Today the certification data suggest that in Mint State the 1912-D is seen about twice as often as the 1912-S, not 36 times as often! The 1912-D is somewhat of a *sleeper* in choice Mint State or finer.

As dozens of die pairs were used, there is no single rule to describe the sharpness, or lack thereof, on a typical 1912-D.

Typically, the dies were spaced slightly too far apart, and most show some lightness—but not to the degree found on 1912-S.

Characteristics and Appearance: Striking varies, and some range from slightly weak (check the ear of corn to the left of the ribbon bow on the reverse) to mushy overall. The luster is subdued or satiny on most, not deeply frosty. Some others are sharp. Cherrypicking is advised.

Mintage and Distribution Notes: Although this was the first nickel to be issued from the Denver Mint, no record of any exceptional public interest has been found—probably because the Liberty Head design was very familiar in circulation by that time, and interest in mintmarked varieties was minimal.

There were 96 obverse dies and 91 reverse dies sent to Denver, suggesting an average of 90,000 or so impressions per die pair, if all were used. Likely, several dozen dies were never employed. The reverses in this instance had unique use for the 1912-D coinage and were not carried over.

1912-D: Circulation Strike

GSID	VG-8	F-12	VF-20	EF-40	AU-50	MS-60	MS-63	MS-65	MS-67
2978	$3.70	$11	$38	$100	$180	$330	$525	$1,150	$18,000

1912-S

Circulation-Strike Mintage:
238,000

Key to Collecting: With its enticingly small mintage figure of just 238,000 coins—far and away the lowest in the series to this point—and its status as the only San Francisco Mint coin of this design, the 1912-S has been popular since day one. In the marketplace, examples are usually either Mint State or well worn. Very few exist at intermediate levels such as Extremely Fine or About Uncirculated.

All examples seen have bulging in the obverse field and are somewhat lightly detailed (see below). Any sharp piece is likely an alteration from a Philadelphia Mint coin, made by adding an S. Such fakes used to be common in collecting circles, but today the leading grading services know how to spot one, and it is a virtual certainty that a certified coin is genuine.

Circulation Strikes

Characteristics and Appearance: All authentic examples have lightness of details on Liberty's hair above her forehead. On most (but not all) on the reverse, the corn ear to the left of the ribbon bow does not show the details of the kernels. However, some others have most kernels visible, but are light on the hair. No Full Details coins have been seen. Both the obverse and reverse field can be somewhat "mushy" and undulating (not flat), this being best seen by holding the coin at an angle to the light. Often, the left obverse field is bulged. Denticles, particularly on the obverse, can be softly struck, blending together in some areas. All 1912-S nickels show weakness; since multiple die pairs were used, this situation can be laid on the shoulders of the press technician, who spaced the dies ever too slightly far apart.

The luster is usually soft and somewhat "greasy," not deeply frosty. Sometimes the luster is greasy on the portrait, but softly lustrous (not deeply frosty) in the fields. Overall, a 1912-S nickel is so distinctive that you can recognize this variety simply by looking at the obverse—no need to check for an S mintmark!

Mintage and Distribution Notes: At the San Francisco Mint in 1912, at least 11 obverse dies were on hand and 10 reverses. However, it seems that some dies remained unused, the reverses being destroyed not because they were unusable, but because the Liberty Head motif had been discontinued. Otherwise, it is likely that just a handful of reverses would have been destroyed, in addition to all of the dated obverses. In his *Annual Report*, Mint Director George E. Roberts stated that the average life of a die for the 1912-S coinage was 23,972 strikes.

He probably used the number of dies made and the total mintage and did some math, not knowing that not all of the dies were used. This theory seems to be borne out by the fact that 160 dies were made at the Philadelphia Mint for a coinage of more than 26 million pieces, which would figure to more than 160,000 coins per die. As noted under the 1912-D commentary, the coinage actually amounted to about 90,000 impressions per die.

One reverse die has the S directly opposite the punctuation dot and equidistant between the dot and the denticles; another has the S slightly right of center and slightly closer to the denticles. Still another has the S close to the dot, ever so slightly to the right of its center, and distant from the denticles.

With a mintage of just 238,000 circulation strikes, in terms of mintage for commerce the 1912-S handily outranks its two closest contenders—the 1885 (1,476,490) and the 1886 (3,326,000). However, in 1885 and 1886 such pieces were not saved as novelties, as collectors simply ordered Proofs, which were made to the extent of several thousand for each year.

I have always found Mint State 1912-S nickels to be more available in the marketplace than the higher-mintage 1912-D issues. In *The Numismatist*, November 1931, William Pukall, of Union City, New Jersey, offered for sale an Uncirculated 1912-D Liberty nickel for $1.25, while a 1912-S of the same grade cost $1. I recall that in the 1950's, it was not unusual to encounter 1912-S nickels in small groups in dealers' stocks, but that this was not true of 1912-D nickels.

While the certification-service data show more Mint State 1912-D coins graded than 1912-S, the ratio is less than 2 to 1. For the 1912-D series, there were 8,474,000 nickels coined, so the mathematical ratio is 36 to 1—clearly an ample verification of the saving of Mint State coins in their era.

1912-S: Circulation Strike

GSID	VG-8	F-12	VF-20	EF-40	AU-50	MS-60	MS-63	MS-65	MS-67
2979	$135	$195	$470	$1,000	$1,450	$1,750	$2,000	$2,600	—

Spotlight on the 1912-S Nickel

Coinage of the 1912-S nickel commenced on December 24, 1912, and lasted just four days.

On December 30, San Francisco Mayor James S. ("Sunny Jim") Rolph Jr. used one of the first-struck coins, provided by Acting Treasurer of the U.S. Sub-Treasury Thomas P. Burns, to launch the city's first electric streetcar. In fact, it was the first in the nation that was owned by a municipality rather than a traction company (as they were called).[7] As part of the inaugural event, trolley cars filled with civil officials went up Geary Street to the St. Francis Hotel, with a crowd estimated at 50,000 watching the proceedings.

An early advertisement for this particular coin appeared in *The Numismatist*, November 1913, and was placed by Burton Fraser, located in Oakland, across the bay from San Francisco. In circus style, the headline included "Nickels. 1912 San Francisco Mint 1912," with the tagline in boldface type: "The first nickels ever coined in the San Francisco Mint and the last of the Lady's Head design." The accompanying text noted the following: "Nickels were made in the San Francisco Mint for the first time December 24, 1912, and were coined but four days. No dealer in the U.S. has any. Strictly Uncirculated specimens 25¢ each. Supply limited. Burton Fraser, 768 Ninth St., Oakland, Cal."

Not much is known about Fraser. If he was a dealer, his business must have been modest. The strong claim that "no dealer in the U.S. has any" seems to reflect a knowledge of the market.

This particular issue has been the subject of a fair amount of numismatic attention. In *Mehl's Numismatic Monthly*, January 1916, the editor commented:

> The 1912 San Francisco nickels are somewhat rare, being coined only four days in the last part of December. The hardness of the metal broke several sets of dies. Nearly every specimen met with in circulation has one or more die breaks on them, and I have one specimen in my collection that has six cracks from the border into the coin on the reverse.

From this we learn that Mehl had at least one 1912-S—with six die cracks—in his personal collection, although the implication is that he had several. Similar to many other dealers, Mehl often acquired examples as novelties in this series, and then sold them when the passion faded.

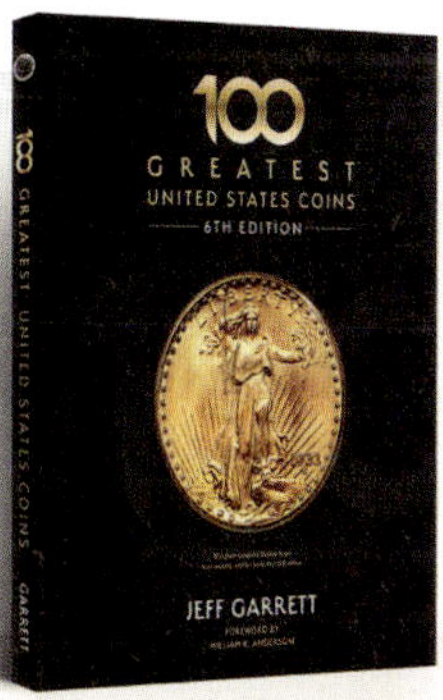

1913

Circulation-Strike Mintage:
4 (estimated)
Proof Mintage:
1 (estimated)

The Rarest of Them All

On the evening of May 21, 1996, with members of the Eliasberg family in the audience, I was at the podium of the auction-sale of part of the Louis E. Eliasberg Sr. Collection.[8] Lot 807, which I had cataloged with a virtually monograph-length description, was coming up for sale. The first few sentences in the introduction read as follows:

The Fabulous 1913 Liberty Head Nickel
Superb Gem Proof
Finest of Only Five Struck
America's Most Famous Rarity

> Lot: 807 • 1913 Liberty Head nickel. Gem Proof-66. Finest known of only five struck and four accounted for, of which two are in museums: equivalent to the finer of two specimens known in private hands. The piece has a glittering mirror surface and, perhaps, is the only specimen with this characteristic. A small planchet lamination is at the rim.

As auctioneer, I called out the starting bid, then took the coin up, and up some more, as several bidder paddles went into the air. In no time at all the prized nickel crossed the million-dollar mark—a stratosphere into which *no* rare coin had ever ventured before! Yet even then, the bids still continued to go up and up, until, finally, the bidding stopped at $1,485,000.

"Sold!" I cried. The buyer was Jasper ("Jay") Parrino.

The million-dollar barrier might not seem all that special today. Indeed, in one afternoon in 2003, American Numismatic Rarities sold *two* rare double eagles for more than $1 million each. But back in 1996, a million-plus price tag was a sensation, just as $50 had been a sensation in 1928.

In connection with this sale, I compiled a roster of the five examples and their past owners. In 2003, Beth Deisher, editor of *Coin World*, picked up on the 1913 Liberty Head nickel and wrote several stories about it, one of which earned her an award from the Numismatic Literary Guild. Eric P. Newman has been most helpful as well. The updated roster given below draws from these sources plus my own conversations with nickel owners from B. Max Mehl, Stephen K. Nagy, and Emery May Holden Norweb onward to those of our own era.

1. Eliasberg Coin

This is the finest example, cataloged as PF-66 in the Eliasberg Collection and now in a PCGS/CAC PF-66 holder. It seems to have been struck from Proof dies, but on an ordinary planchet. Some writers have considered *all* 1913 nickels to be Proofs, but my view is that this is the only one with a claim to that status, and that the others all have or had mint luster (I have examined them all, and carefully).

Numismatic Gallery acquired this coin from numismatist and historian Eric P. Newman in 1948, and on December 14 of that year, Abe Kosoff, a partner in the firm, offered it to Louis E. Eliasberg Sr., who purchased it shortly thereafter for about $2,400.[9] It remained with Eliasberg, then after his passing went to his son, Richard A., who in 1986 consigned it to my company. As described in the opening paragraphs of this section, it sold for $1,485,000—the first coin ever to cross the million-dollar barrier, a sensation. It then continued to change hands, and in 2003 was purchased by Edward C. Lee for about $3 million (who said he expected it to reach a value of $5 million in a matter of a few years).[10]

Lee held it for nearly two years, then in June 2005 announced that title had been transferred to Legend Numismatics (co-owned by Laura Sperber), who earlier had owned example number 4. Typical of quite a few "trophy coins" in recent times, the Eliasberg 1913 Liberty Head nickel has gone from dealer to dealer but has not yet landed in a private collection—which, no doubt, it will do someday. When it does, it will be the prize of prizes.

Provenance:

- Samuel W. Brown and/or Stephen K. Nagy (1913–1920's)
- Stephen K. Nagy, likely on consignment for a time in 1923 and 1924 to August Wagner (early 1920's to 1924)
- Wayte Raymond (1924)
- Colonel E.H.R. Green (1924–1936); Green estate (1936–1941)
- Eric P. Newman (1941–1948)
- Abe Kosoff and Abner Kreisberg, trading as the Numismatic Gallery (1948–1949)
- Louis E. Eliasberg Sr. (1949–1976)
- Eliasberg estate to Richard A. Eliasberg (1976–1996; auctioned by Bowers & Merena)
- Jay Parrino (1996–2001)
- Dwight Manley, for the California Gold Marketing Group (2001–2003)
- Edward C. Lee (2003–2005)
- Bruce Morelan, Laura Sperber, and George Huang (Legend Numismatics; 2006–2007)
- Dr. William Morton-Smith (via Ron Gillio; 2007–2018; auctioned by Stack's Bowers Galleries)
- Gerald Forsythe (2018–2021)
- Bruce Morelan (2021 to date)

2. Walton Coin

This and the McDermott coin are the only two pieces that are flatly struck at the ear of corn to the left of the ribbon bow on the reverse, perhaps indicating they were struck at a different time than the other three. This coin was deaccessioned by Eric P. Newman and acquired by James F. Kelly, a Dayton jeweler and rare coin dealer who was rising to prominence in the early 1940's.

Kelly is thought to have sold it directly to Conway A. Bolt Sr., although accounts are mixed.[11] From there it was said by Bolt to have gone to the R.J. Reynolds family,[12] hence the "Reynolds example" label that was attached to this particular coin for a long time—even though a spokesperson for the family (the Reynolds clan in the tobacco business) says they have no record of having owned such a coin.

In actuality, it seems to have been traded or sold to George O. Walton, a coin dealer and collector from North Carolina, a bachelor who conducted his business without publicity. Walton did not publicly acknowledge ownership of the nickel, but said that he had "access to the coin whenever he wanted to display it." Walton had a fake made (by altering a 1910 nickel) for casual passing around and a real one which he kept as a personal treasure.[13] Walton was pictured holding one of these nickels in the July 1960 issue of the *Appalachian Bulletin*, a local club newsletter, although other publicity concerning it seems to have been sparse.[14]

Walton was killed in a car crash on March 9, 1962, while on his way to a coin show, when an allegedly impaired driver swerved out of the proper lane and hit him head-on. A large number of coins were recovered intact and without damage by local police from the wrecked vehicle, although his watch and ring were nowhere to be found.[15] Among the nickels was the 1913. It was unclear whether this nickel was genuine, and it was taken to the American Numismatic Society,[16] where experts pronounced it to be a fake—logical enough, for Walton had owned a fake. The rarity-studded Walton estate collection was auctioned the next year by Stack's, but the presumed-to-be-fake 1913 nickel was not included.

So where was the *real* one, the "Reynolds" coin?

It was speculated that either the *real* 1913 coin once owned by Walton had been sold by him to a private client, identity unknown; or that Walton had never owned an original. Theories were plentiful, and facts were scarce.

In 2003 Bowers and Merena Galleries, then located in Wolfeboro, New Hampshire, and owned by Collectors Universe (Ray Merena and I having sold our interests), offered $1 million, sight unseen, to buy the authentic coin if it could be found.[17] The owner of the supposed fake, which had passed to Walton's sister, Melva W. Givens, then to others after she died in 1992, took note of the excitement and brought the coin forth to Montgomery, assuming it was Walton's fake (altered from 1910) nickel, but noting that it looked a lot like pictures of a real one! In due course, the Walton example was reexamined by a group of experienced dealers (Montgomery, John Dannreuther, David Hall, Mark Borckardt, Fred Weinberg, and Jeff Garrett), who pronounced it to be genuine. Voila!

The newly re-identified Walton coin was not for sale. It was exhibited along with the other four examples at the 2003 ANA Convention in Baltimore, where the whole suite of coins, never together in one place since Eric P. Newman had them in the little black case in 1941 and 1942, attracted a great deal of attention. Beth Deisher, editor of *Coin World*, took the story and ran with it, landing an award from the Numismatic Literary Guild. The designation *Walton example* seems more appropriate than *Reynolds example* today, and I use it here. It is graded PCGS PF-63.

Provenance:

- Samuel W. Brown and/or Stephen K. Nagy (1913–1920's)

- Stephen K. Nagy, likely on consignment for a time in 1923 and 1924 to August Wagner (early 1920's–1924)
- Wayte Raymond (1924)
- Colonel E.H.R. Green (1924–1936); Green estate (1936–1941)
- Eric P. Newman (1941–1942)
- Burdette G. Johnson (1942)
- James F. Kelly (1942)
- Conway A. Bolt (1942–ca. 1945)
- Private owner named Reynolds, said by some to be the R.J. Reynolds family, although a spokesperson for that family was unaware of any such connection (to 1946); a tenuous, unproven connection
- George O. Walton (ca. 1946–1962)
- Melva W. Givens (1962–1992); Givens estate heirs (1992)
- Givens estate heirs (1992–2003; auctioned by Heritage)
- Jeff Garret and Larry Lee (2013–2018)
- Martin Burns and Ronald Firman (via Bob Paul; 2018 to date)

3. Norweb Coin

The third of the 1913 Liberty Head nickels is the Norweb Collection example, donated to the Smithsonian Institution, where it is a showpiece. By a tiny margin, this seems to have the sharpest details of any of the five coins.

At one time it was a highlight in the fantastic collection of rare coins formed by His Majesty, King Farouk of Egypt, an avid buyer of numismatic rarities in the 1940's and, at the time, the best customer of several American dealers. Along the way, the monarch acquired many exceedingly important and high-quality American rarities that anyone would be proud to own.

On July 26, 1952, Farouk was overthrown by a military junta under Gamal Abdul Nasser and went into exile. The military government took over his possessions and auctioned them in Cairo in early 1954 under the direction of Sotheby's London office. The winning bidder for the 1913 nickel was Mrs. R. Henry Norweb, via an arrangement with bidders Sol Kaplan and Abe Kosoff, who acquired the coin for 1,300 Egyptian pounds (about $3,750, plus a 5% surcharge, or about $3,940) and immediately afterward sold it to Mrs. Norweb at cost.[18]

The Norweb family made several important gifts to numismatic institutions. In 1977, to celebrate their wedding anniversary (which would take place in 1978), Ambassador and Mrs. R. Henry Norweb decided to donate the 1913 Liberty Head nickel to the National Coin Collection at the Smithsonian Institution. The appraisal value was set at $225,000, based upon the price advertised by Robert L. Hughes for his coin (number 4 in this roster) in the summer of 1977. Today, the curators at the Smithsonian earn high marks from the numismatic community for their contributions to numismatic scholarship and the welcome given to collectors.

Among the four nickels other than the Eliasberg Proof, this was considered to be the second finest by Eric P. Newman, an evaluation shared by some others who have viewed them all. However, while in Farouk's possession it was dipped and lacquered. I was mildly surprised to read that the authors of the *Million Dollar Nickels* book consider this coin to be below even the circulated McDermott example (number 5 in the present roster) in quality.[19]

Provenance:

- Samuel W. Brown and/or Stephen K. Nagy (1913–1920's)
- Stephen K. Nagy, likely on consignment for a time in 1923 and 1924 to August Wagner (early 1920's to 1924)
- Wayte Raymond (1924)
- Colonel E.H.R. Green (1924–1936)
- Green estate (1936–1941)
- Eric P. Newman (1941–1942)
- F.C.C. Boyd (1942–1944)
- Numismatic Gallery (1944)
- King Farouk (1944–1952)
- Government of Egypt (1952–1954)
- Strategic partnership of Abe Kosoff and Sol Kaplan (1954)
- Emery May Holden Norweb (1954–1978)
- Smithsonian Institution (1978 to date)

4. Olsen Coin

This particular coin is probably the most highly publicized of the five examples, and has the cachet of being the only example ever handled by B. Max Mehl, for whom the 1913 nickel was central to a famous (or notorious, depending on the point of view) advertising campaign. In the 1930's the nickel gained great fame, and it was said that streetcars slowed as their conductors stopped to check the dates on nickels given by passengers.

In the Fred Olsen sale, 1944, it was sold to King Farouk of Egypt, who found it to be redundant after he acquired the Boyd coin (number 3, above), which he considered to be of higher quality. Rather than pay for the coin, Farouk had it sent to the ANS in New York City, where curator Henry Grunthal, who often did some coin business on the side, was empowered to sell it.[20]

The coin was placed in a May 1946 auction held by Grunthal and his friend Edward Gans, proprietor of Numismatic Fine Arts (in the same city). Although reported as having sold, in fact, it did not, and it went back to Mehl in Texas. In 1947, Mehl tucked it into the catalog featuring the Will W. Neil Collection. This time the stars were in proper alignment, and the coin was sold to Edwin A. Hydeman, owner of Weist's Department Store in York, Pennsylvania.[21]

In 1961 the Hydeman collection, replete with many rarities, was offered at auction by Abe Kosoff. Once again, the coin was publicized as having been sold, even though it had not. It remained on consignment with Kosoff—with no buyers—until in 1972, when it was sold to World-Wide Coin Investments of Atlanta, Georgia, for $100,000, in a deal that was splashed across the various coin newspapers (also discussed earlier). The coin still found no buyer in the form of a serious collector. The anti-coin scenario continued: for every dealer or collector championing the 1913 nickel as a desirable rarity despite its questionable birth, two others would condemn it as not being worth owning.

My company, Bowers and Ruddy Galleries, bought a half-interest in the coin from World-Wide in 1974, but sold the interest back in 1975. The late John J. Ford Jr. was particularly antagonistic toward this nickel and its publicity, and soundly berated me for being involved with such a piece.

Finally, in 1977, it was sold to Robert L. Hughes Enterprises, a division of A-Mark (Steve Markoff) in Los Angeles. From there it went to Superior Galleries, conducted by the Goldberg family, who sold it to a secret buyer later identified as Los Angeles sports team owner Jerry Buss. It remained with Buss for a time, then was auctioned by Superior, with the buyer being Texas numismatist Reed Hawn.

At the sale of the Hawn Collection, by Stack's, it went to Dwight Manley of Spectrum Numismatics. Manley was to distinguish himself later as the founder of the California Gold Marketing Group, distributor of most of the treasure from the SS *Central America*, and in connection with the Dwight Manley Library at ANA Headquarters, for his generous gift. Spectrum placed it with a Nevada investor, retired from the securities business, with whom they had a close connection. Next the coin went to Laura Sperber, then in 2004, Blanchard & Co. acquired it for a private collector in the Midwest whose name was not disclosed. It seems that Laura Sperber missed her 1913 nickel, and in 2005 she captured an even finer one, the Eliasberg example!

This particular nickel was called "dull, scratched Unc." by Walter Breen in his 1988 *Encyclopedia*. In my opinion, and writing as a former owner, I do not consider it to be deserving of such a negative description. Indeed, it has been highly acclaimed by all who have owned it. I consider it to be a very nice coin in a lower Mint State classification. It is graded NGC/CAC PF-64.

Provenance:

- Samuel W. Brown and/or Stephen K. Nagy (1913–1920's)
- Stephen K. Nagy, likely on consignment for a time in 1923 and 1924 to August Wagner (early 1920's to 1924)
- Wayte Raymond (1924)
- Colonel E.H.R. Green (1924–1936)
- Green estate (1936–1941)
- Eric P. Newman (1941–1942)
- Burdette G. Johnson (1942)
- James F. Kelly (1942)
- Fred E. Olsen (1942–1944; collection auctioned by B. Max Mehl)
- King Farouk, most of this time in the possession of Mehl, to whom it was sent on consignment, finally to be sold in 1947 by listing it in the Will W. Neil collection catalog (1944–1947)
- Edwin Hydeman (1947–1972)
- World–Wide Coin Investments (1972–1975)
- Bowers and Ruddy Galleries, Inc., and World-Wide Coin Investments (1974–1975)
- World–Wide Coin Investments (1975–1977)
- Robert L. Hughes Enterprises, a subsidiary of A–Mark (1977)
- Superior Galleries (1977)
- Jerry Buss (1977–1985; auctioned by Superior Galleries)

- Reed Hawn (1985–1993; auctioned by Stack's)
- Bought by Dwight Manley for Spectrum Numismatics and a Nevada investor (1993–2002)
- Laura Sperber, Legend Numismatics (2002–2004)
- Donald W. Doyle Jr., Blanchard & Co., and John Albanese (2004)
- Private Midwestern collection (2004–2010; auctioned by Heritage
- Greensboro Collection, Part V (2010–2014; auctioned by Heritage)
- Unknown collection (2014 to date)

5. McDermott Coin

The fifth example, somewhat circulated due to being mixed with pocket change, is the nickel owned by J.V. McDermott. This and the Walton coin are the only two pieces flatly struck at the ear of corn to the left of the ribbon bow on the reverse, perhaps indicating they were struck at a different time.

After McDermott died on September 29, 1966, his widow Betts consigned it to Paramount International Coin Corporation. Sold at auction in 1967, with James Kelly at the podium, the coin went to Aubrey E. Bebee. Later, Aubrey and his wife Adeline, having retired from their highly successful rare coin business in Omaha, donated it to the ANA Money Museum in Colorado Springs, where it has been a prime drawing card ever since.

Due to its mishandling, this is the least attractive of the five examples. In his 1988 *Encyclopedia* Walter Breen noted that while Kelly had called it "Uncirculated, partly rough," this was flagrant overgrading, for "The coin I saw is EF, nicked, scratched, cleaned; exhibited at hundreds of conventions, reportedly used by McDermott for bar-room betting," Breen wrote. My own view is that "nicked, scratched, and cleaned" is unnecessarily derogatory, and that a simple "Extremely Fine" will do nicely.

Provenance:

- Samuel W. Brown and/or Stephen K. Nagy (1913–1920's)
- Stephen K. Nagy, likely on consignment for a time in 1923 and 1924 to August Wagner (early 1920's to 1924)
- Wayte Raymond (1924)
- Colonel E.H.R. Green (1924–1936); Green estate (1936–1941)
- Eric P. Newman (1941–1942)
- Burdette G. Johnson (1942)
- James F. Kelly (1942)
- J.V. McDermott (1942–1966)
- Elizabeth ("Betts") McDermott (1966–1967; auctioned by Paramount International Coin Corporation)
- Aubrey and Adeline Bebee (1967–1989)
- American Numismatic Association Money Museum (1989 to date)

1913, Liberty Head: Proof Strike

GSID	PF-60	PF-63	PF-64	PF-65	PF-66	PF-67
3074	$1,200,000	$3,000,000	$3,600,000	$4,800,000	$5,400,000	—

APPENDIX A

Pattern Nickel Five-Cent Pieces

Introduction

First, a note on nomenclature. The first *five-cent* pieces were the silver half dismes of 1792, followed by many different dates and mintmarks of half dimes (the *disme* term was discontinued) from 1794 to 1873. Many different types of pattern half dimes were made, but these, regardless of the metals in which they were struck, are related to half dimes, not to nickel five-cent pieces. For legislative background to the nickel five-cent piece see chapter 1.

Pattern nickel five-cent pieces are pattern coins made with dates from 1865 onward in the diameter of the nickel five-cent piece (much wider than the half dime) and related to that series.

The First Pattern Nickels

Although patterns for the nickel five-cent piece exist with the date 1865, no Mint correspondence or other records have been located to verify that any such coinage took place in that calendar year. Indeed, the reverse dies with large numeral 5 could not have been created prior to May 19, 1866, the date this number punch was provided to the Mint by outside supplier S.E. Adamson. Those of 1865 are believed to have been made later as numismatic delicacies, of which more will be said shortly.

After the passage of the Act of May 16, 1866, the nickel five-cent piece became a reality. About that time (or possibly slightly earlier), in anticipation, James B. Longacre prepared several patterns for submission to Secretary of the Treasury Hugh McCulloch. On May 28 these were delivered to McCulloch. Mint Director James Pollock described them in his letter of transmittal:[1]

> **No. 1:** Obverse, the "Union Shield resting on tied arrows," &c. Motto, "In God we trust," and date. Reverse, 13 stars set in rays, U.S. of America, and figure &c. "5 cents." A neat and unique design, and differs from the devices on all of our other

> coinage. This specimen is in my opinion before all the others in artistic beauty, significance, and diversity, I would respectfully recommend its adoption. [pattern later adopted as the regular issue, and not given a Judd number]
>
> **No. 2:** Obverse, "Head of Washington," Motto, "In God we trust," and date &c. Reverse, same as No. 1; a neat and elegant design. [Judd-473]
>
> **No. 3:** Obverse, "Head of Washington," U.S. of America and date. Reverse, Wreath and figure &c. "5 cents." [Judd-461]
>
> **No. 4:** Obverse, "Head of Washington," Motto, "In God we trust," and date. Reverse. Wreath and figure "5." [probably Judd-470]

The obverse of no. 1 was the Union Shield, as noted, somewhat similar in concept to that found on current two-cent pieces, but with different lettering.

The "Head of Washington" used on nos. 2, 3, and 4 was in low relief and from the same model, based on a bust by Jean Antoine Houdon, used to make certain pattern two-cent pieces of 1863. Washington was a popular choice for a motif, in view of the recent campaign to restore Mount Vernon, the opening of the Washington Cabinet at the Mint (February 22, 1860), and a nationwide interest in the first president.

The reverse of nos. 1 and 2 is the With Rays style as adopted for regular coinage. The reverse of no. 3 is probably that seen on Judd-461, with 5 / CENTS, and with IN GOD WE TRUST at the top border. The reverse of no. 4 either is unknown today or is one of the dies described in Judd as B, C, or D.

From this beginning of four die combinations, the field of pattern nickel five-cent pieces soon expanded to include dozens of varieties, mostly made for collectors.

Pattern Nickels "In Every Style"

The August 1866 issue of the recently launched *American Journal of Numismatics* had a pointed commentary regarding the profiteering by Mint officials, "through the agents," in the making and selling of off-metal varieties of the new nickel and, for good measure, copper strikings of the gold dollar:

> Though collectors have long ceased to regard the true issues of the "government copper-head factory," better known, perhaps, as the United States Mint, as of any value, they may be interested in the information that the ugliest of all known coins, the new five cent piece, is out, as oysters are served in some places "in every style."
>
> Though specimens [of pattern coins, restrikes, and off-metal strikings] are refused to societies and individuals, they are readily procured in Philadelphia through the agents of the young gentleman at the head of that department. At present the price of a set of four, struck in "putty" and various metals, with copper gold dollar included, is $35, though the expected purchaser is informed in every case, that as the owner is *very anxious to sell* (somebody?) he will take $30.
>
> Collectors are advised to wait a little, when it is expected *the owner's* anxiety will increase to such an extent that he will be glad to take any amount, however small, above their legal value. Are we to be afflicted with any more of these horrible little composition counters—called coins by courtesy, whose ugliness is only equaled by

> their intrinsic worthlessness; and whose whole appearance, both in design and execution, is so despicable, that even the pious cant with which the new director has contrived to have them plastered over, fails to redeem them from utter contempt?
>
> There is considerable difficulty at the Mint in putting on coins the motto "In God we Trust." The officers are afraid that everybody will read it "In Gold we Trust"—which is much nearer the fact.

At the time, privileged Mint employees were having a field day making "numismatic delicacies" for their own profit, with no records being kept, and with no benefit to either the Mint or the government. This activity had commenced with vigor in spring 1859, before the time of the nickel five-cent piece. By 1866 it was in high gear.

A report of the Francis S. Hoffman Collection sale held in New York City, April 24 to 27, 1866, included this remark: "Pattern pieces, which have been constantly going down since the United States Mint passed into the hands of the present *family*, showed the actual falling off only in a more marked degree."[2]

As Don Taxay put it in his *U.S. Mint and Coinage*, 1966, the Mint was in effect a workshop for the private gain of officials and key employees. Just about anything went, so long as they didn't get caught in the act. Meanwhile, when questioned by numismatists over a period of time, officials such as A. Loudon Snowden, W.E. DuBois, and Dr. Henry R. Linderman lied through their teeth. All of these shenanigans made it possible for the essence of the present chapter!

In 1887, Mint Director James P. Kimball, who had been in office since July 1885, sought to learn more about patterns, restrikes, and the like, and the only thing he was able to find was a commentary that in 1868 some Proof sets had been struck in aluminum (for details see the listing under 1868 in the following pages). He soon proposed to go on a numismatic witch-hunt, to declare all earlier patterns illegal in view of their unofficial nature. Fortunately for numismatists, this effort came to naught.

An Overview of Patterns

The field of pattern nickels includes those dated from 1865 through the early 20th century. The main popular source for information is Dr. J. Hewitt Judd, *United States Pattern Coins* (10th edition). Much in-depth research data are in Andrew W. Pollock's 1994 study, *United States Patterns and Related Issues.* The website uspatterns.com is maintained by Saul Teichman and is regularly updated with information of numismatic interest.

While many patterns were made to test new designs or concepts (such as the use of aluminum), most of the die combinations known today were made for collectors. Not making matters any easier to understand, at least at casual view, is the fact that certain nickel dies were taken outside the Mint, and fantasy items (such as the combination of a nickel five-cent die with a $5 die) were produced. Only by studying the characteristics of the coins themselves can we make conclusions, and even then certain mysteries remain.

As a general rule of thumb, Shield and Liberty Head nickels struck from regular Proof dies in metals other than nickel alloy are numismatic delicacies, as are combinations of two obverse or two reverse dies (e.g., patterns dated 1865). This is only a partial list.

Outside the Mint Walls

As if Mint-produced delicacies were not enough, certain other patterns seem to have been made privately by persons unknown, who somehow acquired Mint dies. George J. Fuld's "Some Restruck Patterns," published in *The Numismatist,* May 1988, with later annotations by Saul Teichman on the website www.uspatterns.com, treats this category. The following are a few excerpts selected to represent nickels (for the article covered other series as well), here slightly modified:

> An unusual group of coins, generally accepted as part of regular United States pattern coinage . . . really belongs in a category of its own. . . . Although these coins are struck from genuine United States Mint dies, they are not Mint products, but rather fantasy patterns produced by individuals outside the Mint. One such specimen (Judd 516) is an 1866-dated Washington pattern struck over a regular-issue 1867 Shield nickel, a most spectacular fantasy first reported in B. Max Mehl's 1944 Belden Roach Sale (Lot 2903). . . .
>
> Besides the absurdity of two-headed nickels or a 5-cent obverse artfully combined, or "muled," with a half-eagle reverse, the most obvious difference between these and normal Mint patterns is that none are known in true Proof strikings. Experts at the coin grading services must shudder when classifying one of these issues as a Proof! The mules under consideration here . . . made with 11 ex-Mint dies, are struck on off-size planchets of varying diameter; most are considerably oversize. Even in their as-struck state they could not be mistaken for true Uncirculated or Proof specimens.
>
> As further evidence that these mules were struck outside the Mint, consider their composition. Their content varies, as shown by the brass flakes on some copper or bronze specimens. The official Mint patterns of Washington made in 1866 occur mainly in nickel and copper, and occasionally in bronze. Nickel (the regular fabric) and copper or bronze were used to strike the Mint-produced nickel patterns. However, the mules occur not only in nickel and copper, but also in silver, white metal, steel, lead and brass—materials never used previously for a nickel pattern and not at all commonly used by the Mint.
>
> The diameter of the regular-issue nickel, .808 to .811 inch, is tightly controlled. Unfortunately, the diameters of the mules are sparsely recorded in the auction literature, but the four published figures are .850, .853, .854 and .856 inch. This enlarged diameter of the mules is considerably outside Mint tolerances. Direct observation over the past 45 years shows that they generally are larger than called for in Mint regulations. In addition, die alignments vary from variety to variety.
>
> The weights of the mules also tend to be much higher than the authorized nickel weight of 76.16 grains. . . . On the other hand, the mules struck in nickel have recorded weights of 72.1, 84.3, 86.1 and 96.3 grains. These are far from the normal tolerance of 2 grains allowed by Mint standards. Silver mules have recorded weights of 72.1, 83.2 and 88.3 grains—quite a variation; white-metal mules have a wide range of weights—59.6, 84.5, 86.7 and 92.9 grains. Copper mules also vary widely from patterns made at the Mint. . . .
>
> It is difficult to completely document the origin of the 11 ex-Mint dies involved.

The first appearance of many of these pieces was in John W. Haseltine's sale titled the Sylvester S. Crosby Collection, 1883. However, as Fuld suggests, perhaps these did not belong to the highly esteemed Crosby, but were simply advertised as such—Haseltine's way of bringing them into the market.

Generally, the non-Mint productions described by Fuld (delineated individually in following listings) elicit neither the same attention nor the same market price as do numismatic delicacies made within the walls of the Philadelphia Mint. Concerning the latter, collectors can be silently thankful for the officers and insiders at the Mint who produced thousands of patterns in various series, mostly unofficially, from spring 1859 until early 1885, with much of this era overlapping the time when the nickel five-cent piece was being made. Absent these shenanigans, there would be very few pattern coins available for numismatists today.

Suggestions for Collecting Nickel Patterns

There are so many odd and curious limited-production pattern nickels that it is a puzzlement as to what a numismatist should do to collect them. There are several strategies short of trying to obtain one of each (an impossible task). Quite doable, and interesting, is acquiring examples to illustrate each of the different *dies* described below. While some are elusive, most are offered with frequency on the market. Of course, in many instances a single coin will serve to represent two different die designs, simplifying the search.

Another way would be to seek one of each in the category of Rarity-6 or less. These represent coins that were widely distributed (officially as well as privately) in the numismatic market in the 19th century, and exclude the rarities. My own preference would be to try to obtain an example from each die, in nickel alloy.

Generally, patterns produced officially or unofficially by the Mint were struck in Proof finish. Examples on the market today tend to be attractive if struck in nickel alloy, of mixed quality if in aluminum (many have been cleaned), and a mixed bag for copper and bronze. Most of the last two have been cleaned at one time or another, or recolored. For any and all, a degree of connoisseurship is needed to find a piece with excellent eye appeal. If you stay with the issues of R-6 or less, in time you will be able to build a fine display. If you seek the great rarities, *opportunity* is the most important consideration, and you may not have the luxury of being choosy about quality. As to patterns made outside the Mint, as described by George J. Fuld, for the most part these are rather unattractive in appearance, and this is to be expected. Such pieces have their own interest if taken for what they are.

Introduction to the Listings

The following is a discussion of nickel five-cent patterns year by year, for the dates 1865 through 1913. The varieties listed are those that have been recorded in the Judd or Pollock texts or have been described on Saul Teichman's uspatterns.com website, combining to yield in the present text the most detailed pattern-nickel ever to appear in print in a single place.

Likely, certain other patterns were made, but none are known today. Some listings are from traditional texts and may represent coins that never existed or have been misdescribed (these listings are thus noted). Research is ongoing.

Methodology and Research Notes

To a degree, the approximate time that certain patterns were struck can be estimated by studying the die characteristics. This is particularly useful for patterns of the 1860's that employ either the With Rays or the Without Rays style of reverse. The known styles of obverses and reverses for Shield nickels, Obverse Styles 1a through 1c and Reverse Styles A through F, are described in detail in chapter 4, to which please refer.

Certain of the illustrations in the Adams-Woodin, Pollock, and Judd books are composites used to "create" representations of designs of varieties and are not necessarily from actual coins of that variety. The same is true for a minority of illustrations (which are described as such) on uspatterns.com. The attributions of die characteristics in the following listings are a trial effort. In time, as more pieces are closely examined, additional conclusions can be made as to the order in which certain pieces were struck. All illustrations in the present text are of actual coins.

In the following listing, *copper* means copper or bronze. All have plain edges unless specifically stated otherwise. The rarity ratings (R-7, for example) are explained under "How to Use This Book" at the end of the Introduction.

Pattern Nickels of 1865

As confirmed by the use of an obverse die style first regularly employed in 1872, it is demonstrated that those patterns dated 1865, and known to present-day numismatists, were made in 1872 or later.[3] Because these patterns are of the same styles regularly used in 1866 and 1867, they are exceptionally popular with collectors today. Generally, they are referred to as *transitional* patterns, although in this case they were made after the fact.

Five-Cent Die Combinations of 1865

Judd 416 and 417

Obverse: Regular shield design, Style 1c, as first used in 1872, arrowhead compact and distant from shield border.

Reverse: Regular With Rays design as adopted in 1866 (Style A). At least two different reverse dies of this type were used, one with center dot and repunched 5 (J-417), as employed on regular-issue Proofs, and the other lacking the center dot (J-416).[4]

J-416 • Nickel alloy • High Rarity-6

It is likely that most known examples of this variety were struck in 1872 or later, although strikings made in 1867 or earlier may exist (see introduction to this year); if so, they would be from a different obverse die than that described above.

Pattern 1865 Shield nickel in copper, from an obverse die believed to have been made no earlier than 1872. The reverse is the same With Rays die as used to coin regular-issue *1866* Proof Shield nickels (with two center dots and the 5 lightly double punched), created in May 1866.

Pattern 1865 Shield nickel, in nickel metal, from the same obverse as J-417, but here in an earlier state, indicating this issue was struck first. The reverse is Style F, from a die in existence by 1870 and used in 1870 to strike regular-issue Proofs. The die is heavily relapped and has several incomplete letters. In recent decades the science and art of numismatic forensics, if it can be called that, has revealed the true striking-times of many pattern coins, which often differ from the dates on them.

J-417 • Copper • Low Rarity-7

This variety was another later production. Die relapped with weak shaft to arrowhead; raised diagonal die line through feather.

Judd 418 and 419

Obverse: Same die as used on J-416. Early state, no relapping.

Reverse: Regular Without Rays design as adopted in 1866, Style F.

J-418 • Nickel alloy • High Rarity-6

This variety was struck from a particular reverse die with broken letters that was also used to strike J-687 to 689 (1869), J-805 (1870), and regular 1870 Proof Shield nickels (see listing under 1870 in chapter 6).

J-419 • Copper

No example confirmed by modern specialists.

Pattern Nickels of 1866

Patterns of this date are a free-for-all, or so it seems. The Mint produced a few patterns in 1866, to which were added mulings and restrikes made at later dates, plus some fantasies made outside the Mint. Many of the last were poorly struck on imperfect planchets and today are, shall I say, *unprepossessing* in appearance.

In time, the study of die characteristics may make it possible to know which varieties were available in the summer of 1866, like "oysters in every style" (per the earlier quoted *American Journal of Numismatics* comment), and which were made or restruck later.

Today, this excerpt from "Rules" and the preface thereto issued by Director Pollock on July 1, 1866, may be called "numismatic humor" in the face of what he was *really* doing![5]

> [Pattern coins] have hitherto been given out, or withheld, by no rule whatsoever, although they by degrees attained a very considerable importance, on account of the eagerness of many collectors to obtain them. There is, indeed, a pretty strong

reason why these should be used only for their special purpose; namely to aid the Treasury Department, or a Congressional Committee, in forming an idea of the size, appearance, and practicability of any newly proposed coin, or of any changes of devices of an old one.

But it has been found impossible to put this rigid limit upon them. If we strike only a few, the ambitious collector will have one at any price; and a competition is created, out of all proportions to the merit of the prize. It seems better, therefore, avoiding the error of making such pieces too plentiful, to give some scope to the acquisition of them.

The whole department will be under the supervision of the Director of the Mint, and all inquiries and requests, with or without money, must be addressed to him. The medals and coins will be in the responsible custody of one of his clerks, who will also attend to the orders, reply to letters, and keep the accounts. . . .

These arrangements, though internal, are here openly stated, with a view to assure the public that there is a system of suitable checks and guards against undue or secret issues. . . .

It may be said, however, in regard to the rule against striking a coin or pattern after its proper date, that while it seemed desirable that some patterns of former years which are very scarce or curious should be repeated, yet we could not issue them impartially, without giving out an indefinite number. And if some kinds are thus struck, there would be a call for other kinds; there would be no knowing where to begin or end.

Pieces struck out of date bear a falsity on their face, and have not the interest or value of a synchronous issue. An uncertainty is also kept up, as to the extent of the supply. And, as in the case of regular coinage, they so far falsify the Mint Records and Tables as to the amount of coinage and delivery, or as to the very fact of such and such pieces having been coined in any given year.

On the whole, therefore, it seemed a plain course to let the past go and to begin afresh. . . .

Rules

1. No coins, nor pattern pieces, shall be struck after the year of their date; and to insure this, the dies shall be rendered unfit for their use.
2. No coins, nor patterns, are to be issued in any but their proper metal.
3. Any experimental or pattern piece can be obtained at the Mint, within the year of its date, but not after. Standing orders for such pieces will be registered and attended to. Any patterns that remain on hand at the end of the year must be defaced. . .

4. The price of a pattern coin, in any but precious metal, will be three dollars in currency; if in gold or silver, the value of the metal is to be added. But when a pattern piece is adopted and used in the regular coinage, in the same year, it will then be issued as a Proof, at a price near its current value. The Director reserves the right to send a pattern piece, without charge, to any incorporated Numismatic Society within the United States. In such cases, if the pattern is in gold or silver, the value of the metal will be expected.

5. The price of a regular Proof set of gold will be forty-three dollars in gold; the Proof set of silver and copper, three dollars in silver as heretofore. To suit the convenience of many, payment may be made in the currency equivalent.[6]
6. The profits of this whole department are reserved to the Medal Fund, which is a part of the public moneys; and are not to be perquisite to any person holding a place in the Mint. All such persons are expected to refrain from dealings in this line, or affording aid to friends or dealers outside. If this expectation is counteracted, it will call for serious notice.

Rule 6 is especially funny to read today! Rules notwithstanding, those in charge of dies and certain equipment put the making of fancy pieces into overdrive, the momentum of which continued unabated and unabashed for nearly the next two decades, until the summer of 1885.

Returning to 1866, this was the first year of regular issue of the Shield nickel and also the first year in which regular Proof dies were used to make off-metal strikings (J-510 to 512).

The Lincoln portrait patterns, J-486 and later, are perhaps the most distinctive Mint-issued patterns of this year. The several Washington dies are all adapted from the 1785 bust by Jean Antoine Houdon, this being the most widely used of all portraits of our first president (and seen in somewhat altered form on current quarter dollars). As there was no interest in changing the recently adopted IN GOD WE TRUST motto to anything else, it is presumed that all GOD AND OUR COUNTRY issues are items made solely for the numismatic trade. Also drawing attention is the 1866 Without Rays transitional pattern, style of 1867, J-507. The first Without Rays die is thought to have been made very late in 1866 or early in 1867.

The following die details are adapted from those used in the Judd text and are a useful key to the variety descriptions.

Five-Cent Obverse Dies of 1866

Obverse die 1866-1a: Washington portrait, UNITED STATES OF AMERICA. *Low*-relief portrait facing right. *D in UNITED leans slightly right*; base of D, if extended to the left, will be above baseline of adjacent E. The base of O in OF is stronger and the center has more space than on 1b. These are slight differences and require study to detect. Used with J-526.

Obverse die 1866-1b: Washington portrait, UNITED STATES OF AMERICA. *Low*-relief portrait facing right. *D in UNITED is upright*; base of D, if extended to the left, will be on the same level as the baseline of adjacent E. O in OF thin or weak at base. On the late die state there is a raised dot or "island" centered below N in UNITED. The 1b die was also used outside of the Mint to create many unusual mulings and other pieces. This die and Obverse Die 1866-C were donated to the Boston Numismatic Society circa 1869 to 1878, where their use, if any, is undocumented. In spring 1956, Edmund A. Rice, a dealer from Cranbury, New Jersey, sold George J. Fuld some special strikings, leading to the discovery that one silver bar and nine in aluminum had been impressed with each of these dies by the then-curator of the BNS, who admitted to same. The dies and impressions were seized by the government and destroyed.[7] (Note:

Dies 1866-1a and/or 1b used with J-461 to 463, J-513 to 528, and J-547. Also used on J-579 of 1867. Study is ongoing.)

Obverse die 1866-2: Washington portrait, IN GOD WE TRUST. *Low*-relief portrait facing right. Used with J-464 to 479, J-529, J-530, and J-545; also used on J-580 and 581 of 1867, as well as outside the Mint. See note under Obverse die 1866-1b above.

Obverse die 1866-3: *High*-relief portrait of Washington, facing right, inscription GOD AND OUR COUNTRY around border, date 1866 below. The appearance of this die is quite unlike that of any other in the series. Used with J-480 to 485, all of which are great rarities.

Obverse die 1866-4: Lincoln portrait, facing right, UNITED STATES OF AMERICA around, date 1866 below. Used with J-486 to 488a.

Obverse die 1866-5: "Shield design, but ball divides date." Shield nickel similar to regular die, but with differences (placement of point of pattee cross, spacing, etc.) except the date divided by the ball at the bottom of the shield. Exists in two die states: (1) early, with two prominent outlines between the left side of the shield frame and the field, above the arrow feather; and (2) late, with die relapped and certain lower-relief features gone, including these two lines. Used with J-489 to 500.

Obverse die 1866-6: Regular Shield nickel die of the year. Used with J-501 to 512, and J-531 and 531a.

Five-Cent Reverse Dies of 1866

Reverse die 1866-A: Large, bushy wreath, open at top, 5 / CENTS. Above is IN GOD WE TRUST in small letters. Used with J-461 to 463, J-486 to 488, J-531, J-533.

Reverse die 1866-B: Dutch 5. Small wreath enclosing "Dutch"-style 5 with large knob at upper right of numeral. UNITED STATES OF AMERICA around border. Reverses 1866-B and C are probably by the same engraver. Used with J-464 to 466a, J-480, J-489 to 491.

Reverse die 1866-C: Tall 5. Small wreath enclosing tall 5 with pointed top of numeral. UNITED STATES OF AMERICA around border. Reverses 1866-B and C are probably by the same engraver. Used with J-467 to 469, J-481 and 482, J-492 and 493, J-501 to 503, J-527.

Reverse die 1866-D: Short 5 with large, bushy open wreath enclosing 5 / CENTS. Leaves at the bottom of the wreath are especially prominent and bushy. UNITED STATES OF AMERICA in tall letters at border. Used with J-470 to 472, J-483 to 485, J-494 to 496, J-504 to 506, J-528.

Reverse die 1866-E: Regular With Rays design. Proof die with two center dots, slight repunching of 5. Used with J-473 to 475, J-497 to 499, J-510 to 515.

Reverse die 1866-Fa: Regular design Without Rays as adopted in 1867. This die is thought to have been made in late 1866 or very early in 1867. *Used for regular-issue Proofs made early in 1867.* Stars point under upright of E and at center of A. *Two center dots from a compass point.* Repunching on the upper and lower left sides of the numeral 5.

Reverse die 1866-Fb: Regular design Without Rays as adopted in 1867. *Used for regular issues 1867 to 1869, but about 10% of 1868 are of Style E.* Stars point under right serif of E and between A and M.

Reverse die 1866-Fc: Regular design Without Rays as adopted in 1867. *Used for regular issues 1869 to 1883.* Stars point under right serif of E and at interior of M just left of center.

Reverse die 1866-G: Large 5 / CENTS in straight line. Large open wreath enclosing 5 / CENTS, with CENTS in a straight line. IN GOD WE TRUST in small letters at top border. Used with J-529, J-530.

Five-Cent Die Combinations of 1866

Judd 461–463

Obverse: Obverse die 1866-1b (Washington portrait; UNITED STATES OF AMERICA).
Reverse: Reverse die 1866-A (large wreath, motto above).

An example of the popular J-461 variety struck in nickel alloy. The obverse portrait by (presumably) Longacre is taken from the 1785 Jean-Antoine Houdon bust of Washington. This particular die was taken out of the Mint and used to make illogical mulings and rarities. In the 1870's it was in the hands of the Boston Numismatic Society. The reverse, with 5 / CENTS within a particularly luxuriant wreath, was used on several varieties of patterns during this era.

J-461 • Nickel alloy • Rarity-5

J-462 • Copper • Low Rarity-7

J-463 • Copper-nickel • Rarity-8

Die variety not studied (1866-1a or b). Example sold by New England Rare Coin Galleries in April 1980.

Judd 464–466

Obverse: Obverse die 1866-2 (Washington portrait, *low* relief, facing right; IN GOD WE TRUST).
Reverse: Reverse die 1866-B (Dutch 5).

J-464 • Nickel alloy • High Rarity-7

J-465 • Copper • Rarity-8
Except by elemental analysis, it is not possible to differentiate between J-465 and J-466.

J-466 • Bronze • High Rarity-7
Comments same as for J-465.

Judd 466a

Obverse: Obverse die 1866-2 (Washington portrait, *low* relief, facing right; IN GOD WE TRUST).
Reverse: Reverse die 1866-A (large bushy wreath, open at top, 5 / CENTS; above this, IN GOD WE TRUST in small letters).

J-466a • Silver
No example confirmed by modern specialists; may be a misdescription of another variety (cf. Haseltine sale of September 1876, Lot 425). *Any* nickel five-cent pattern struck in silver is a numismatic delicacy or fantasy, not a Mint product (see research of George Fuld).

Judd 467–469

Obverse: Obverse die 1866-2 (Washington portrait, *low* relief, facing right; IN GOD WE TRUST).
Reverse: Reverse die 1866-C (tall 5).

J-467 • Nickel alloy • High Rarity-7

This popular obverse die features the portrait of Washington with IN GOD WE TRUST above. On the reverse (also used on other patterns of this era), the leaves and the numeral 5 show a particularly deep "sculptured" effect; also, the berries have highly unusual stems. During this period several talented engravers assisted Longacre, and perhaps this distinctive reverse was created by one of them. Illustration is of J-468.

J-468 • Copper • Rarity-8
Except by elemental analysis, it is not possible to differentiate between J-468 and J-469.

J-469 • Bronze • Low Rarity-7
See J-468.

JUDD 470–472

Obverse: Obverse die 1866-2 (Washington portrait, *low* relief, facing right; IN GOD WE TRUST).
Reverse: Reverse die 1866-D (Short 5).

The 1866-2 Washington die is used on J-470 with a distinctive reverse. The wreath is very heavy, and its ends are tipped slightly inward at the top to permit UNITED STATES OF AMERICA to fit. Letters of this style, with heavy uprights, are sometimes attributed to engraver Anthony C. Paquet, who did work for the Mint as an employee and, at times, a private contractor.

J-470 • Nickel alloy • Low Rarity-6

J-471 • Copper • Rarity-8

Except by elemental analysis, it is not possible to differentiate between J-471 and J-472.

J-472 • Bronze • Low Rarity-7

See J-471.

JUDD 473–475

Obverse: Obverse die 1866-2 (Washington portrait, *low* relief, facing right; IN GOD WE TRUST).
Reverse: Reverse die 1866-E (regular With Rays design; die with center dot and repunched 5). Also used to make regular-issue Proofs.

To create J-473 the popular 1866-2 die with Washington and IN GOD WE TRUST was paired with the reverse die used to coin regular Proof 1866 With Rays nickels.

J-473 • Nickel alloy • Low Rarity-6

J-474 • Copper • Rarity-8

Except by elemental analysis, it is not possible to differentiate between J-474 and J-475.

J-475 • Bronze • Rarity-8

See J-474.

Judd 476–479

Obverse: Obverse die 1866-2 (Washington portrait, *low* relief, facing right; IN GOD WE TRUST).
Reverse: Reverse Die 1866-Fc (regular Without Rays style as adopted in 1867).
None of this combination are Mint products.

J-476 • Nickel alloy • Possibly unique

Ex Crosby sale (1883) to T. Harrison Garrett. 84.3 grains. I cataloged the Garrett patterns for The Johns Hopkins University as part of four sales, the nickels crossing the block in Garrett II held in March 1980. This coin opened at $3,500 and sold for $13,500.

J-477 • Copper • Rarity-8

Specific reverse die not studied. Édouard Frossard sold a "brilliant Proof" in October 1884 (Lot 416), possibly the same as Superior, October 1992, Lot 1204, "Proof-62."

J-478 • Brass

Specific reverse die not studied. None confirmed by modern specialists.

J-479 • White metal • Rarity-8

Stars point under right serif of E and at interior of M just left of center. Broadstruck example illustrated in Rulau-Fuld, page 49, with the notation "three known specimens." Not a Mint product. The Garrett II coin, ex Haseltine's 1883 Crosby sale, was sold in March 1980 for $7,500. In 1883, T. Harrison Garrett, of Baltimore, was America's largest private buyer of coins and had the most extensive collection.

Judd 480

Obverse: Obverse die 1866-3 (Washington portrait, *high* relief, facing right; GOD AND OUR COUNTRY around border; date 1866 below).
Reverse: Reverse die 1866-B (Dutch 5).

J-480 • Nickel alloy • Unique

Judd 481 and 482

Obverse: Obverse die 1866-3 (Washington portrait, *high* relief, facing right; GOD AND OUR COUNTRY around border; date 1866 below).
Reverse: Reverse die 1866-C (tall 5).

J-481 • Nickel alloy • Low Rarity-7

J-482 • Copper • Rarity-8

Judd 483–485

Obverse: Obverse die 1866-3 (Washington Portrait, *high* relief, facing right; GOD AND OUR COUNTRY around border; date 1866 below).
Reverse: Reverse die 1866-D (short 5).

J-483 • Nickel alloy • Rarity-8

J-484 • Copper • Rarity-8

Except by elemental analysis, it is not possible to differentiate between J-484 and J-485.

J-485 • Bronze • High Rarity-7

See J-484.

Judd 486–488a

Obverse: Obverse die 1866-4 (Lincoln portrait).
Reverse: Reverse die 1866-A (large wreath, motto above).

J-486 to 488a are the only 18th-century patterns to feature the portrait of the Great Emancipator (as he was called). The obverse letters are the heavy style attributed to Paquet. These and related Lincoln patterns were never made available to numismatists openly, but were filtered into the market through local dealer William Idler and others with connections to the Mint. Today, all are rarities. Illustrated is J-487.

J-486 • Nickel alloy • Low Rarity-7

As the only use of Lincoln's portrait on a 19th-century federal coin, J-486 and metallic variations have always been in incredible demand. It is highly unlikely that a circulating coin featuring Lincoln would have been considered seriously, for this was the age of Reconstruction, Lincoln's memory was detested in the South, and an effort was being made to heal the country.

J-487 • Copper • Low Rarity-7

Except by elemental analysis, it is not possible to differentiate between J-487 and J-488.

J-488 • Bronze • High Rarity-7

See J-487.

J-488a • Brass

Example not seen in recent times and not subjected to elemental analysis. This listing may be a misdescription of J-488; the citation comes from the Lohr Collection, 1960, and may represent a J-488 with unusual toning.

Judd 489–491

Obverse: Obverse die 1866-5 ("Shield design, but ball divides date").
Reverse: Reverse die 1866-B (Dutch 5).

The distinctive obverse die used for J-489 and related patterns features the shield motif moved downward on the coin, and the date was divided by a ball, as 18•66. This reverse is known as the *Dutch 5* and features "sculpted" leaves and unusual berry stems as also seen on the reverse of 1866-C. No doubt the same engraver created both.

Judd 489 • Nickel alloy • Low Rarity-6

Early die state with extra outlines to left side of shield.

J-490 • Copper • Low Rarity-7
Later die state from relapped die, extra outlines not visible. Except by elemental analysis, it is not possible to differentiate between J-490 and J-491.

J-491 • Bronze • Low Rarity-7
See comments for J-491.

Judd 492 and 493

Obverse: Obverse die 1866-5 ("Shield design, but ball divides date").
Reverse: Reverse die 1866-B (Dutch 5).

J-492 • Nickel alloy • Unique
Ex Peter Gschwend sale, Thomas L. Elder, June 1908, Lot 242; later in Farouk (1954, Lot 1800) and the Kreisberg-Schulman auction of February 1958 (Lot 2481).

J-493 • Copper • Unique
Ex Peter Gschwend sale, Thomas L. Elder, June 1908, Lot 243; later in the Edwin Hydeman sale, Abe Kosoff, 1961, Lot 861. Not seen in modern times.

Judd 494–496

Obverse: Obverse die 1866-5 ("Shield design, but ball divides date").
Reverse: Reverse die 1866-D (short 5)

J-494 • Nickel alloy • Rarity-8

J-495 • Copper • High Rarity-7
Except by elemental analysis, it is not possible to differentiate between J-495 and J-496.

J-496 • Bronze • High Rarity-7
See J-495.

Judd 497–499

Obverse: Obverse die 1866-5 ("Shield design, but ball divides date").
Reverse: Reverse die 1866-E (regular With Rays design).

J-497 combines the shield obverse with ball dividing the date with the regular reverse used to coin Proof 1867 With Rays nickels. In this year, with A. Loudon Snowden as chief coiner and Henry Linderman as Mint director, the game was to make as many rarities as possible—a policy that continued into later times. However, this particular issue, at least for the nickel-alloy striking, seems to be a true pattern.

J-497 • Nickel alloy • High Rarity-7

Early strikings have a deep impression of the shield-motif punch into the working die, with extra outlines to left side of shield. This gives a good idea of what the motif would have looked like—with very bold features—if deeply impressed into working dies for regular issues, and not relapped. Likely, J-497 became a stock-in-trade item for certain Mint employees, and examples were made at later times in response to numismatic demand. Later strikes are from a relapped obverse die.

J-498 • Copper • High Rarity-7

Obverse: Later die state from relapped die, extra outlines not visible. Except by elemental analysis, it is not possible to differentiate between J-498 and J-499.

J-499 • Bronze • High Rarity-7

Die state not studied. Except by elemental analysis, it is not possible to differentiate between J-498 and J-499.

Judd 500

Obverse: Obverse die 1866-5 ("Shield design, but ball divides date").
Reverse: Reverse Style C (handmade die; No Rays; stars point under upright of E and at center of A).

J-500 • Nickel alloy • Unique

Judd 501–503

Obverse: Obverse die 1866-6 (regular Shield nickel die of the year).
Reverse: Reverse die 1866-C (tall 5).

J-501 • Nickel alloy • Rarity-8

J-502 • Copper • Rarity-8

Except by elemental analysis, it is not possible to differentiate between J-502 and J-503.

J-503 • Bronze • Rarity-8

See J-502.

Judd 504–506

Obverse: Obverse die 1866-6 (regular Shield nickel die of the year).
Reverse: Reverse die 1866-D (short 5).

J-504 • Nickel alloy • Low Rarity-7

J-505 • Copper • Rarity-8

Except by elemental analysis, it is not possible to differentiate between J-505 and J-506.

J-506 • Bronze • Rarity-8

See J-505.

Judd 507–509a

Obverse: Obverse die 1866-6 (regular Shield nickel die of the year).
Reverse: Reverse die 1866-Fa (regular design Without Rays as adopted in 1867; stars point under upright of E and at center of A).

The distinctive obverse die used for J-489 and related patterns features the shield motif moved downward on the coin, and the date was divided by a ball, as 18•66. This reverse is known as the *Dutch 5* and features "sculpted" leaves and unusual berry stems as also seen on the reverse of 1866-C. No doubt the same engraver created both.

J-507 • Nickel alloy • Rarity-5
Transitional pattern; regular obverse and reverse of the 1867 Without Rays type, but dated a year earlier. One of the more plentiful nickel patterns of this era, J-507 played to a strong collector demand in its time.

J-508 • Copper • High Rarity-6
Except by elemental analysis, it is not possible to differentiate between J-508 and J-509.

J-509 • Bronze • High Rarity-6
See J-508.

J-509a • White metal • Unique
Specific die not studied. Sold in the Pine Tree Auction Co. sale of September 1974.

Judd 510–512

Obverse: Obverse die 1866-6 (regular Shield nickel die of the year).
Reverse: Reverse die 1866-E (regular With Rays design). Die with center dot and repunched 5 also used to make regular Proofs.

J-510 • Copper • Rarity-8
Status uncertain. George Fuld considered this and the following to be made outside the Mint, but some scholars (Saul Teichman, for one) disagree.

J-511 • Bronze • Rarity-8
Absent elemental analysis, this is impossible to differentiate from J-510.

J-512 • Steel or pure nickel (magnetic) • Unique
Ex J.W. Haseltine's sale of September 1876, Lot 562, segueing quickly into Edward Cogan's A.S. Jenks sale, November 1877, Lot 209, then to Lorin B. Parmelee and a string of later owners. Sold by Bowers and Merena, March 1996; no elemental analysis performed. Saul Teichman comment: "May be a Mint product, as it was known as early as 1876, before any of the restrike mules were reported. However, George Fuld thought it might be a restrike from dies held at one time by Joseph J. Mickley. Could be pure nickel. Examination would be helpful."

Judd 513–515

Obverse: Obverse die 1866-1 (type of 1866-1a/1b—exact die not known; Washington portrait, *low* relief, facing right; UNITED STATES OF AMERICA).
Reverse: Reverse die 1866-E (regular With Rays design).

J-513, J-514, J-515 • Nickel alloy, copper, and brass, respectively
None confirmed by modern specialists; may not exist.

Judd 516–520

Obverse: Obverse die 1866-1b (Washington portrait, *low* relief, facing right; UNITED STATES OF AMERICA; *D in UNITED is upright;* base of D, if extended to the left, will be on the same level as the baseline of adjacent E).
Reverse: Reverse die 1866-Fc (regular design Without Rays as adopted in 1867; stars point under right serif of E and at interior of M just left of center).

J-516 • Nickel alloy • Rarity-8
Not a Mint product. The coin illustrated in Rulau-Fuld, page 51, is clearly overstruck on a regular Shield nickel dated 1867. Ex Belden Roach Collection (B. Max Mehl, 1944) and Lenox R. Lohr Collection (Q. David Bowers and James F. Ruddy, 1960). Another example, not overstruck, is rumored.

J-517 • Copper • High Rarity-7
One has the die alignment medal-wise (Lemus Collection), another has the reverse double struck. Thick- and thin-planchet varieties offered in the 1883 Crosby sale.

J-518 • Silver
Not confirmed by modern specialists; may not exist. None in the 1883 Crosby sale (although such was erroneously reported later).

J-519 • Brass • Rarity-8 or unique
Multiple citations from Crosby (1883) to modern times may be the same coin; *Rare Coin Review* numbers 21 and 22 listed it in 1974.

J-520 • Lead • Rarity-8
Crosby (1883) was laden with three pieces! Apparently all three have a cracked reverse die (see Saul Teichman).

Judd 521–524

Obverse: Obverse die 1866-1b (Washington portrait, *low* relief, facing right; UNITED STATES OF AMERICA).
Reverse: Obverse die 1866-2 (Washington portrait, *low* relief, facing right; IN GOD WE TRUST).

J-521 • Silver • High Rarity-7 or R-8
Muling of two *obverse* dies. None of this die combination are Mint products. Pieces in various metals first appeared in Haseltine's Crosby sale, 1883. An example of J-521, ex Haseltine-Crosby, appeared in the Garrett II sale, March 1980, and sold for $11,000. Weight: 88.1 grains.

J-521a • Nickel alloy • Rarity-8

J-522 • Copper • Rarity-8

J-523 • Brass • Rarity-8
The Garrett II coin, ex Haseltine-Crosby in 1883, realized $8,500 in 1980.

J-524 • White metal • Unique
Described at uspatterns.com as being "in white metal, copper plated, then brass plated over white metal. Specific gravity 11.15."[8]

Judd 525 and 526

Obverse: Obverse die 1866-1a (Washington portrait, *low* relief, facing right; UNITED STATES OF AMERICA).
Reverse: Obverse die 1866-1b (Washington portrait, *low* relief, facing right; UNITED STATES OF AMERICA).

This double-headed J-526 is thought to have been made outside the Mint, but who knows? In any event, it is a numismatic delicacy created for collectors. Three of them appeared in J.W. Haseltine's 1883 sale featuring the collection of the highly esteemed S.S. Crosby (author of *Early Coins of America*), but it is most likely that Haseltine added these and certain other pattern rarities from another source.

J-525 • Copper • Unique
Muling of two almost identical obverse dies. Not a Mint product. Ex Crosby 1883 sale. Weight: 86 grains. In Garrett II, March 1980, this coin sold for $6,000. Later it was featured in Superior's section of Auction '82, Lot 1492.

J-526 • White metal • Rarity-8
Three were in Haseltine's 1883 Crosby sale. Two were in the Lohr Collection (1960). Two examples weighed by Fred Weinberg were 59.6 and 86.7 grains, on thin and thick planchets.

Judd 527

Obverse: Obverse die 1866-1 (type of 1866-1a/1b—specific die not known; Washington portrait, *low* relief, facing right; UNITED STATES OF AMERICA).
Reverse: Reverse die 1866-C (tall 5).

J-527 • Nickel alloy of unknown mixture
Existence unconfirmed.

Judd 528

Obverse: Obverse die 1866-1 (type of 1866-1a/1b—exact die not known; Washington portrait, *low* relief, facing right; UNITED STATES OF AMERICA).
Reverse: Reverse die 1866-D (short 5).

J-528 • Nickel alloy
Not confirmed by modern specialists; may not exist.

Judd 529

Obverse: Obverse die 1866-2 (Washington portrait, *low* relief, facing right; IN GOD WE TRUST).
Reverse: Reverse die 1866-G (large 5 / CENTS in straight line).

J-529 • Nickel • Rarity-8
Obverse misdescribed in the eighth edition Judd book, corrected for the seventh edition of Judd.

Judd 531

Obverse: Obverse die 1866-6 (regular Shield nickel die of the year).
Reverse: Reverse die 1866-A (large 5 / CENTS in curved line).

The J-531 variety is extremely rare today. The obverse is the regular Proof Shield nickel die of the year. The motto IN GOD WE TRUST appears on both sides of the coin, an illogical situation—but, then, logic played no part in the creation of many patterns of this era.

J-531 • Nickel • Rarity-8
This represents the only use of this reverse die, a very unusual situation. The motto IN GOD WE TRUST appears on both sides of this coin. George J. Fuld considered this variety to be made outside the Mint, and it is indeed curious. However, its appearance is more like that of a Mint product.

Judd 531a

Obverse: An obverse die used for a *$3 gold* coin of this era.
Reverse: Obverse die 1866-6 (regular Shield nickel die of the year).

J-531a • Nickel • Unique
Multidenomination muling of two obverse dies, a particularly unusual numismatic delicacy, probably made outside the Mint. An example was described in the J.F. McCabe Collection sale, Chapman brothers, June 1905; another was in the inventory of Bowers and Ruddy Galleries in the late 1970's. Further study is indicated.

Judd 532

Obverse and Reverse: A muling of two dies of the regular design Without Rays as adopted in 1867. Circulation strike (not Proof) dies, one die cracked.

J-532 • White metal • Unique

Not a Mint product. At least two dies of this general style were used off-premises. Sold by Superior Galleries in the Walter Lee Crouch Collection sale, June 1977.

Judd 533

Obverse: Regular design Without Rays as adopted in 1867. Specific die not studied.
Reverse: Reverse die 1866-A (large 5 / CENTS in curved line).

J-533 • Copper

Not confirmed by modern specialists; may not exist.

Judd 534

Obverse: Obverse die 1866-2 (Washington portrait, *low* relief, facing right; IN GOD WE TRUST).
Reverse: $5 reverse die of the pre-1866 type without motto.

J-534 • White metal • Unique or nonexistent

Not a Mint product. Broadstruck, without a collar. Sold by Bowers and Ruddy Galleries in May 1974. Saul Teichman comment: "An absurd combination of a 5-cent obverse with a half eagle reverse. Crudely struck. Taxay called it a 'private restrike.' This example may no longer exist; rumor has it that it melted when it was heated to inhibit corrosion."

Pattern Nickels of 1867

In many ways the patterns of 1867 can be compared to those of the preceding year. Some legitimate issues were made to test new concepts (such as the use of aluminum) or to explore new designs. In addition, there were quite a few numismatic delicacies, including weird mulings believed to have been struck outside the Mint. The result is a playground for numismatic research, much of which is still ongoing.

R.W. Julian contributed the following from his notes:

> Although dissatisfaction with the obverse design led officials to order a series of pattern dies for the nickel between 1867 and 1871, not all of the impetus was merely the desire to find a more pleasing design. Mint officials were seriously concerned over the continued heavy usage of dies despite the improvement obtained in early 1867 when the reverse design was altered to remove the rays between the stars.
>
> It is probable that the new die life (after January 1867) was in the general range of 20,000 or 21,000 pieces per pair of dies. As late as 1882 the average was only slightly over 26,000 pieces per pair, though it really is not known what, if any, improvement in die life was made between 1867 and 1882. Coinages were still very heavy in 1868 and 1869, thus leading to the patterns being made.
>
> Another important reason for the series of pattern nickels struck in 1867 was the desire to test aluminum as a coining metal. There was a great deal of interest during

> the 1860s in this particular metal, especially in the U.S. Mint at Philadelphia, and the patterns were the natural result of this curiosity. The most important argument for aluminum coinage, from a technical standpoint, was the ease of coining and the long die life that would result. The proposed metal was fairly soft and one could assume that dies would last a minimum of 100,000 pieces.
>
> A secondary reason was the value of aluminum in 1867, which was not far from that of silver. The Mint paid $2.50 per ounce in greenbacks for the limited quantities necessary for patterns, and contemporary observers rated this price as nearly equivalent to the current value of silver in the depreciated post-war circulating currency. The nominal value of one troy ounce of silver was $1.29 if bought with silver or gold coins, more if with depreciated paper.[9]

The actual depreciation for the year 1867 varied from $132 in paper needed to buy $100 in gold coins on January 3, to $146.37 on September 12. On this basis an ounce of silver, purchasable for $1.29 in gold, would have cost from $1.70 to $1.88 in paper money.

Chief Engraver James B. Longacre was personally interested in the possibility of using aluminum, perhaps to quiet criticism about die wear and breakage, as noted by Julian. On June 12, 1867, he wrote to Secretary of the Treasury Hugh McCulloch in Washington, care of Mint Director Henry R. Linderman, enclosing a supply of aluminum pattern five-cent pieces, likely of the Judd-561 variety, with a completely new head of Liberty, and the die proudly signed, LONGACRE. In favor of the use of aluminum, he mentioned the following in his letter to McCulloch:

> 1. The facility and certainty with which it can be distinguished from all other metals in use or known, arising from its remarkable place among the specific gravities of metals; its extreme lightness, presenting a greater safeguard against adulteration or spurious imitation, than even the opposite quality of gold, which may be regarded as occupying nearly the other end of the scale of metallic gravities.
> 2. It is less liable to discoloration from mere atmospheric exposure than any other metal used as a circulating medium except gold.
> 3. It is malleable and fusible at a modest heat.
> 4. Its relative value, which would give for the value of five cents, intrinsically; a piece of the size of the Half Eagle; one of the most desirable sizes of coin for extensive circulation, for which there would be no danger of mistaking it, even in the dark, to say nothing of color.
> 5. These considerations have induced me to prepare for the purpose from dies designated and engraved by myself, the accompanying specimens, corresponding in size with the coin above mentioned, in order to exhibit fully and fairly under the usual process of coining, the fitness of the metal for the requisite operations.[10]

While Longacre's petition may have contained elements of logic, it overlooked two major issues:

First, neither the Mint nor the Treasury Department had any interest in having "fractional currency" (a term for minor *coins*, not the Fractional Currency paper bills in circulation) coined from precious metals. Ever since the early days of the Mint in the 1790's, the facility made handsome profits on minor coins by striking them in metals of low intrinsic value. Called *seignorage*, this profit was a great source of revenue, for the coinage of silver and gold yielded but a tiny profit in the handling, and hardly anything on seignorage.

Second, Longacre failed to take into account the connections that Joseph Wharton had forged with just about everyone who counted in the Mint and Congress.

Director Linderman sabotaged the effort by sending a note to McCulloch, along with Longacre's letter, to the effect that the market price and availability of aluminum were both uncertain and that metal of high intrinsic value was not desired for minor coins. Historian Don Taxay, in *U.S. Mint and Coinage*, commented as follows:

> It seems that the Director was already committed to the nickel interests. After admitting in his first annual report that the copper-nickel three- and five-cent planchets had worn out the Mint's machinery and broken an enormous number of dies, Linderman framed a bill to create copper-nickel cents and dimes. All of these coins were to have uniformly proportioned weights, and an alloy of not less than 25 per cent nor more than 33 per cent nickel. Linderman's willingness to increase the proportion of nickel by eight per cent, after he had already complained of the alloy's intractability and advised a modest value for the minor coins, throws some doubt on his official motives.[11]

Further, R.W. Julian notes that "Linderman did authorize the selling of aluminum patterns to numismatists but at . . . a high figure ($5 each). . . . One suspects that the price was a deliberate ploy by the director to further tarnish the reputation of aluminum as a coining metal."

Five-Cent Obverse Dies of 1867

Obverse 1867-1: Indian Princess head. Head of Liberty with feathered headdress, facing left, ribbon inscribed UNION & LIBERTY on hair, four stars to right, signature LONGACRE F. below portrait, UNITED STATES OF AMERICA around (slightly unbalanced in its orientation), 1867 below, curved along the border. Likely, this is the key pattern issue of the year, the coin that figured in Longacre's letter and in many discussions. Used with J-561 to 565.

Obverse 1867-2: Coronet Head, no star. Head of Liberty facing right, no star on coronet. Coronet inscribed LIBERTY. Around border, UNITED STATES OF AMERICA, 1867 below. Used with J-566 and 567, J-569, J-574 to 581.

Obverse 1867-3a: Coronet Head, with star; 7 distant from curl. Head of Liberty facing right, with star on coronet below the word LIBERTY. Around border, UNITED STATES OF AMERICA, 1867 below. This die was also used outside the Mint.[12] Five-dollar patterns (J-601 and 601a, J-778) were made with this obverse, but are not discussed here. This general type (without respect to the obverse die *variety*) used with J-568, J-570 and 571, J-582, J-583.

Obverse 1867-3b: Coronet Head, with star; 7 close to curl. Head of Liberty facing right, with star on coronet below the word LIBERTY. Around border, UNITED STATES OF AMERICA, 1867 below. Used with J-570 and 571.

Obverse 1867-4: Regular Shield nickel die of the year. Used with J-572 to 573a.

Five-Cent Reverse Dies of 1867

Reverses B, E, F, and G of 1866 were also used on 1867 patterns and are so designated. Reverses 1867-C and 1867-D are new and introduce the V as a mark of denomination.

Reverse 1867-C: V on shield. Large V on shield with ornamented frame surrounding, IN GOD WE TRUST in small letters above. Used with J-561 to 564.

Reverse 1867-D: V within wreath. Large V within very heavy wreath of oak and olive, connected at the top by scrolls and ornamented with a six-pointed star. Used with J-565.

Reverse 1867-H: Large 5 / CENTS in curved line. Large open wreath, rather "bushy" in appearance, enclosing 5 / CENTS, with CENTS in a curved line; 5 repunched at top right of flag; IN GOD WE TRUST in small letters at top border.[13] Used with J-569 to 571 of 1867, and J-623 of 1868.

Five-Cent Die Combinations of 1867

Judd 561–564

Obverse: Obverse 1867-1 (Indian Princess head).
Reverse: Reverse 1867-C (V on shield).

J-561, the signature coin (literally) among Longacre's pattern five-cent pieces, was made to test the feasibility of aluminum as a coinage metal.

J-561 • Aluminum • Plain edge • Rarity-5
This employs one of two new reverses used on patterns of 1867. This variety was made in significant numbers and was no doubt widely distributed to demonstrate the use of aluminum. This is also one of Longacre's most distinctive designs, with his surname spelled out in full on the die, with a new portrait of Liberty, and an unusual motto. J. Colvin Randall, Philadelphia dealer of the era, stated that 100 were struck.

J-562 • Aluminum • Reeded edge • Low Rarity-7
The use of a reeded edge is unusual on a pattern in this series, although there are a few others. This and the next two variations were made as numismatic delicacies.

J-563 • Copper • Plain edge • High Rarity-7

J-564 • Copper • Reeded edge • High Rarity-7

Judd 565

Obverse: Obverse 1867-1 (Indian Princess head).
Reverse: Reverse 1867-D (V within wreath).

J-565 • Nickel alloy • Rarity-8

This is the only use of this distinctive new reverse die. Saul Teichman records just two, one being the Lorin G. Parmelee coin, sold in 1890, now in the Durham Western Heritage Museum, Omaha, Nebraska; and the other being the George D. Woodside coin, sold by New York Coin & Stamp Co. (April 1892), to Judson Brenner (and exhibited at the ANS in 1914), through various owners including Dr. J. Hewitt Judd, to B&M in June 1984, to Superior in February 1987, to the Ed Rector Collection. In addition, an example in Mehl's January 1942 sale may be the Woodside coin; if not, it is a third example. The variety was first brought to market in 1870 through—who else?—William K. Idler, who had connections with the Mint.

Judd 566 and 567

Obverse: Obverse 1867-2 (Coronet Head, no star).
Reverse: Reverse die 1866-G (large 5 / CENTS in straight line).

J-566 displays Longacre's Coronet Head, without a star in the tiara. The die was unfinished when this coin was struck, and extensive preparation lines can be seen. The reverse die is from 1866.

J-566 • Nickel alloy • Low Rarity-6

J-567 • Copper • Low Rarity-7

Judd 568

Obverse: Obverse 1867-3a (Coronet Head, with star; 7 distant from curl).[14]
Reverse: Reverse die 1866-G (large 5 / CENTS in straight line).

J-568 • Nickel alloy

This may not exist. At minimum, it has not been seen by modern specialists.[15]

Judd 569

Obverse: Obverse 1867-2 (Coronet Head, no star).
Reverse: Reverse die 1867-H (large 5 / CENTS in curved line).

J-569 • Nickel alloy

Existence not confirmed by modern scholars.

Judd 570 and 571

Obverse: Obverse 1867-3a (Coronet Head, with star; 7 distant from curl).
Reverse: Reverse die 1867-H (large 5 / CENTS in curved line).

The J-570 variety features Longacre's Coronet Head with a star in the tiara. Two obverse dies were made of this general style, 1867-3a (as here, with the 7 in the date distant from the curl) and 1867-3b (with the 7 close). The reverse die is one of several left over from 1866.

J-570 • Nickel alloy • Rarity-5

This seems to be a regular pattern made as an alternative to the Shield design. It is said that the Mint struck 50 pieces, but the actual number is anyone's guess.

J-571 • Copper • Low Rarity-7

J-570, obverse variation • Nickel alloy • Rarity-8

Obverse 1867-3b (Coronet Head, with star; 7 close to curl). Reverse die 1867-H (large 5 / CENTS in curved line). Rarity estimate may be too high, as some examples of J-570 have not been examined for their die characteristics.

J-571, obverse variation • Copper • Rarity-8

Same obverse and reverse dies as J-570, obverse variation.

Judd 572

Obverse: Obverse 1867-4 (regular Shield nickel die of the year).
Reverse: Reverse die 1866-E (regular With Rays design; Proof die with two center dots, slight repunching of 5).

J-572 • Copper • Low Rarity-7

The Garrett II coin weighed 73 grains.

Judd 573

Obverse: Obverse 1867-4 (regular Shield nickel die of the year).
Reverse: Reverse die 1866-Fa (regular design Without Rays as adopted in 1867, thought to have been made in late 1866 or very early in 1867; stars point under upright of E and at center of A).[16]

This variation of J-573 has a different reverse die, with stars pointing under the right serif of E in STATES and between A and M in AMERICA. The obverse is that of the regular Proof die of the year.

J-573 • Copper • Rarity-7 [Pollock-649]

J-573, reverse variation • Copper • High Rarity-6 [Pollock-650]

Reverse die 1866-Fb (regular design Without Rays as adopted in 1867; stars point under right serif of E and between A and M). The Garrett II coin, Lot 998, March 1980, was of this variety.

Judd 573a

Obverse: Obverse 1867-4 (regular Shield nickel die of the year).
Reverse: Reverse die 1866-G (large 5 / CENTS in straight line).

J-573a • Copper • Rarity-8

Judd 574

Obverse: Obverse 1867-2 (Coronet Head, no star).
Reverse: Reverse die 1866-E (regular With Rays design; Proof die with two center dots, slight repunching of 5).

J-574 • White metal • Unique

Not a Mint product. One owned by Waldo C. Newcomer of Baltimore (cf. Don Taxay). Not traced today.

Judd 575

Obverse: Obverse 1867-2 (Coronet Head, no star).
Reverse: Reverse die 1866-F (regular Without Rays design as adopted in 1867). Specific die variety not known.

J-575 • Nickel alloy

Not seen by any consultant to this book; however, PCGS lists an Extremely Fine coin certified. Reverse style may be the result of an early misdescription, but examination of the PCGS coin could answer that. If it exists it never saw the interior of the Mint.

Judd 576

Obverse: Obverse 1867-2 (Coronet Head, no star).
Reverse: Reverse die 1866-B (Dutch 5) or 1866-C (tall 5; *tentative*).

J-576 • Nickel alloy • Unique

The conventional illustrations of this variety, including in the Judd text, may show the incorrect reverse die. More study is required.[17]

Judd 577

Obverse: Obverse 1867-2 (Coronet Head, no star).
Reverse: Reverse die 1866-G (large 5 / CENTS in straight line).

J-577 • Nickel alloy

Unconfirmed by modern specialists.

Judd 579

Obverse: Obverse 1867-2 (Coronet Head, no star).
Reverse: Obverse die 1866-1b (Washington portrait, *low* relief, facing right; UNITED STATES OF AMERICA; *D in UNITED is upright;* base of D, if extended to the left, will be on the same level as the base line of adjacent E).

J-579 • Silver • Unique
Nonsensical combination of two obverse dies with two different dates. Not a Mint product.

Judd 580 and 581

Obverse: Obverse 1867-2 (Coronet Head, no star).
Reverse: Obverse die 1866-2 (Washington portrait, *low* relief, facing right; IN GOD WE TRUST).

J-580 • Nickel alloy
Not a Mint product. Existence not confirmed by modern specialists.

J-581 • White metal • Unique
Not a Mint product. Ex William H. Woodin, Judson Brenner (exhibited at the ANS in 1914), Lenox R. Lohr.

Judd 582 and 583

Obverse: Obverse 1867-3a (Coronet Head, with star; 7 distant from curl).
Reverse: Reverse die 1866-Fc (regular design Without Rays as adopted in 1867; stars point under right serif of E and at interior of M just left of center).

J-582 • Nickel alloy • Unique
Not a Mint product. The George D. Woodside coin (April 1892, Lot 212), to Woodin, then Brenner (cf. Don Taxay).

J-583 • Silver • Rarity-8
Not a Mint product. The Haseltine-Crosby coin, 1883, was double struck, later appearing in the Lohr Collection (1960). Another was in the F.C.C. Boyd Collection, to Farouk.

Judd 584

Obverse: Obverse 1867-3 (Coronet Head, with star; date position not known).
Reverse: Obverse die 1866-1b (Washington portrait, *low* relief, facing right; UNITED STATES OF AMERICA; *D in UNITED is upright*; base of D, if extended to the left, will be on the same level as the base line of adjacent E).

The J-584a muling is most curious, being not only a two-headed coin, but bearing two different dates! This whimsical production is believed to have been made outside the Mint. No records have been found as to who made novelties in this general category, or when they were struck; and today what we know is pieced together from examining the coins themselves. At one time this example belonged to T. Harrison Garrett, the Baltimore numismatist and scion of the family that controlled the Baltimore & Ohio Railroad.

J-584 • White metal
Unconfirmed in white metal. Another nonsensical muling of two obverse dies with *two different* dates. This (if it exists) and the following are not Mint products.

J-584a • Nickel alloy • Unique

Obverse 1867-3a (Coronet Head, with star; 7 distant from curl). Obverse with several prominent raised die-finish lines in the left field. Reverse with denticles crumbling at lower right. From the Garrett II sale, March 1980, Lot 999, at $7,000.

J-584b • Silver • Unique

Date position not known. Same general type as preceding, though struck in silver. Sold by B&M, January 1996.

Judd 585

Obverse: Obverse 1867-3a (Coronet Head, with star; 7 distant from curl).
Reverse: Obverse die 1866-2 (Washington portrait, *low* relief, facing right; IN GOD WE TRUST).

J-585 • White metal • Rarity-8

Another illogical combination of two obverse dies of two different dates. Not a Mint product.

Pattern Nickels of 1868

The pattern nickels of 1868 comprise just six basic design types, three of which use reverse dies from earlier years. Judd 633 is significant as the five-cent entry in a projected series of uniform designs for the cent, nickel three-cent, and nickel five-cent coins, a proposal engineered through the influence of (once again) Joseph Wharton. The March 1868 bill, introduced by Representative Kelley (Pennsylvania),

> had three main objectives. The first was to extend the use of nickel. The measure permitted a large increase in the nickel content of the 5 cent piece, an increase in both the size and the nickel proportion of the 3 cent piece, and the substitution of a nickel cent for the bronze 1 and 2 cent pieces. . . . A second objective was to adopt metric weights for all the minor coins, as a first step, Kelley said, in the establishment of a universal coinage. The third objective was uniform legal tender and redeemability for minor coins.[18]

Ultimately, the bill was rejected due to complications introduced by Missouri nickel interests. As Carothers noted, these patterns for a uniform nickel coinage (described below) were never made as regular issues.

In 1868, as in certain earlier years, off-metal strikings were produced from the Proof dies of various denominations, with special attention being paid in 1868 to aluminum. "To demonstrate how exceedingly excellently aluminum coined in any dies, several Proof sets were struck in aluminum of the regular dies of the 16 denominations of the year, presented to Dr. Linderman, Director of the Mint," Judd related, picking up this comment from the Eavenson Sale catalog, 1903, Lot 242. At least two sets were intended to be sent overseas, one to the Bank of England and the other to France.[19]

This seems to be the only time that the Mint actually kept a record of special off-metal Proof sets' being made. Years later, in 1887, after the 1859 to 1885 era of private restriking and rarities had ended, a new administration at the Mint sought to find out what had happened, and this set was the only one that could be verified! Illogically, when the Linderman estate coins were put up for auction in 1887, the government seized certain patterns and such, including a full aluminum Proof set of 1868.[20]

As an interesting side note, *The Numismatist* (June 1962) reported that a curator of the Iowa State Department of History and Archives had, in July 1961, discovered a set of 1867-dated coins: "all die trial pieces struck in copper. . . . two pieces of each coin struck in the year 1867, with the exception of the two quarter eagles and one eagle." This marvelous find was "still in [its] original housing consisting of a thick cardboard, eight by ten inches, with recessed holes for each piece and covered on the back with coarse plain paper. . . . [and the] front . . . covered with an imitation velvet material of a faded royal purple." Apparently, John Kasson, a former member of Congress and a prominent Iowa citizen, had presented them to the state as a gift.

Five-Cent Die Combinations of 1868

Judd 623–629a

Obverse: Coronet Head, no star.
Reverse: Reverse die 1867-H (large 5 / CENTS in curved line).

The J-623 features a Coronet Head, no star, and is by Longacre. On this die the date is closer to Liberty's neck than to the border denticles (the position of the 1 provides easy reference). The reverse is from a sturdy die first employed in 1866.

The J-624 variety is similar to the preceding, except that the obverse die has a different placement of the date, here closer to the border denticles than to the neck of Liberty. Perhaps one die broke, and another had to be made up as a replacement. This is on a broad planchet, and while the dies are the same diameter as for J-623, this is wider overall, with extra metal at the border.

J-623 • Nickel alloy • Plain edge • Low Rarity-6
On obverse, 1 in 1868 closer to *neck* than to *denticles*.

J-624 • Nickel alloy • Broad planchet • Plain edge • Low Rarity-6
On obverse, 1 in 1868 closer to *denticles* than to *neck*.

J-625 • Nickel alloy • Reeded edge
Obverse die variety not known. Existence not confirmed by modern specialists.

J-626 • Copper • Plain edge • High Rarity-7
Obverse die variety not known.

J-627 • Copper • Broad planchet • Plain edge • Low Rarity-7
On obverse, 1 in 1868 closer to *denticles* than to *neck*.

J-628 • Copper • Broad planchet • Reeded edge • High Rarity-7
On obverse, 1 in 1868 closer to *denticles* than to *neck*.

J-629 • Aluminum • Plain edge • Rarity-8
Obverse die variety not known.

J-629a • Aluminum • Broad planchet • Plain edge
Obverse die variety not known. Existence not confirmed by modern specialists. This entry is based on a listing by Don Taxay.

Judd 630

Obverse: Coronet Head, no star, 1 (1868) closer to *neck* than to *denticles.*
Reverse: Reverse 1867-C (large V on shield with ornamented frame surrounding; IN GOD WE TRUST in small letters above).

The J-630 variety employs one of the two Coronet Head, no star, dies of 1868, this with the 1 in 1868 closer to the neck than to the denticles. The reverse die is the one used on Longacre's Indian Princess aluminum pattern of 1867.

J-630 • Nickel alloy • High Rarity-7

Judd 631

Obverse: Coronet Head, no star, 1 in 1868 closer to *neck* than to *denticles.*
Reverse: New design with thin laurel wreath enclosing V; at top of wreath, a small ribbon inscribed IN GOD WE TRUST; small Maltese cross in field above WE.

J-631 • Nickel alloy • Rarity-8

Judd 632 and 632a

Obverse: Coronet Head, no star, 1 in 1868 closer to *neck* than to *denticles.*
Reverse: Reverse 1867-D (large V within very heavy wreath of oak and olive, connected at the top by scrolls and ornamented with a six-pointed star).

J-632 • Copper • High Rarity-7

J-632a • Aluminum • Unique
Obverse die variety not known.

Judd 633 and 634

Obverse: Coronet Head, with star.
Reverse: New design as used on J-631 (thin laurel wreath enclosing V; atop wreath, a small ribbon inscribed IN GOD WE TRUST; small Maltese cross in field above WE).

J-633 introduces the 1868 Coronet Head die with star. Adding large stars to coronets seems to have been pleasing to Chief Engraver Longacre, for they are seen on many other pattern dies, ranging from the 1860 $5 gold piece (J-271) through the Standard Silver issues at the end of the decade. The reverse is new this year and is from a particularly well-executed die.

J-633 • Nickel alloy • Rarity-5

Certain of these were sold in cased sets for $9, with accompanying J-608 cent and J-618 three-cent piece (see Stack's Floyd Starr Collection sale).

J-634 • Copper • High Rarity-7

Judd 635 and 636

Obverse: Regular Proof dies of the year.

The die pair that was employed to strike J-635 (presumably) and J-636 was also used to make regular Proof coins this year. Illustrated is J-636 in aluminum.

J-635 • Copper

Reverse die characteristics not known. Existence not confirmed by modern specialists.

J-636 • Aluminum • Low Rarity-7

Reverse die 1866-Fb (regular design Without Rays as adopted in 1867; stars point under right serif of E and between A and M). Certain of these were issued as part of full aluminum Proof sets of 1868, some of which were distributed in cases.

Pattern Nickels of 1869

Chief Engraver James B. Longacre died on January 1, 1869, ending a career at the Mint that had commenced with his appointment on September 16, 1844. However, many of his dies were continued in use. He was soon succeeded in the post by William Barber, who held the position until his death in late summer 1879.

The Medal Department of the Mint went into even higher gear in 1869 with the production of numismatic delicacies for unofficial sale to collectors. However, most of this activity centered on the Standard Silver patterns of higher denominations, and just seven basic design combinations are known in the nickel series for this year, of which two are illogical double-headed mulings.

Five-Cent Die Combinations of 1869

Judd 683

Obverse: Coronet Head, with star.

Reverse: Reverse die 1867-C (large V on shield with ornamented frame surrounding; IN GOD WE TRUST in small letters above).

The obverse of J-683 features a Coronet Head with star in the tiara, while the reverse reprises a die used in 1867, then in combination with Longacre's Indian Princess design.

J-683 • Nickel alloy • Low Rarity-7

Judd 684 and 685

Obverse: Coronet Head, with star.

Reverse: Same die as used on J-631 and J-633 of 1868 (thin laurel wreath enclosing V; atop the wreath, a small ribbon inscribed IN GOD WE TRUST; small Maltese cross in field above WE).

J-684 combines the 1869 Coronet Head, with star, die with a reverse first used in 1868. This seems to be the only variety of 1869 pattern nickel five-cent piece made in quantity, probably over 100 pieces.

J-684 • Nickel alloy • Rarity-5

This is the only readily collectible pattern nickel of 1869, as the others are all rarities.

J-685 • Copper • Rarity-8

Judd 686

Obverse: Coronet Head, with star.

Reverse: Reverse die 1866-G (large 5 / CENTS in straight line; large open wreath enclosing 5 / CENTS, with CENTS in a straight line; IN GOD WE TRUST in small letters at top border).

J-686 • Nickel alloy

Existence not confirmed by modern specialists.

Judd 687–689

Obverse: Regular Shield nickel Proof dies of the year.

Reverse: Regular Shield nickel Proof dies of the year, but—for all metals in this group—very highly polished so as to remove some of the details of the letters, such as from the tops of D, S, S, F, and R in UNITED STATES OF AMERICA, and the bottom of the S in CENTS.

J-687 • Copper • Rarity-8

This reverse die, with broken letters, was also used to strike J-418 (1865), J-687 to 689 (1869), J-805 (1870), and regular 1870 Proof Shield nickels.

J-688 • Aluminum • High Rarity-7

A notation in the George D. Woodside Collection, April 23, 1892, under Lot 235, suggested that 15 full Proof sets were struck in aluminum from regular Proof dies.

J-689 • Steel or pure nickel • Unique

Judd 690

Obverse: Coronet Head, with star.

Reverse: Reverse die 1866-C (small wreath enclosing tall 5 with pointed top of numeral; UNITED STATES OF AMERICA around border).

J-690 • Nickel alloy

Existence not confirmed by modern specialists.

Judd 690a

Obverse: Coronet Head, with star.

Reverse: Obverse die 1866-2 (Washington portrait, *low* relief, facing right; IN GOD WE TRUST).

J-690a • Nickel alloy • Unique

Illogical two-headed muling. Not a Mint product. Ex Garrett Collection, March 1980, earlier from Haseltine's 1883 "Crosby sale." 96.8 grains.

Judd 691

Obverse: Regular Shield nickel Proof die of the year.

Reverse: Obverse die of an 1869 Indian Head cent.

J-691 • Nickel alloy • Unique

Illogical double-headed, double-denomination muling (possibly a Mint error?). A very curious coin! The pedigree includes the Jenks Collection (Cogan, April 1877), Lorin G. Parmelee Collection (N.Y. Coin & Stamp Co., 1890), Judson Brenner (who displayed it at the ANS in 1914), Waldo C. Newcomer, Fred Olsen, King Farouk, and Dr. James O. Sloss.

Pattern Nickels of 1870

The pattern nickels of this year consist of impressions from the regular Proof Shield nickel dies of the year. Relating to patterns in general, this commentary—E.B. Mason Jr.'s review of his recent Fewsmith Collection sale—appeared in *Mason's Coin & Stamp Collector's Magazine*, (vol. 4, November 1870):

> The result of the public sale of the Fewsmith cabinet of coins and medals, in New York, last month, was satisfactory to owners and purchasers; if we except the pattern pieces, which were slaughtered in cold blood! *Purchasers*, no doubt, were pleased at the latter result; but, as *owners*, we protest earnestly against the *cause* which produced this *effect*.
>
> Pattern pieces coming from a private collection formed by nearly a lifetime of anxious care, should not be classed (as they were in the case of this coin sale), with pieces *said to be* recently struck, surreptitiously, at the United States Mint. "Down with the patterns," has been the numismatic war-cry with those who fortunately disposed of all such pieces previous to taking up arms against them.
>
> We assert, that the day will come when pattern pieces will command fabulous prices; already they have touched bottom in regard to price and rebounded at least twenty-five percent higher than prices realized at the last public sale. Here, in Philadelphia, we know the truth in regard to pattern pieces; we know that the dies of all such pieces are destroyed up to 1869;[21] and we know further that nearly all the patterns thrown upon the market have come from the collections disposed of by auction and otherwise; including the cabinets of Randall, Haseltine, Thatcher, Hodge and Fewsmith. The supply will one day fall short of the demand, and lucky is he, who, disregarding the false reports of large quantities of pattern pieces in circulation for a market, has quietly snapped up the bargains recently offered by public sales and "salted" them for future speculative purposes.

Five-Cent Die Combinations of 1870

Judd 805–808

Obverse: Regular Proof dies of the year.

Reverse: The same die, with broken letters, that was used to strike J-418 (1865), J-687 to 689 (1869), J-805 (1870), and regular 1870 Proof Shield nickels.

J-805 is simply a striking in copper (or bronze) from the regular Proof Shield nickel dies of the year. Several letters on the reverse are broken or incomplete, due to overpolishing.

J-805 • Copper • High Rarity-7

J-806 • Aluminum • Rarity-8

J-807 • Nickel alloy • Very thin planchet • Rarity-7

Possibly a mint error, not a pattern. The reverse is *not* from the die with broken letters.

J-808 • Steel or pure nickel • Unique

Pattern Nickels of 1871

The nickel patterns of this year include runs with two different Coronet Head obverses, both with the same portrait punch and wreath punch, but J-1050 to 1052a on a broader die (giving more open field area), and J-1053 to 1055 on a narrower die.[22]

Five-Cent Die Combinations of 1871

Judd 1050–1052a

Obverse: Coronet Head. The 1 in 1871 is midway between neck tip and denticles.
Reverse: Laurel wreath enclosing V / CENTS, the V being erroneously shaded on the right, rather than on the left, and presenting a curious appearance. J-1050 through 1052a are all larger diameter than J-1053 through 1055.

The J-1050 pattern is especially popular due to the backward-shaded V on the reverse. Quite a few (probably more than 100) of these were made, making them readily collectible today (in the context of generally scarce patterns).

J-1050 • Nickel alloy • Low Rarity-6

J-1051 • Copper • Low Rarity-6

J-1052 • Aluminum • Low Rarity-7

J-1052a • Aluminum • Broader planchet • Unique

Reported to be at the Connecticut State Library, but not examined by specialists.[23]

Judd 1053–1055

Obverse: Coronet Head, different die. The 1 in 1871 is high and very close to neck tip. There are other topological differences from the preceding (J-1050 to 1052a), including smaller planchets.
Reverse: Laurel wreath enclosing 5 / CENTS, the last letters in a curve. Same wreath features as on J-1050 to 1052a.

J-1053 and related issues are from a different obverse die with the date high and with different spacing of other features. The portrait punch is unfinished, and there are raised lines on the neck. The obverse field is not completely finished, either. On the reverse the wreath is similar to the preceding, but with different lettering.

J-1053 • Nickel alloy • Low Rarity-6

J-1054 • Copper • Low Rarity-6

J-1055 • Aluminum • Low Rarity-7

Judd 1056–1058

Obverse: Regular Proof Shield nickel dies of the year.
Reverse: Regular Proof Shield nickel dies of the year; reverse letters not broken, unlike 1870.

J-1056 • Copper • Rarity-8

J-1057 • Aluminum • Rarity-8

J-1058 • Steel or pure nickel • Unique
An example was owned by Judson Brenner circa 1913.

Pattern Nickels of 1872

The only patterns for 1872 are off-metal strikes from regular Shield nickel Proof dies.

Judd 1189 and 1190

Obverse and Reverse: Regular Proof Shield nickel dies of the year.

J-1189 • Copper • High Rarity-7

J-1190 • Aluminum • Rarity-8

Pattern Nickels of 1873

The only patterns for 1873 are off-metal strikes from regular Shield nickel Proof dies.

Judd 1264 and 1265

Obverse and Reverse: Regular Proof Shield nickel dies of the year with Closed 3 in date.

J-1264 is a striking in copper from the regular Proof dies of the year with Closed 3 in the date.

J-1264 • Copper • High Rarity-7

J-1265 • Aluminum • Rarity-8

Pattern Nickels of 1874

The only patterns for 1874 are off-metal strikes from regular Shield nickel Proof dies.

Judd 1350 and 1351

Obverse and Reverse: Regular Proof Shield nickel dies of the year.

J-1350 • Copper • Rarity-8

J-1351 • Aluminum • Rarity-8

Pattern Nickels of 1875

The only patterns for 1875 are off-metal strikes from regular Shield nickel Proof dies.

Judd 1387 and 1388

Obverse and Reverse: Regular Proof Shield nickel dies of the year.

J-1387, a copper impression from regular Proof dies of the year, was distributed, at least in part, with copper Proof sets that included the gold denominations.

J-1387 • Copper • High Rarity-7

J-1388 • Aluminum • High Rarity-7

Pattern Nickels of 1881

In 1881 the focus was on creating a uniform set of Liberty Head designs for the cent, three-cent piece, and nickel five-cent piece, the background of which effort is given in chapter 7. Charles E. Barber, who in 1880 had succeeded his late father in the post of chief engraver, created the obverse motif, featuring what eventually became a famous portrait on the Liberty Head nickels of 1883 and later. In the meantime, pattern issues with varying obverse inscriptions were created. Two reverses are known to have been paired with Liberty Head obverses in 1881.

This inaugurated an illustrious series of pattern nickels that extended through 1883.

Five-Cent Die Combinations of 1881

Judd 1671–1673

Obverse: Liberty Head. UNITED STATES OF AMERICA / 1881 around the border. ***Reverse:*** Open wreath of wheat and cotton enclosing the Roman numeral V.

The J-1671 is important in the chronicle of nickel five-cent pieces, as it represents the beginning of an extensive series of patterns that led to the regular-issue Liberty Head nickel of 1883.

J-1671 • Nickel alloy • High Rarity-6

Produced in fair quantities for a pattern, J-1671 is regularly offered today.

J-1672 • Copper • High Rarity-6

J-1673 • Aluminum • Low Rarity-7

Judd 1674a

Obverse: Liberty Head. UNITED STATES OF AMERICA / 1881 around the border.
Reverse: Similar to that for J-1671 through 1673, but with IN GOD WE TRUST in small letters above the wreath.

J-1674a • Nickel alloy • Unique
In the Smithsonian Institution. This reverse die created a rarity in 1881, but was liberally used in 1882.

Pattern Nickels of 1882

The diversity of the patterns of 1882 reflects the early years of the denomination, such as 1866 and 1867. However, this time around there are fewer "impossible" rarities and numismatic delicacies. Although some metal variations are rare, a basic set of most of the die combinations is a realistic pursuit for the specialist.

Emphasis continues on Charles E. Barber's Liberty Head, again with various treatments of stars and inscriptions. The first die described, with UNITED STATES OF AMERICA around (used on J-1675–1686), exists in at least two die varieties, one on which the 1 in 1882 touches the neck, the other on which it does not touch the neck. Some Judd varieties, such as J-1677, are known from both dies; this is the first publication of the differences, and little is known as to the distribution of the dies across the issues.

Several reverse dies were used. An especially popular transitional pattern (J-1690) features the obverse and reverse style as actually adopted in the year following, 1883. Two rare varieties of this year, J-1683 and J-1697, have five raised ridges on their edges and are known as the *Blind Man's Nickel.*

Five-Cent Die Combinations of 1882

Judd 1675 and 1676

Obverse: Liberty Head by Charles E. Barber; UNITED STATES OF AMERICA / 1882 around the border.
Reverse: Die used for J-1671 in 1881 (open wreath of wheat and cotton enclosing Roman numeral V).

J-1675 • Nickel alloy • Rarity-8
Three known, per Saul Teichman. The one in the Garrett II sale, March 1980, sold for $10,000. T. Harrison Garrett had purchased it from the collection of Dr. Edward Maris. 78.1 grains.

J-1676 • Copper • Unique
Die not examined. In the Lenox R. Lohr Collection, 1960, Bowers and Merena, 2005, at $46,000.

Judd 1677–1679

Obverse: Liberty Head style by Charles E. Barber; UNITED STATES OF AMERICA / 1882 around the border.
Reverse: Similar to that for J-1675 and 1676, but with IN GOD WE TRUST in small letters above the wreath. This die was used on J-1674a of 1881.

J-1677 combines an 1882 Liberty Head die similar to that of 1881, with UNITED STATES OF AMERICA surrounding. The reverse die is from 1881 and has the motto IN GOD WE TRUST.

J-1677 • Nickel alloy • Low Rarity-7

J-1678 • Copper • Low Rarity-7
Die not examined.

J-1679 • Aluminum • Low Rarity-7
The 1 in 1882 touches the neck.

Judd 1680–1683

Obverse: Liberty Head style as for J-1677 through 1679.
Reverse: Open wreath of wheat and cotton enclosing the Roman numeral V, with E PLURIBUS UNUM in small letters above the wreath; 22 mm average diameter. Concerning denticles see commentary under J-1684.

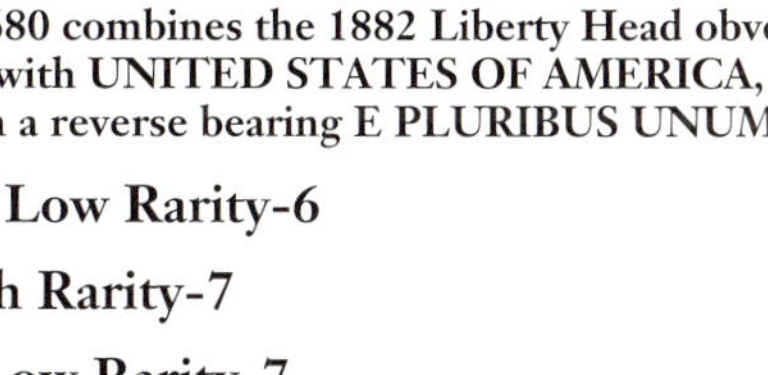

J-1680 combines the 1882 Liberty Head obverse die with UNITED STATES OF AMERICA, with a reverse bearing E PLURIBUS UNUM.

J-1680 • Nickel alloy • Low Rarity-6

J-1681 • Copper • High Rarity-7

J-1682 • Aluminum • Low Rarity-7

J-1683 • Nickel alloy • Rarity-8
Five equally spaced bars or ridges on the outer edge. The first variety of the so-called Blind Man's Nickel (also see J-1697). The curious edge of this variety in combination with its nickname have made this a numismatic favorite for a long time. It might be a point of debate today as to whether an example should be encapsulated in a holder where the edge cannot be seen. One is in the Mitchelson Collection, Connecticut State Library.

Judd 1684–1686

Obverse and Reverse: Dies similar to the preceding (J-1680–1683) but with smaller denticles at the borders of the obverse and reverse. Average diameter 21 mm. The aspect of denticle length on J-1684 through 1686 in comparison to J-1680 through 1683 has been studied only lightly.

J-1684 • Nickel alloy • Low Rarity-6

J-1685 • Copper • Rarity-8

J-1686 • Aluminum • High Rarity-7
One coin attributed as "J-1686" has long denticles on the obverse and short denticles on the reverse.

Judd 1687–1689

Obverse: Liberty Head by Charles E. Barber (IN GOD WE TRUST above; seven stars left; six stars right; date 1882 below; head high on the coin, distant from lower border, allowing more space for the date).
Reverse: Open wreath of cotton and corn enclosing Roman numeral V, UNITED STATES OF AMERICA / E PLURIBUS UNUM around border. This Without CENTS reverse die is the same used for some Proof regular issues in early 1883. The S in PLURIBUS repunched on all.

The obverse of J-1687 has stars and IN GOD WE TRUST around the obverse border. The reverse die is the style of the regular Without CENTS nickel of 1883 and is from the same die used to produce a few of the regular-issue 1883 Proofs, being distinguished by having the S (PLURIBUS) sharply repunched to the right.

J-1687 • Nickel alloy • Low Rarity-6

J-1688 • Copper • Unique
The only citation located by Saul Teichman is in the Thomas L. Elder sale of October 17, 1908, Lot 227, with a handwritten notation that it is in copper.

J-1689 • Aluminum • Rarity-7

Judd 1690–1692

Obverse: Liberty Head by Charles E. Barber (13 stars surrounding, date below; type adopted in 1883, but with slight differences in the position of the stars).
Reverse: Same die as for J-1687 through 1689; "Without CENTS" adopted in 1883 and used on some Proofs of this year. Repunched S in PLURIBUS.

Famous and highly desired transitional pattern. The Garrett II coin, March 1980, soared to $19,000. Walter Breen, in his 1988 *Encyclopedia*, comments: "Specimens of this adopted design, dated 1882, went to [Secretary of the Treasury] Folger and various other officials, who spent them, kept them for pocket pieces, or possibly used them for barroom betting; whatever the reason, most survivors are circulated." While *some* survivors are circulated, most seen are PF-60 or finer, with PF-63 being typical. Diameters of certain reported examples vary from 21.0 mm to 21.1 mm, or slightly smaller than the 22 mm later used on regular Liberty Head nickels.[24]

One of the most famous and most desired patterns in the nickel series, although not a great rarity, is J-1690, the transitional issue with obverse and reverse style of the 1883 Liberty Head nickel Without CENTS.

J-1690 • Nickel alloy • Rarity-5

J-1691 • Copper • High Rarity-6

J-1692 • Aluminum • Rarity-7

JUDD 1693–1696

Obverse: Shield nickel design, modified to remove the ball from the base of the shield in an effort to extend the life of the dies.[25]
Reverse: Regular die of the year.

J-1693 is similar to the regular-issue Shield nickel except that there is no ball above the date. The reverse is from a regular Proof die of the era.

J-1693 • Nickel alloy • Rarity-7

J-1694 • Copper • Low Rarity-7

J-1694a • Copper • Thin, small planchet (a cent planchet?) • Rarity-8
This has not been examined by modern scholars. An example from the Farouk Collection was sold by Superior Galleries in the Walter Lee Crouch Collection sale, June 1977.

J-1695 • Aluminum • Rarity-7

J-1696 • White metal • Unique
Ex Judson Brenner, loan to the ANS Exhibition, 1914; later in the Major Lenox R. Lohr Collection, there described as "oxidized."

Judd 1697

Obverse and Reverse: Regular Proof dies of the year, but with five raised ridges on the edge, second variety of the "Blind Man's Nickel" (also see J-1683).

J-1697 • Nickel alloy • High Rarity-7

Don Taxay, in *Scott's Comprehensive Catalogue* (1971), stated that just three were struck. One was in J.W. Haseltine's March 1883 sale. These were never openly distributed to collectors. One is in the Mitchelson Collection, Connecticut State Library.

Pattern Nickels of 1883

The year 1883 is particularly remarkable for its interesting panorama of pattern nickels. All feature Barber's Liberty Head designs, but some have variations in the star placements and inscriptions. The reverses include four that state their metallic compositions, but in actuality many were made in alloys different from the inscriptions. Elemental analyses have not been conducted by modern scholars, and the composition of the alloys actually used is not known for those that have a general appearance of nickel.[26] The possibilities of variant metals are exemplified by the obvious J-1706, stated to be PURE / NICKEL, but struck in aluminum! Shenanigans were still going on at the Mint, and coins such as this were never available to collectors directly. Instead, supplies were privately sold by Mint officials through dealers, most notably John W. Haseltine of Philadelphia.

A few patterns were indeed struck in pure nickel and can be differentiated from nickel alloy in that pure nickel coins are magnetic. Certain patterns with the regular Without CENTS reverse are from an early hub (see note under J-1714).

Judd 1704–1706

Obverse: Liberty Head by Charles E. Barber. UNITED STATES OF AMERICA / 1883 around the border.

Reverse: Open wreath of wheat and cotton enclosing PURE / NICKEL. Around border: FIVE above, CENTS below, seven stars left, and six stars right.

J-1704 is the first of four reverse-die combinations using Barber's pattern 1883 Liberty Head die, UNITED STATES OF AMERICA surrounding, with a reverse die lettered PURE / NICKEL. No comment is needed on why certain of these were struck in *aluminum*!

J-1704 • Pure nickel (magnetic) • Low Rarity-6

Weight about 81 grains. Apparently, these were given out in fair numbers, for examples in nickel are the most often seen of this die combination.

J-1705 • Nickel alloy • Unique

Only one example, ex Dr. Judd Collection, is recorded by Andrew W. Pollock III in his study.

J-1706 • Aluminum • High Rarity-7

Judd 1706a

Obverse: Same die as for J-1704 through J-1706.

Reverse: The regular Without CENTS die introduced this year.

J-1706a • Nickel alloy • Unique

Judd 1707–1709

Obverse: Same die as for J-1704 through J-1706.

Reverse: Open wreath of wheat and cotton enclosing 75 N. / 25 C. Around border: FIVE above, CENTS below, seven stars left, and six stars right.

J-1707 combines the Liberty Head die as preceding with a reverse lettered 75 N. / 25 C., a composition that would have warmed the heart of Joseph Wharton had it been adopted.

J-1707 • Pure nickel (magnetic) • Low Rarity-6

Average weight is about 88 grains.

J-1708 • Nickel alloy • High Rarity-7

J-1709 • Aluminum • High Rarity-7

Judd 1710 and 1711

Obverse: Same die as for J-1704 through J-1706.

Reverse: Open wreath of wheat and cotton enclosing 50 N. / 50 C. Around border: FIVE above, CENTS below, seven stars left, and six stars right.

The reverse of J-1710 suggests an alloy of half nickel and half copper.

J-1710 • Nickel alloy • Rarity-5

J-1711 • Aluminum • Low Rarity-7

Judd 1711a

Obverse: Regular Liberty Head die of the year.
Reverse: As preceding, with open wreath of wheat and cotton enclosing 50 N. / 50 C. Around border: FIVE above, CENTS below, seven stars left, and six stars right.

J-1711a • Nickel alloy • Unique

Judd 1712 and 1713

Obverse: Same die as for J-1704 through J-1706.
Reverse: Open wreath of wheat and cotton enclosing 33 N. / 67 C. Around border: FIVE above, CENTS below, seven stars left, and six stars right.

The last of four dies in this interesting series was used on J-1712 and is inscribed 33 N. / 67 C.

J-1712 • Nickel alloy • Low Rarity-6

J-1713 • Aluminum • High Rarity-7

Judd 1714–1716

Obverse: Charles E. Barber's head of Liberty wearing a necessarily *plain* coronet so as not to be redundant with the word LIBERTY appcaring above the head and near the border. Six stars left and seven stars right, date 1883 below.
Reverse: Regular die of the year without CENTS, but early hub variation with long leaf over upper left of V, with the upright of the R in AMERICA placed so that, if extended downward, it would touch the point of a leaf.

J-1714 has no inscription on the coronet, so as not to be redundant with LIBERTY at the border. The reverse is the style of the regular 1883 Without CENTS.

J-1714 • Nickel alloy • Low Rarity-6

J-1715 • Copper • High Rarity-7

J-1716 • Aluminum • High Rarity-7

Judd 1717–1719

Obverse: Regular Liberty Head die of the year.
Reverse: Similar to the regular issue, but with the word CENTS added on a curved ribbon across the V. This reverse must have been a very early proposal to correct the omission of the word CENTS on coins made for circulation, a situation that had led certain people to gold-plate pieces and pass them as $5 gold coins.

The J-1717 to 1719 patterns are particularly significant, for although they incorporate the word CENTS on the reverse, its style differs from that soon adopted for regular coinage. This is a rare aluminum striking of the die combination J-1719.

J-1717 • Nickel alloy • High Rarity-6

J-1718 • Copper • Unique

J-1719 • Aluminum • Rarity-7

Judd 1719a

Obverse: Regular Liberty Head die of the year.
Reverse: Variation of the regular die With CENTS.

J-1719a • Copper • Unique
July 1989, Auction '89, Stack's, Lot 1856. Cleaned, according to Tom DeLorey.[27]

Judd 1720

Obverse: Regular Liberty Head die of the year.
Reverse: Similar to regular style With CENTS, but with differences, including bent-back tassels in relation to the tops of the arms of V, and the position of the I in PLURIBUS in relation to the upright of the E in STATES; a different die from that used for J-1719a.

J-1720 • Aluminum • Rarity-8
Seeking this reverse die on a regular Proof impression struck in nickel alloy might be rewarding!

Pattern Nickels of 1884

The pattern scenario for this year features one-cent and five-cent pieces popularly known as the Eastman Johnson "holey designs," from the hole at the center. Eastman Johnson was an artist of the era, and these apparently followed certain of his suggestions made in the form of sketches in May 1879. The holes in the coins were intended to make them more easily distinguishable from higher denominations and thereby "remedy the inconvenience of similarity in our small coin."

Johnson (1824–1906), with a Maine family heritage, worked as an artist in New York and Paris for about half a century and did many paintings relating to American life. At the 1876 Centennial Exhibition held in Philadelphia he displayed paintings (*What the Sea Says*, *The Prisoner of State*, and *The Old Stage-Coach*) in group 27, a category of various art and architectural items. He was given an award (as were most exhibitors, simply for exhibiting!), his being titled, "Artistic excellence in genre." Earlier, some of his pieces were adapted to prints by Currier & Ives.

The "holey" cents and nickels were struck on perforated planchets; metal was squeezed inward during the minting process and created holes of irregular outline. It is doubtful whether there was any serious interest in issuing circulating coins with perforated centers, as decades earlier such patterns had caused problems in planchet preparation and striking. However, now and again the Mint produced pieces following the usually naive suggestions of outsiders (Dana Bickford's $10 coin of 1874 being another example). Likely, the "holey" coins were made for private profit (to dispel any lingering doubt, see commentary under the "improved" version of 1885).

Copper strikings from Proof dies are reported of this year's various denominations, including the rare trade dollar, but no citation has been found for a five-cent piece.

Judd 1724–1726

Obverse: FIVE above, CENTS below, shield to each side. Open field at center with an irregular perforation.
Reverse: UNITED STATES OF AMERICA / 1884 around border enclosing circle of 13 stars. Open field at center enclosing irregular perforation.

The several metallic versions, here aluminum, of J-1725 (Eastman Johnson's "holey nickel" proposal), would seem to have no logical basis. As with other patterns in the series, such coins are eagerly desired by numismatists.

J-1724 • Nickel alloy • Low Rarity-6

"Holey nickel." One example is said to have been struck on a thin planchet.

J-1725 • Aluminum • Low Rarity-7

J-1726 • White Metal • Unique

Important variation of the preceding, with raised rims around a circular hole. Ex Judson Brenner (coin illustrated in the 1914 ANS Exhibition catalog), later in the Farouk Collection, there purchased by Abe Kosoff, 1954.

Pattern Nickels of 1885

Patterns for the 1885 represent the swan song of Mint-created rarities for no other purpose than to enrich the officials involved. Now we have an "improved" version of Eastman Johnson's illogical "holey" proposal, but with the perforations uniform and surrounded with interior rims containing denticles, and struck in *silver*. To put the icing on the cake, the other pattern this year is from regular Proof dies, but struck in aluminum.

In July 1885 James P. Kimball became director of the Mint, and the secret fun and games that had begun in the spring of 1859 under Director James Ross Snowden, and had continued uninterruptedly through several changes of officers since that time, came to a quiet end. More than just a few of the rarities from this era remained "underground" for a long time and were not disclosed until the early 20th century, by John W. Haseltine and his then business partner, Stephen K. Nagy (later of 1913 Liberty Head nickel connection).

Judd 1742

Obverse: Similar to *reverse* of J-1724 of 1884, but with date 1885. UNITED STATES OF AMERICA / 1885 around border enclosing circle of 13 stars. Open field at center except for border of denticles surrounding perforation.
Reverse: FIVE CENTS above, shield flanked by branches below. Open field at center except for border of denticles surrounding perforation

J-1742 • Silver • High Rarity-6
"Holey nickel." Said to have been struck on a thin planchet, not seen by Saul Teichman, in addition to the regular thickness.

Judd 1743

Obverse and Reverse: Struck from regular Proof dies.

Without doubt, J-1743 has to be the crème de la crème of off-metal strikings in the nickel series, combining as it does the popular date of 1885 (a key issue in the regular series) with great rarity. This marks the end of the "numismatic delicacies" secretly made at the Mint and privately sold into the market.

J-1743 • Aluminum • Rarity-8

PATTERN NICKELS OF 1896

The patterns of 1896 comprise two different denominations, each with a single die-design combination, but in die varieties among those designs, and also in a bewildering array of metal possibilities (more than a dozen alloys). The dies were by Charles E. Barber. Each featured a shield design on the obverse and a wreath on the reverse, a motif not particularly attractive to the modern eye, and certainly not seriously considered for replacing the Liberty Head nickel (also by Barber, and generally considered to be among his better works) in use at the time. These were engendered by a House resolution (passed June 9, 1896) requesting the Secretary of the Treasury to report on the advantages and disadvantages of various alloys, and to authorize the making of patterns as necessary.

In compliance with the resolution, the Mint struck experimental one- and five-cent pieces from pure nickel; pure aluminum; an alloy of 66% copper, 18% nickel, and 16% zinc; and three different aluminum alloys. These technical aspects of the alloys are reported in the Judd text;[28] the upshot of these experiments seems to be that the aluminum alloys were too soft, and the pure nickel, too hard. Further experimentation revealed that the main problem with nickel was that the blanks hadn't been correctly annealed. When annealed properly, the blanks were "malleable and received the impression from dies without any pressure greater than that required to strike the regular-issue minor coins."[29]

Although hundreds of pattern cents and nickels were ultimately produced, few reached numismatic circles until years later. In 1909 a large group of remainders was part of an exchange involving A. Loudon Snowden (and/or the Mint itself), John Haseltine, and William H. Woodin. Woodin turned over to the Mint Collection the two die varieties, each unique, of the $50 gold "half union" coins of 1877 that he had recently acquired from Haseltine and Stephen K. Nagy. Per Haseltine, the coins supposedly traced their pedigrees to the William Idler estate—but as Haseltine often distorted the truth, and as documents from this era can be misleading, that may not have been the case. At least one of those half union coins had been part of the Mint Cabinet until 1893, when *Haseltine* had persuaded the curator (R.A. McClure) to deaccession it (i.e., remove it from the collection and sell it) and to use the money for other things.

Woodin's possession of the half unions—both presumed to have been former Mint Cabinet treasures—had been considered outrageous by many. In reply to a letter from U.S. Attorney Henry W. Wise, Woodin's attorney gave an "official" summary of the situation. On June 7, 1910, Woodin's attorney wrote:

> Col. Snowden, who had originally purchased these coins from the Director of the Mint in Philadelphia by depositing the bullion value and the charge for pattern pieces to save them from being melted down, in the course of negotiations between himself and Dr. [A. Piatt] Andrew, Director of the Mints, came to an agreement with the latter over all matters in dispute between them, and proposed to Mr. Woodin to repay him the $20,000 he had paid for these pieces, in order that he might carry out his arrangement with Dr. Andrew.
>
> Mr. Woodin after numerous visits to Philadelphia and Washington and conference with Dr. Andrew, both there and in this city, decided to accept this offer, returned the 50's to Col. Snowden, and I thereupon notified Mr. Pratt, as did Mr. Woodin, that the incident was closed, and we requested a letter from your office

> confirming the same. In view of the trouble and expense to which Mr. Woodin was put to facilitate Dr. Andrew in the adjustment of a very difficult situation, your letter seems a little unfair, in that it would tend to create the appearance of a record some time in the future that Mr. Woodin had been compelled to give up something of which he was improperly in possession.[30]

However, others such as Stephen K. Nagy and Robert K. Botsford recalled that Woodin had also received thousands of unsold pattern coins—some dating back to Gobrecht issues restruck from the late 1850's to the 1870's—in the exchange. Further, the above correspondence does not explain how the two half unions, with a stated value totaling $20,000, had found their way back into the Mint Cabinet.

Botsford, a well-known dealer in Nescopeck, Pennsylvania, knew Woodin personally, and told me that Woodin had acquired quantities of unsold issues. R.W. Julian suggests that these patterns may have come from Colonel A. Loudon Snowden, erstwhile director of the Mint, which seems logical enough. As to whether there was an exchange of $20,000, after which Woodin bought the cache of patterns, or exactly what happened, will probably never be known.

Though many pieces from this remarkable hoard were sold by Woodin himself (and furnished the raison d'être or his 1913 book on patterns with Edgar H. Adams), a large quantity remained in his estate after his death on May 4, 1934. These coins went to F.C.C. Boyd, Abe Kosoff, and, residually, to Botsford. Curiously, some varieties that were called *unique* in the 1913 book were represented by multiple examples in the Woodin estate! Hundreds of the 1896 patterns were sold in the 1940's and early 1950's.

The following listing is simplified; for specific alloys coined, see the ninth edition of Judd (pp. 260–261).[31]

Five-Cent Die Combinations of 1896

Judd 1770–1772

Obverse: Charles E. Barber's design. At the center is a shield, across which is a ribbon inscribed LIBERTY, incuse. Crossed poles behind support a liberty cap and an eagle. E PLURIBUS UNUM above, 1896 below, seven stars left, six right, all within circle of dots.
Reverse: Olive wreath enclosing 5 / CENTS. Around the border inside a circle of dots is UNITED STATES OF AMERICA.

Many different alloys were used for this die combination. J-1770, shown here, was made in pure nickel.

J-1770 • Pure nickel (magnetic) • Low Rarity-6

J-1771 • Aluminum alloy • Low Rarity-6

An example subjected to elemental analysis yielded this content: aluminum 88%, nickel 2.7%, copper 2.5%, manganese 2.2%, zinc 1.8%, silicon 1.6%, iron 0.6%, silver 0.4%.[32]

J-1771a • Copper • High Rarity-7

J-1772 • Aluminum • High Rarity-6
Many of these from the Woodin estate are somewhat oxidized from damp storage.

Patterns of 1909

At the Mint, thought was given to revising the design of the five-cent piece, under the new administration of President William Howard Taft. Against the wishes of Chief Engraver Charles E. Barber, the previous administration (Roosevelt's) had sought designs for coin motifs from several private-sector artists, notably Augustus Saint-Gaudens for the $10 and $20 coins of 1907, Bela Lyon Pratt for the $2.50 and $5 coins of 1908, and Victor D. Brenner for the new 1909 Lincoln cent.

In 1909, Mint Director Frank A. Leach saw the portrait of George Washington as the logical choice for another change in the design of a denomination—the five-cent piece.[33] Director Leach was an admirer of Barber's work (obviously a happy circumstance for the chief engraver). Barber would be replacing his own Liberty Head nickel motif with another of his own designs, so the situation promised to be more pleasant than if an outside artist were to be hired.

Barber created a preliminary design (seemingly hasty in its conception), modeled after the 1896 pattern nickel, then seven versions of Washington portrait coins. It seemed that such coins could be ready for circulation by the end of 1909, and some newspaper notices appeared to that effect. Leach resigned in July 1909, however, effectively ending the matter (although a related pattern nickel would be made in 1910).

The patterns of 1909 were struck in very small numbers. These coins were saved from destruction by numismatist William H. Woodin, who had seen them during a visit with Leach's successor, Mint Director A. Piatt Andrew, in the summer of 1910, and who wrote on June 13, 1911, to Andrew's successor, Director George E. Roberts:

> May I be permitted to offer a suggestion in regard to some designs of nickels that have been executed by Mr. Charles Barber, in the Mint in Philadelphia? In company with Dr. Andrew, a year ago, last summer, I had the pleasure of seeing these, and I understand that none of them have been placed in the Mint cabinet in Philadelphia.
>
> Whether these designs are accepted or not, it seems to me very important that one specimen of each design should be placed in the coin cabinet, as these pieces were designed by the chief engraver and coiner of the United States Mint, and a metallic record of this ought to be put in the government's pattern collection. I am emboldened to write this to you for fear that these pieces might be destroyed.

Accordingly, examples were preserved in the Mint Cabinet. Today they are part of the National Numismatic Collection at the Smithsonian Institution. No Washington-head five-cent pieces were ever made for circulation.

Five-Cent Die Combinations of 1909

Judd 1933

Obverse: Charles E. Barber's design. Shield in the center with a scroll across inscribed LIBERTY (incuse), crossed poles behind supporting a liberty cap on one and eagle on the other, 13 stars around, date 1909 below.

Reverse: Olive wreath enclosing 5 / CENTS, UNITED STATES OF AMERICA above at border, E PLURIBUS UNUM at bottom border in very small letters. Stylistically similar to the reverse of J-1770 of 1896.

This is the only known example surviving from what must have been a limited coinage of J-1933. Chief Engraver Charles E. Barber produced these and several other varieties, in what is thought to have been an effort to dissuade the Treasury Department from seeking an outside artist to redesign the nickel.

J-1933 • Nickel alloy • Unique

Judd 1934

Obverse: Bust of George Washington facing right, LIBERTY above in small letters, date 1909 below, seven stars left, six stars right. Obverses vary among J-1934 through J-1936, as noted.

Reverse: Olive wreath enclosing 5 / CENTS, UNITED STATES OF AMERICA above at border with E PLURIBUS UNUM at bottom border in very small letters. Stylistically similar to the reverse of J-1770 of 1896.

J-1934, Chief Engraver Barber's idea of what George Washington should look like on a five-cent piece.

J-1934 • Nickel alloy • Unique

Judd 1935

Obverse: Similar to that for J-1934, but with date smaller.

Reverse: Same die as that for J-1934.

J-1935 • Nickel alloy • Unique

Judd 1936

Obverse: Similar to that for J-1935, but with LIBERTY to right at border in front of bust.
Reverse: Same die as that for J-1934.

J-1936 • Nickel alloy • Unique

Judd 1937

Obverse: Similar to that for J-1934, but with L**I**B**E**R**T**Y* at border.
Reverse: Same die as that for J-1934.

J-1937, another Barber concept for Washington, this one perhaps setting a record for the spacing of the word LIBERTY around the border of a coin.

J-1937 • Nickel alloy • Unique

Judd 1938

Obverse: Large bust of Washington facing left, 1909 in front of bust, LIBERTY behind at border.
Reverse: Same die as that for J-1934.

J-1938, another Barber creation, has Washington facing to the left.

J-1938 • Nickel alloy • Unique

Judd 1939

Obverse: Similar to that for J-1938, but with date in different style.
Reverse: Large outlined 5, crossed by the word CENTS, within two laurel branches. At top border is UNITED STATES OF AMERICA, with E PLURIBUS UNUM beneath in smaller letters.

J-1939 is similar to the preceding, but has the date differently styled.

J-1939 • Nickel alloy • Rarity-8
Two known, both in the Smithsonian Institution.

Patterns of 1910

In 1910 a pattern nickel five-cent piece was struck, an adaptation of a style by Charles E. Barber used in 1909 (J-1939), but with different placement of the date.

Judd 1942

Obverse: Large bust of Washington facing left, LIBERTY at border in front of bust, 1910 at border to right.
Reverse: Large outlined 5, crossed by the word CENTS, within two laurel branches. At border, UNITED STATES OF AMERICA, with E PLURIBUS UNUM beneath in smaller letters. IN GOD WE TRUST in minute letters at bottom of border.

J-1942 has resemblances to J-1939, but with different arrangement of the obverse letters and with the date 1910.

J-1942 • Nickel alloy • Rarity-8
Two known, both in the Smithsonian Institution.

APPENDIX

B

Shield and Liberty Head Nickel Mint Errors

Mint errors in the Shield and Liberty Head nickel series are fairly scarce in comparison to those of the later Buffalo and (in particular) Jefferson nickel errors. Most often seen are off-center strikings, such as a Liberty Head nickel with part of the design off the planchet, and with areas of blank planchet still remaining.

Most of the pieces illustrated here are courtesy of specialist Fred Weinberg, as are the descriptions.[1] As very few mint errors are the same, the valuations given here are apt to vary in actual transactions. The Combined Organizations of Numismatic Error Collectors of America (CONECA) publishes *Errorscope*, and is a meeting place for those interested in this specialty.

1866 Shield nickel With Rays, struck 50% off-center. EF-45 (PCGS). Although not quite as rare as off-metals, off-center Shield nickels are quite hard to find, and the nice example here is one of very few far off-center pieces known. Because mechanical errors were neither appreciated nor fully understood in the 19th century, they were not saved by numismatists at that time. Many of the known off-centers of 5% to 20% are well circulated, although a few high-grade examples do exist.

1866 Shield nickel With Rays, struck 25% off-center. VF-35 (NGC). This example is a variation on the preceding theme, but not as much off center. (Private collection)

1873 Shield nickel struck on a bronze one-cent planchet. MS-62 (PCGS). This beautiful example of an off-metal strike is from the Zabriskie Sale of 1909 (Henry Chapman Auction); it later reappeared in the Olsen Sale conducted by B. Max Mehl, and went into the King Farouk collection. Off-metal Shield nickels are extremely rare, with only 8 to 10 reported on cent, three-cent, or half dime planchets. The pattern listed as J-807 (see appendix A) may be an error of this type, on a nickel three-cent-piece planchet.

1893 Liberty Head nickel, double struck. MS-64 (PCGS). Never the most popular design for nickel-error collectors, Liberty nickels do exist in off-metal and off-center strikes ranging in grades from VG to choice Mint State. This 1893 nickel was struck a second time, 85% off-center, and is a high-grade Mint State example.

1906 Liberty Head nickel struck on a bronze one-cent planchet. MS-63. There are approximately two dozen known Liberty Head nickels struck on cent planchets, and these range in grade from Fine to MS-63. More easily found are the Liberty Head nickels struck on slightly smaller, nickel five-centavos planchets from Colombia, Nicaragua, and Haiti, which slipped into circulation in the United States. Today these are found well circulated from VG to EF grades. (Saul Teichman)

NOTES

Chapter 1

1. Also see commentaries about Wharton in *Walter Breen's Complete Encyclopedia of United States and Colonial Coins* (1988, pp. 243, 244); in several places in Neil Carothers, *Fractional Money: A History of Small Coins and Fractional Paper Currency of the United States*; and in Don Taxay, *U.S. Mint and Coinage*, this being a short list, not to overlook appendix A of the present text. Another opportunist par excellence under the Lincoln administration was John Cisco, who managed the Treasury's affairs at its facility in New York City and in the process became a very wealthy man.
2. *Congressional Globe*, 39th Congress, 1st Session, pp. 1452, 1875, 2520.
3. Carothers, *Fractional Money*, pp. 205, 206.
4. Sometimes the true significance of the diameter of a coin cannot be understood if it is simply expressed in inches (the usual practice) or millimeters in a coin reference book.
5. Any chronicle of the finances of the state of Indiana in the era of state-chartered banking must of necessity mention him in many important contexts, including the issuance of paper money. In the federal service he was also instrumental in the implementation of the National Banking Act of 1863.

Chapter 2

1. *Annual Report of the Director of the Mint*, issues 1863 to 1866; Carothers, *Fractional Money* (p. 205).

Chapter 4

1. Adapted from my sketch in *United States Three-Dollar Gold Coins 1854–1889*.
2. See the chapter titled "A Workshop for Their Gain" in Taxay, *U.S. Mint and Coinage*.
3. Senate document dated May 23, 1856.
4. Waldo Abbott, "Making Money: The Mint at Philadelphia" (1861).
5. The two best coin- (not bank note–) related biographies of Longacre are F.C.C. Boyd, "Engravers of the U.S. Mint in Philadelphia" (1940) and Thomas DeLorey, "Longacre, Unsung Engraver of the U.S. Mint" (1985). The definitive article on Longacre's models, inspirations, and family history is Joy Goforth's "Longacre's Goddess of Liberty" (1983). *Longacre's Ledger*, journal of the Flying Eagle and Indian Cent Collectors Society (founded in 1990 by Richard Snow and Larry Steve), bears his name.
6. David W. Lange, personal communication, July 30, 2005.
7. Spindel, personal communication, August 3, 2005.
8. In my delineation, I employ the standard numismatic form (popular since the days of S.S. Crosby's *Early Coins of America*, 1875) of assigning numbers to obverses and letters to reverses. This differs from the method in Edward L. Fletcher Jr.'s *Shield Five Cent Series* (1994), in which letters are used for obverses and numbers for reverses. Gloria Peters and Cynthia Mohon, in *The Complete Guide to Shield and Liberty Head Nickels* (1995), follow the numbered-obverse and lettered-reverse style.

9. Douglas L. Kurz, personal communication, June 19, 2005.
10. During the course of writing this book, I corresponded extensively with specialists and enthusiasts, who added ideas. Mark Slotkin (personal communication, September 2005) contributed this thought: "It is a distinct possibility that the reverse with its stars and bars resembled and reminded the North of the Confederate flag. The North had no love for the South and, being in control, decided to eliminate the bars (rays) from the coin. This is not such a far-fetched theory because approximately 15,000,000 of the With Rays nickels were minted and circulated in 1866 and 1867. One wonders how this many nickels could be made if there were such production problems. Why did they continue production with rays? Mass quantities combined with the politics of the day do not wash with Chief Coiner Snowden's complaints that the rays must be removed due to the dies' failure to take the metal flow correctly. Further, Snowden did not go through the normal channel of communication, which would have been to deal with the problem with Mint Director Millward. Instead he chose to discuss it directly with the secretary of the Treasury, bypassing Millward, who would have had the real knowledge if there was a production problem."
11. R.W. Julian, personal communication, June 2005.
12. Thomas K. DeLorey, personal communication, July 30, 2005.
13. Opinions differ on this. Howard Spindel, for one, suggests that galvanos were used early in the reverse hub-and-die sequence (personal correspondence, August 5, 2005). My belief is that punches and devices, not large models or galvanos, were used.
14. See J. Hewitt Judd, *United States Pattern Coins: Complete Source for History, Rarity, and Values* (2005), and Andrew W. Pollock III, *United States Patterns and Related Issues* (1994).
15. Saul Teichman, personal communication, June 17, 2005.
16. Listing J-573 covers two different reverses, P-649 and P-650.
17. Teichman, personal communication, June 17, 2005.
18. See note 17.
19. Julian, personal communication, June 2005.
20. Ken Hill, personal communication, August 6, 2005.
21. Carothers, *Fractional Money* (pp. 207, 208); also *Annual Reports.*
22. As quoted by Carothers in *Fractional Money* (pp. 208, 209).
23. A student of the Shield nickel series, not to be named here, commented to the author: "I have several different dates of these 'German silver' Shield nickels. Some are quite well executed! I consider them among the best of the contemporary counterfeits, as far as accuracy in die execution, as they are handmade dies, of course."
24. Citations provided by Katherine Jaeger.
25. Quoted by Rusty Goe, *The Mint on Carson Street* (2003, p. 37).
26. With the advent of the two-cent piece in 1864, *sets* came into being. Earlier, Proof one-cent pieces had been sold separately.
27. Julian, personal communication, June 2005.

28. Ibid. Also, John Dannreuther, "1867 With Rays Nickel, Proof, New Obverse Die Discovered."
29. Dannreuther to the author, July 14, 2005.
30. To this day, this article has never been rebutted.
31. Kurz, personal communication, September 10, 2005.

Chapter 5

1. Spindel, personal communication, August 3, 2005. Also see the detailed description of this reverse given earlier.
2. To verify that this was still the case, I did some "field testing" by examining hundreds of Proof Shield (and also Liberty Head) nickels in 2005.
3. Spindel, personal communication, August 5, 2005.
4. Including suggestions by Howard Spindel, personal communication, August 3, 2005.

Chapter 6

1. R.W. Julian, "2004 Five-Cent Nickel Last 'New' U.S. Coin Created" (2004).
2. John Dannreuther to author, January 15, 2005, and extensive later correspondence through August 2, 2005.
3. Photographic overlay study conducted by Howard Spindel at the suggestion of J.T. Stanton.
4. Douglas L. Kurz to author, June 28, 2005.
5. Spindel, personal communication, August 3, 2005.
6. Howard Spindel comments, "Shield nickel folk believe this to be a lathe reduction line" (correspondence, August 5, 2005).
7. Spindel, personal communication, August 5, 2005.
8. Spindel, personal communication, August 3, 2005.
9. Hill, personal communication, August 6, 2005.
10. Chris Pilliod, "What Error Coins Can Teach Us About Die Settings" (1996). Also, Pilliod, correspondence, April 12, 1996.
11. Personal communication, July 30, 2005.
12. Quadruple per Howard Spindel (personal communication, August 3, 2005); usually listed as triple punched.
13. R.W. Julian, "2004 Five-Cent Nickel."
14. Bill Fivaz, personal communication, August 5, 2005. Fivaz has a circulation strike, as does Ken Hill.
15. Observation by Howard Spindel, personal communication, August 6, 2005.
16. Spindel, personal communication, August 4, 2005.
17. Hill, personal communication, August 6, 2005.
18. Updated figure supplied by Ken Hill (see note 16).
19. For many years, the editors of *A Guide Book of United States Coins* preferred Close 3, since the knobs on the 3 are close to one another but are not fully closed—a distinction that is not commonly made in the marketplace. In keeping with collector usage, the editors reverted to Closed 3 for all listings in the 79th edition.
20. Spindel, personal communication, August 6, 2005.
21. From Fletcher, *Shield Five Cent Series.*

22. Michael Wescott, "Shield Nickel Overdates: Fact or Fiction" (1992). Howard Spindel agrees with Bill Fivaz (personal communication, August 5, 2005).
23. Personal communication, June 19, 2005.
24. Personal communication, August 17, 2005.
25. Julian, personal communication, September 11, 2000.
26. David W. Lange, "Grading Shield Nickels" (1998).
27. Further information about this deception can be found at www.shieldnickels.net.
28. Julian, personal communication, September 11, 2005.
29. Lange, "Grading Shield Nickels."
30. Personal communication, July 30, 2005.
31. Personal communication, September 10, 2005.
32. Personal communication, August 29, 2005.
33. Personal communication, September 10, 2005.
34. Possibility raised by John Dannreuther, personal communication (August 27, 2005), based on certain research he has done with Proof *gold dollars.*
35. Thanks to Douglas Kurz, John Dannreuther, Howard Spindel, ANR, and others. The opinion of Ron Howard, of PCGS, was sent by John Dannreuther.
36. Julian, personal communication, August 29, 2005.
37. Dannreuther, personal communication, September 11, 2005.
38. Julian, personal communication, August 29, 2005.
39. Ibid.
40. Ibid.
41. Spindel, personal communication, August 2005.
42. Ibid.
43. Ibid.
44. Ibid.
45. Ibid.
46. Ibid.
47. R.W. Julian, information from Mint archives, personal communication to the author, September 10, 2005.

Chapter 7

1. For most of this time the *director* of the Mint, with charge of all of the mints, was Horatio C. Burchard, whose office was in the Treasury Building in Washington, D.C.
2. The full text was published in *Mason's Coin & Stamp Collector's Magazine*, volume 6, January 1872.
3. Quoted by Charles Davis, Armand Champa Library II, Lot 1005. In a copy of the 1913 Adams-Woodin work on patterns, Chapman made the notation under AW 61-63, "Mules by the 'Snowden-Thatcher' (?) gang 1874–1880."
4. Certain of the information regarding Barbers, Morgan, and Linderman was provided by Roger W. Burdette, personal communication, 2005.
5. Roger W. Burdette, "Mr. Morgan's New Silver Dollar" (manuscript copy to the author, 2005).
6. Correspondence furnished to the author by Roger W. Burdette.

7. Burdette information based upon Mint records.
8. On March 4, 1875, Barber married Martha E. Jones. the union produced one child, Edith (who married William T. Moseley of Wilmington, Delaware). Martha died in 1898, and on December 3, 1902, Barber married Caroline Gaston. Barber died on February 18, 1917. George T. Morgan became chief engraver soon afterward.
9. Variety known to T.L. Comparette, curator of the collection in 1912 (when it was located in Philadelphia), but subsequently listed as J-1674, with E PLURIBUS UNUM on the reverse. The attribution error was noticed by "Butch" Vosloh while inspecting coins in the Smithsonian collection. Today the correct variety is listed as J-1674a and Pollock-1876; J-1674 does not exist (discrepancy found by Saul Teichman).
10. R.W. Julian, "Depicting Liberty, Barber's Liberty Head Nickel Endured Early Design Changes" (2004).
11. Details from *Mason's Monthly Illustrated Coin Collector's Magazine* (June 1884, vol. 1, p. 3).
12. Citation furnished by Richard Winslow III.
13. Charles J. Folger, 34th secretary of the Treasury, served from 1881 to 1884.
14. Certain information in this account is adapted from that presented in extenso in my *More Adventures With Rare Coins*. The correspondence involving Finnegas was provided by Robert D. Leonard Jr. from government archives.
15. For additional comments about debunking the "Josh story," see Mark M. Hooten, "Racketeers Turn 5¢ Into $5: CENTS-less Nickel Provides Golden Opportunity" (2005).
16. During the 19th century there was little call for one-cent or five-cent pieces for general commerce in California. However, the new 1883 Liberty Head nickel created nationwide attention, and thousands were shipped to the West Coast.
17. Information furnished by Robert D. Leonard Jr. from government archives.
18. *The Numismatist*, October-November 1908.
19. R.W. Julian to the author, 2005.
20. Soon afterward, Bosbyshell sold many rare pattern 1877 half dollars and other rarities to George W. Cogan (son of dealer Edward Cogan), who sold many of them to T. Harrison Garrett, the Baltimore numismatist. Correspondence is given in my *History of United States Coinage as Illustrated by the Garrett Collection*, 1979.
21. Peters and Mohon, *Complete Guide* (p. 106).

Chapter 8

1. Description courtesy of Mark M. Hooten (correspondence, September 7, 2005).

Chapter 9

1. Julian, "Depicting Liberty."
2. Julian, personal communication, August 29, 2005.
3. Carothers, *Fractional Money* (p. 273).
4. Julian, personal communication, August 29, 2005.
5. Correspondence, September 7, 2005.
6. *Annual Report of the Director of the Mint for the Fiscal Year Ending June 30, 1900*, as part of a discussion of a loss that took place in 1897.

7. In the *Pacific Coast Numismatic Society Journal*, April 1986, David W. Lange's article, "Sunny Jim and the 12-S Nickel," told of the distribution of the coin and is one of the sources used here.
8. Credits for this section include these: Probably the first truly realistic and comprehensive view of this rarity was in 1971, when Courtney Coffing, Clyde Mervis, and others on the staff of the Amos Press (publisher of *Coin World* and, at that time, the *Numismatic Scrapbook Magazine*) delved into the subject in depth. An excellent article, "Liberty 1913 Nickel Offers Mystic Aura," in the *Scrapbook*, was the result. This study served as a foundation for what I later wrote in *Adventures With Rare Coins*, with some new ideas added by Courtney Coffing, who kindly reviewed my manuscript. Eric P. Newman kindly furnished his files on the 1913 Liberty Head nickel. Beth Deisher's articles in *Coin World* have been useful as well. The recently published (July 2005) book *Million Dollar Nickels: Mysteries of the Illicit 1913 Liberty Head Nickels Revealed* (by Paul Montgomery, Mark Borckardt, and Ray Knight, 2005) furnished information, particularly for the Walton example.
9. "Abe Kosoff Remembers," *Coin World*, December 14, 1977.
10. Montgomery, Borckardt, and Knight, in *Million Dollar Nickels* (pp. 271–277), give a slightly different version (none of the three authors of that book were present at the event) from my own recollection, which is fine. Indeed, that is what the history of the 1913 Liberty Head nickel is all about! That text has it that Laura Sperber intended to showcase her coin to prospective *buyers* at the event, and that John Snyder was surprised by the Manley coin commentary. However, my scenario had been cleared and enthusiastically approved by Steve Geppi, lead partner in Diamond International. No matter, it was a night to remember for the glitterati of Baltimore and some of the most important figures on the American numismatic scene.
11. Kelly to Bolt is the scenario given by Montgomery et al. in *Million Dollar Nickels* (p. 169).
12. "Abe Kosoff Remembers," *Coin World*, December 14, 1977.
13. Ibid.
14. Picture rerun in *Numismatic News*, July 15, 2003.
15. Montgomery et al., *Million Dollar Nickels* (p. 208).
16. Ibid. (p. 210).
17. The story of this program is told in fascinating detail in *Million Dollar Nickels.*
18. Emery May Holden Norweb, recollection to the author.
19. Montgomery et al., *Million Dollar Nickels* (p. 331). Their roster, from the finest downward: Eliasberg, Olsen, Walton, McDermott, and Norweb examples, a different order than any other I have ever encountered (pre-2003 opinions lacked an evaluation of the Walton coin). For enlightenment, amusement, or whatever, reading the changing grading opinions on the 15 known examples of the 1804 silver dollar is an interesting exercise; see the detailed roster in Bowers, *The Rare Silver Dollars Dated 1804 and the Exciting Adventures of Edmund Roberts* (1999).
20. A related account of this appears in "Abe Kosoff Remembers," *Coin World*, February 7, 1977.
21. "Abe Kosoff Remembers," *Coin World*, October 25, 1972.

Appendix A

1. Reiterated from chapter 1.
2. *American Journal of Numismatics*, June 1866. The sale was cataloged by W. Elliot Woodward and was held at the salesrooms of Leavitt, Strebeigh & Co.
3. Saul Teichman, comment to the author, July 9, 2005: Some patterns of nickel five-cent pieces could have been made by spring 1867. If so, these have not been seen by specialists today, but if located could be identified by obverse characteristics. Teichman cites W.E. Woodward's sale of the Mickley Collection, commencing on April 30, 1867, Lot 2241, where under patterns a piece is described as "Five cent piece, 1865, nickel, Proof." The buyer was a Mr. Dudley, who paid 20 cents for it.

   Perhaps this was J.F. Dudley, whose collection was auctioned in April 1882 by William Seemuller of Baltimore. There is the possibility that this was a striking in nickel alloy from regular *half dime* dies. We do know that regular *dime* dies were used to make nickel strikings (J-422).
4. See Pollock, *United States Patterns.*
5. Don Taxay, *Counterfeit, Mis-Struck, and Unofficial U.S. Coins* (1963, pp. 96 ff).
6. Paper money was valued at a sharp discount from gold and silver coins. The prospective buyer desiring to buy coins from the Mint had the choice of either (a) going to a bullion dealer or exchange office and buying coins at a premium, or (b) checking conversion tables (regularly published in city newspapers) to determine how much extra in paper money had to be sent in place of gold or silver coins.
7. Details can be found in George J. Fuld's "A Group of Restruck Patterns" (1988).
8. See Fuld, "Group of Restruck Patterns."
9. R.W. Julian to the author, 2005, these notes forming the matrix for various articles he has prepared over the years. Here adapted.
10. As cited by Taxay, *U.S. Mint and Coinage.*
11. Much more on the political clout of Wharton ("the nickel interests") and various machinations can be found in Carothers, *Fractional Money.* However, numismatists can be collectively grateful to the rascally Wharton, without whom there might be no nickel five-cent pieces.
12. Pollock's *United States Patterns* (p. 157, figs. 255 and 256) illustrates the varieties.
13. In the eighth edition of the Judd text this die was misdescribed as *Reverse H of 1866.*
14. Tentative attribution, per Pollock-637 (J-568).
15. Teichman, personal communication, July 9, 2005.
16. Pollock, *United States Patterns* (p. 158, figs. 262 and 263).
17. Teichman, personal communication, July 9, 2005.
18. Carothers, *Fractional Money* (pp. 209–211). The legislative history of the bill is in the *Congressional Globe*, 40th Congress 2nd session, and 41st Congress 1st and 2nd sessions. Also see Taxay, *Counterfeit, Mis-Struck, and Unofficial U.S. Coins*, passim (regarding Wharton's machinations).
19. Pollock, *United States Patterns* (p. 163).
20. Taxay, *Counterfeit, Mis-Struck, and Unofficial U.S. Coins* (p. 99).

21. This 1869 die-destruction information was from a false statement by Chief Coiner A. Loudon Snowden, to the effect that he had discovered many old dies in a vault, and with the approval of the Mint director, each and every one was destroyed. In fact, many of these dies were therewith used to make restrikes and rare patterns for collectors.
22. Pollock, *United States Patterns* (p. 226) with credit to Tom DeLorey.
23. Teichman, personal communication, July 9, 2005.
24. Pollock, *United States Patterns* (p. 345).
25. R.W. Julian from Mint correspondence, communication to the author, September 10, 2005.
26. Teichman, personal communication, July 9, 2005.
27. Pollock, *United States Patterns* (p. 352).
28. Judd, *United States Pattern Coins* (p. 261).
29. Lee F. Hewitt, "The Experimental Coins of 1896" (1950, pp. 9–14), based on original report.
30. Certain correspondence on the matter, by Woodin, was preserved by John J. Ford Jr. and came on the market in the early 21st century. The papers are now in a Southern collection. This citation is from the Ford Library I sale by George F. Kolbe.
31. To these can be added an unlisted variation, Pollock-1988, of nickel-copper-iron alloy: 74.5% copper, 12.6% nickel, and 12.9% iron. PE. This was discovered by Devonshire Coin Galleries, authenticated by Rick Montgomery, and publicized in *Coin World* on January 4, 1993.
32. Teichman, personal communication, July 19, 2005.
33. Certain information and Mint-document copies are from Roger W. Burdette, in the manuscript for the forthcoming book, "Renaissance of American Coinage 1909–1915."

Appendix B

1. Fred Weinberg to the author, January 2005. Photographs by Douglas Plasencia of American Numismatic Rarities.

Credits and Acknowledgments

Creative Director and Cover Designer, Matt Jeffirs
Editorial Director, Diana Plattner
Graphic Designers, Matt Heller and Thinh Bui
Pricing Editors, John Feigenbaum and Patrick Ian Perez

Photo updates in the second edition of this book were provided by Heritage Auctions, NGC, PCGS, and Stack's Bowers Galleries. Close-ups of varieties are largely from the *Cherrypickers' Guide to Rare Die Varieties of United States Coins*, sixth edition, volume 1, by Bill Fivaz and J.T. Stanton.

The following individuals were invaluable help in the production of the first edition of this book, and the author would like to acknowledge and thank them for their contributions.

For assisting with research, writing, data compilation, and editing, and for providing other support: the American Numismatic Association, ANACS, Wynn Bowers, Kenneth E. Bressett, Roger W. Burdette, Jane Colvard, John Dannreuther, Thomas K. DeLorey, Dr. Richard Doty, Bill Fivaz, Edward L. Fletcher Jr., Krystal Fontaine, Roberta French, Kathryn Fuller, Ken Hill, Mark Hooten, James Hughes, Katherine Jaeger, R.W. Julian, Douglas L. Kurz, David W. Lange, Stephen K. Nagy, Eric P. Newman, Numismatic Guaranty Company (NGC), *Numismatic News*, *The Numismatist*, Chris Pilliod, Professional Coin Grading Service (PCGS), the Smithsonian Institution, Howard Spindel, David M. Sundman (Littleton Coin Company), Saul Teichman, and Fred Weinberg.

For providing photographs, offering coins and other objects for photography, and/or providing clerical and other support: Jerry Alkire, Jim Bunte, Tom Denly, Wayne Dunn, Danny Fey, Michael S. Fey, Edward L. Fletcher Jr., Kevin Flynn, Kenneth Goldman, Randy Inman Auctions, John M. Kauffman Jr., Jenna King, Douglas L. Kurz, Tom Mulvaney, Melissa Plasencia and Douglas Plasencia (American Numismatic Rarities), Bill Roberts, Scott Schechter (NGC), Shield Nickel Viewer (shieldnickels.net), Mark Slotkin, Howard Spindel, Stack's, David M. Sundman (Littleton Coin Company), Superior Galleries, Steve Tanenbaum, Saul Teichman, Robert Van Ryzin, Frank Van Valen, Fred Weinberg, Robin Wells, and Richard Winslow III.

About the Author

Q. David Bowers got his start in the rare-coin business when he was a teenager in 1953. He is co-founder of Stack's Bowers Galleries in New York and New Hampshire. For many years he was numismatic director at Whitman, and he is editor emeritus of *A Guide Book of United States Coins* (popularly called the *Red Book*).

Bowers is a recipient of the Pennsylvania State University's Distinguished Alumnus Award (1976). He has served as president of both the American Numismatic Association (1983–1985) and the Professional Numismatists Guild (1977–1979). A recipient of the highest honor bestowed by the ANA (the Farran Zerbe Award), Bowers was the first ANA member to be named Numismatist of the Year (1995), and he has been inducted into the Numismatic Hall of Fame at ANA headquarters in Colorado Springs.

Bowers is a recipient of the Professional Numismatists Guild's highest honor, the Founder's Award, and has received more honors from the Numismatic Literary Guild than has any other writer. In 2000 he was the first annual recipient of the Burnett Anderson Memorial Award, an honor sponsored jointly by the American Numismatic Society, the American Numismatic Association, and the Numismatic Literary Guild.

He is the author of more than 50 books, hundreds of auction and other catalogs, and several thousand articles in numismatic publications such as *Coin World* and *Numismatist.* He is an award-winning columnist for *Paper Money* magazine, and his "Joys of Collecting" column has run in *Coin World* for more than 50 years, making it the longest-running column by any author in the history of numismatics. He has written about Morgan and other dollars in hundreds of articles and catalogs and as part of several books, and his two-volume study *Silver Dollars and Trade Dollars of the United States: A Complete Encyclopedia* (1992) has become a standard in the field.

Selected Bibliography

Abbott, Waldo. "Making Money: The Mint at Philadelphia." *Harper's New Monthly Magazine*, March 1861.

Akers, David W. *United States Gold Patterns: A Photographic Study of the Gold Patterns Struck at the United States Mint From 1836 to 1907*. Racine, WI: Western Publishing, 1975.

Altman, Charles I. "History of the United States Nickel Five-Cent Piece." *The Numismatist*, January 1949.

American Journal of Numismatics (American Numismatic and Archaeological Society, later renamed the American Numismatic Society), various issues since 1866.

Annual Report of the Director of the Mint, various years (especially 1865–1913).

Bowers, Q. David. *Adventures With Rare Coins.* Los Angeles, CA: Bowers and Ruddy Galleries, 1979. Later printings by Bowers and Merena Galleries, Wolfeboro, NH.

———, *The History of United States Coinage as Illustrated by the Garrett Collection.* Los Angeles, CA: Bowers and Ruddy Galleries, 1979. Later printings by Bowers and Merena Galleries, Wolfeboro, NH.

———, *Abe Kosoff: Dean of Numismatics.* Wolfeboro, NH: Bowers and Ruddy Galleries, 1985.

———, *The Rare Silver Dollars Dated 1804 and the Exciting Adventures of Edmund Roberts.* Wolfeboro, NH: Bowers and Merena Galleries, 1999.

———, *More Adventures With Rare Coins.* Wolfeboro, NH: Bowers and Ruddy Galleries, 2002.

———, *United States Three-Cent and Five-Cent Pieces.* Wolfeboro, NH: Bowers and Ruddy Galleries, 2005.

———, *United States Three-Dollar Gold Coins 1854–1889.* Wolfeboro, NH: American Numismatic Rarities, 2005.

Boyd, F.C.C. "Engravers of the U.S. Mint in Philadelphia." *The Numismatist*, July 1940.

Breen, Walter H. *Walter Breen's Encyclopedia of United States and Colonial Proof Coins, 1792–1977.* Albertson, New York: FCI Press, 1977.

———, *Walter Breen's Complete Encyclopedia of U.S. and Colonial Coins.* New York: Doubleday,1988.

———, *Walter Breen's Encyclopedia of United States and Colonial Proof Coins, 1792–1989.* Wolfeboro, NY: Bowers and Merena Galleries, 1989.

Bressett, Kenneth E., ed. *A Guide Book of United States Coins.* Florence, AL: Various modern editions.

Bressett, Kenneth E., and Q. David Bowers. *The Official American Numismatic Association Grading Standards for United States Coins*, 7th ed. Florence, AL: Whitman, 2024.

Burdette, Roger W. "Mr. Morgan's New Silver Dollar." Manuscript, 2005.

———, "Renaissance of American Coinage 1909–1915." Manuscript in process.

CAC Rare Coin Market Review (Virginia Beach, VA), various issues since 2000.

Carothers, Neil. *Fractional Money: A History of Small Coins and Fractional Paper Currency of the United States.* New York: John Wiley & Sons, 1930.

Coffing, Courtney, Clyde Mervis, et al. "Liberty 1913 Nickel Offers Mystic Aura." *The Numismatic Scrapbook Magazine.*

Coin Values (Sidney, OH: Amos Press), various issues since 2003.

Coin World (Sidney, OH: Amos Press), various issues since 1960.

Coin World Almanac. Sidney, OH: Coin World, 2000.

Coinage Laws of the United States 1792–1894. Reprint, with modern foreword by David L. Ganz. Wolfeboro, NH: Bowers and Merena Galleries, 2001.

Comparette, T. Louis. "On the Utility of a Cabinet of Historic Coins." *The Numismatist*, March 1906.

Crosby, S.S. *Early Coins of America.* Boston: Author, 1875.

Dannreuther, John. "1867 With Rays Nickel, Proof, New Obverse Die Discovered." Revised July 14, 2005. Manuscript.

Davis, R. Coulton. "Pattern and Experimental Issues of the United States Mint." *Coin Collector's Journal*, May 1886.

DeLorey, Thomas. "Longacre, Unsung Engraver of the U.S. Mint." *The Numismatist*, October 1985.

Doty, Richard. *America's Money, America's Story.* Atlanta, GA: Whitman Publishing, 2008.

Elder, Thomas L. *Hobbies*, February 1943.

Errorscope (Santa Rosa, CA: CONECA), various issues. Information available at conecaonline.org/errorscope.

Evans, George G. *Illustrated History of the United States Mint.* Philadelphia: Evans, 1883. Reprinted 1885, 1889, and 1893.

Fivaz, Bill, and J.T. Stanton. *The Cherrypickers' Guide to Rare Die Varieties* (6th ed.), vol. 1. Atlanta, GA: Whitman, 2025.

Fletcher, Edward L., Jr. *The Shield Five Cent Series.* Ormond Beach, FL: Dead End Publishing, 1994.

Flynn, Kevin, and Bill Van Note. *Treasure Hunting Liberty Head Nickels* (2nd ed.). Brooklyn, NY: Brooklyn Gallery, 2005.

Flynn, Kevin, and John Wexler. *Over Mintmarks and Hot Repunched Mintmarks.* Brooklyn, NY: Brooklyn Galleries Coins & Stamps, Inc., 2003.

Fuld, George J. "A Group of Restruck Patterns." *The Numismatist*, May 1998. Republished based on data supplied by Saul Teichman, 1995. uspatterns.store.turbify.net/groupofrespa.html.

Goe, Rusty. *The Mint on Carson Street.* Reno, NV: Southgate Coins and Collectibles, 2003.

Goforth, Joy. "Longacre's Goddess of Liberty." *Mint Press*, November 1983. Reprinted in *Coin World*, January 4, 1984.

Hewitt, Lee F. "The Experimental Coins of 1896." *The Numismatic Scrapbook Magazine*, January 1950.

Hooten, Mark M. "Proof Liberty Head Nickels Pleasingly Engaging: Among Overlooked Coins From Late 19th, Early 20th Centuries." *Coin Values*, April 2005.

———, "Racketeers Turn 5¢ Into $5: CENTS-less Nickel Provides Golden Opportunity." *Coin Values*, April 2005.

Judd, J. Hewitt. *United States Pattern Coins: Complete Source for History, Rarity, and Values* (10th ed.). Florence, AL: Whitman, 2024.

Julian, R.W. "Notes on U.S. Proof Coinage: Silver and Minor." *Numismatic Scrapbook Magazine*, March 1966. Cited in *Walter Breen's Encyclopedia of U.S. and Colonial Proof Coins, 1792–1977.* Albertson, New York: FCI Press, 1977. Updated edition by Bowers and Merena Galleries, Wolfeboro, NH, 1989.

———, "1866 5¢." Unpublished research and historical notes about the Shield nickel, 1990's.

———, "2004 Five-Cent Nickel Last 'New' U.S. Coin Created." *Numismatic News*, April 24, 2004.

———, "Depicting Liberty: Barber's Liberty Head Nickel Endured Early Design Changes." *Coins*, September 2004.

Kagin, Donald. *Private Gold Coins and Patterns of the United States*. New York: Arco, 1981.

Kosoff, Abe. "Abe Kosoff Remembers." Column in *Coin World*, various issues.

Lange, David W. "Sunny Jim and the 12-S Nickel." *Pacific Coast Numismatic Society Journal*, April 1986. Reprinted in *The Numismatist's Bedtime Companion*, Bowers and Merena Galleries, Wolfeboro, NH.

———, "Grading Liberty Head Nickels." *The Numismatist*, December 1997.

———, "Grading Shield Nickels." *The Numismatist*, April 1998.

Liberty Nickels Collectors Society. libertynickels.org.

Mangels, William F. *The Outdoor Amusement Industry From Earliest Times to the Present.* New York: Vantage Press, 1952.

McCullough, Edo. *Good Old Coney Island.* New York: Charles Scribner's Sons, 1957.

Monthly Greysheet. (Virginia Beach, VA), various issues since 1963.

The Numismatist (Colorado Springs, CO, and other addresses: American Numismatic Association), various issues since 1888.

Peters, Gloria, and Cynthia Mohon. *The Complete Guide to Shield and Liberty Head Nickels.* Virginia Beach, VA: DLRC Press, 1995.

Pilliod, Chris. "What Error Coins Can Teach Us About Die Settings." *The Numismatist*, April 1996.

———, "A Motto's Impact on Conscience and Coinage." *The Numismatist*, October 2001.

Pollock, Andrew W., III. *United States Patterns and Related Issues.* Wolfeboro, NH: Bowers and Merena Galleries, 1994.

Raymond, Wayte. *Standard Catalogue of United States Coins and Paper Money.* New York: Scott Stamp & Coin Co. (among others), editions from 1934 to 1957 (titles vary).

Rulau, Russell. "People Admired or Hated 'Witch of Wall Street.'" *Numismatic News*, April 6, 2004.

Rulau, Russell, and George Fuld, in consultation with Q. David Bowers. *Medallic Portraits of Washington* (2nd ed.). Iola, WI: Krause Publications, 1999.

Sanders, Mitch. "Houdon and U.S. Coin Design." *The Numismatist*, March 2000.

Snow, Richard. *Coney Island: A Postcard Journey to the City of Fire.* New York: Brightwaters Press, 1984.

Spindel, Howard. "The Shield Nickel Viewer." Online database. Latest version, 2005. shieldnickels.net/snv/snv.html.

Stride, H.G. *Nickel for Coinage.* London: Hutchinson & Co., 1964.

Taxay, Don. *Counterfeit, Mis-struck, and Unofficial U.S. Coins.* New York: Arco Publishing, 1963.

———, *U.S. Mint and Coinage.* New York: Arco Publishing, 1966.

———, *Scott's Comprehensive Catalogue of United States Coinage.* New York: Scott Publications, 1970 (cover date 1971). Revised ed. 1976, updated by Joseph Rose and H. Hazelcorn.

Van Ryzin, Robert R. *Twisted Tails, Sifted Fact, Fantasy and Fiction From U.S. Coin History.* Iola, WI: Krause Publications, 1995.

Vermeule, Cornelius. *Numismatic Art in America.* Atlanta, GA: Whitman Publishing, 2007.

Wescott, Michael. *The United States Nickel Five-Cent Piece: A Date-by-Date Analysis and History.* Wolfeboro, NH: Bowers and Merena Galleries, 1991.

———, "Shield Nickel Overdates: Fact or Fiction." *The Numismatist*, March 1992.

Young, Richard G., and Wade J. Wilkin. *Racketeer Nickel and Its Many Mysteries.* Published by the authors, 2004.

Washington Quarters
1965-1998
Date and Mintmark Set
Washington Quarters 1965-1998
Washington Quarters 1932-1964
State, DC, and
Territories Quarters
1999-2009
Date and Mintmark Set
State, DC, and Territories Quarters 1999-2009

INDEX

T

U

V

W

Y